RAIDERS
from the
SEA

RAIDERS
from the
SEA

**The Story of the Special
Boat Service in WWII**

John Lodwick

With a New Foreword by Lord Jellicoe

Naval Institute Press, Annapolis

Published and distributed in the United States of America
by the Naval Institute Press, Annapolis, Maryland 21402.

This edition is authorized for sale only in the United States
and its territories and possessions.

Library of Congress Catalog Card No. 90–60493

ISBN 1–55750–525–X

Publishing History
Raiders from the Sea was first published as
The Filibusters: The Story of the Special Boat Service
in 1947 (Methuen & Co. Ltd., London) and is reproduced
now exactly as the original edition, complete and unabridged,
with the addition of a new Foreword by Lord Jellicoe.

Quality printing and binding by
Billing & Sons Limited, Hylton Road, Worcester WR2 5JU, England

FOREWORD

I am delighted to have been invited to contribute a foreword to this book by my old companion the late John Lodwick: his lively account of the SBS in the Mediterranean. It is high time that his book was republished.

I had the honour to command the SBS for less than two years. However, those years are etched indelibly in my memory.

It was, like the SBS today, never a large unit. Even when it was dignified with the title of Regiment for the last year or two of the war, its strength never amounted to more than 300 or so at the most. But it made up in quality and versatility what it may have lacked in quantity.

'No names, no pack drill' is usually a good rule. But I would like to single out, almost at random, just a few of those who made up its star-studded cast. They come alive in John Lodwick's racy prose. David Sutherland, professional to his fingertips who succeeded me in command and whose epic raid on Rhodes Lodwick vividly describes; Jock Lapraik, another real pro who contributed, like David, so much to the SBS, both during and also after the war; Ian Patterson, a brilliantly intelligent as well as a brave officer, tragically killed in a wartime flying accident; Ambrose McGonigal, later a senior judge in Northern Ireland; Walter Milner-Barry, our veteran and a wise and dear companion. And Lodwick's prose brings back most vividly of all in my mind's eye the memory of Anders Lassen – Andy, whose career was crowned with a sadly posthumous VC – the young Dane of whom David Sutherland has justly written, 'I do not expect to see his like again.' The other ranks, as varied and distinct a bunch of individuals as you could wish for, were the equals in quality of their officers. I was very lucky to command them.

Curiously, we had a surprising amount of literary talent in the unit. Fitzroy Maclean, of Yugoslav fame, who was with us for a short spell. He needs no introduction. John Verney, who has described with an amused and ironical eye our interlude of training in Palestine in *A Dinner of Herbs*. And Eric Newby who travelled much with the SBS in wartime, and who has travelled much more since then in peacetime, and whose capture in Sicily and subsequent escape are described with wit and charm in that lovely book *Love and War in the Appenines*. Not least, John Lodwick himself. We did not lack for chroniclers.

And then there were those others who, in one way or another, touched our lives, often very directly. David Stirling, the founder of the SAS and in many ways our father figure. David Lloyd Owen and his valued companions in the Long Range Desert Group. Colonel Tsigantes, the commander of the Greek Sacred Regiment, and rightly the most celebrated of Greek officers in the Second World War. And the sailors who ferried us around the Aegean and the Adriatic – brilliant navigators like Lieutenant-Commander John Campbell, Adrian Seligman of the Levant Schooner Flotilla and those submarine and MTB commanders who hazarded themselves and their ships embarking and disembarking us.

These men, and many more, John Lodwick evokes in his pages. He also, and rightly, pays tribute to the Greeks with whom we were inevitably involved in our operations, especially that special brand of Greek, the Cretans. We were there in a way to help them. But often we found ourselves more helped than helping. They gave us invaluable information. They fed us. Often they sheltered us. And, sometimes, indeed too frequently, they sacrificed themselves for us. We owed a tremendous lot to them – usually simple fisherman and peasants and their indomitable ladies.

As I write these words, looking out from my study towards the placid Wiltshire Downs, these are some of the memories which Lodwick's prose brings back to me. He describes, describes well, the excitement, indeed the exhilaration, of raids well executed. But he rightly does not spare the reader from the disappointments, the frustrations and the tragic loss in life inseparable from war.

Was it all worth while one asks? I think it was. The SBS in those wartime years inflicted a great deal of damage on the enemy – and with a reasonable economy of resources. What is more, by the unit's ceaseless activity in the Eastern Mediterranean it helped to pin down Axis forces in the Aegean and the Balkans which were badly needed on other fronts. If I had a quarrel with John Lodwick's book it would be with his original publisher's choice of title. *The Filibusters* was doubtless good copy. But the title served, I feel, to disguise the serious purpose behind the unit's wartime exploits, as serious in purpose as those of its successor some forty years later in South Georgia and the Falklands.

John Lodwick, sadly, died prematurely in a car accident in the late 1950s. Otherwise I am sure he would have achieved a considerable reputation as a writer. In any event in this fine book he has a good tale to tell and he tells it with panache and, just possibly, with a touch of the apocryphal at times. For example, I am inclined to wonder whether after his remarkable escape from German captivity in the Balkans I really said, 'Ah, you're back. Damned slow about it, weren't you!'

But let that be. John was a good writer. He was also a good soldier – 'inventive, operationally imaginative with a fertile mind as a planner', to quote David Sutherland. And he was also durable, as shown by his service in the Foreign Legion, the SBS and his remarkable escape. I am sure, too, that this splendidly evocative book will likewise endure.

JELLICOE

ILLUSTRATIONS

Appearing between pages 96 & 97

Dick Harden. Against a Turkish background
Macris, a great Greek. Govier at Megara
Guerrillas—Samos. Turkish friend. M. and V.
Sutherland and friend. Lassen's Sergeant Nicholson.
   Trooper Crouch (*killed in action*)
Base. Manhunting in Jugosalvia. Waiting for a cupper
Folboats away. Leros. Greek conference
Base. Hide-out. Lying up
On the way
Brigadier Turnbull
Jellicoe and friend. Rough passage
Sean O'Reilly. Trophy. A rare shave
Ski interlude
Jellicoe. Lassen and Casulli
Captured craft. Find the ship—*Fairmiles* under camouflage
Homeward bound. Port Deremen
Leros gets it. The stores come in

Maps on pages 10/11, 165, 177, 213 *and* 227

9

LEGEND

• *Places raided*

━━ *Patterson 1944*

Scale of Miles

Richard Cribb

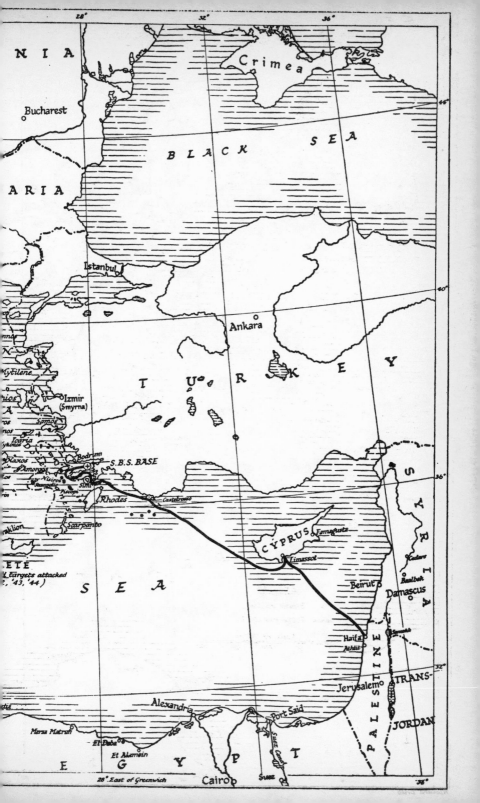

CHAPTER ONE

A few minutes before ten o'clock on an evening in June the submarine surfaced. She lay four miles offshore. The sea was calm, and there was a slight mist—but no moon. The moon would not rise for another two hours.

The two men were sitting in the ward-room eating ham sandwiches when this occurred. When they had eaten seven or eight ham sandwiches they lit cigarettes and inhaled deeply and deliberately for they would not be smoking again for some time. Presently, the captain called down that all was in readiness. The two men extinguished their cigarettes and, carrying their collapsible canoe and stores, mounted the steel steps to the conning-tower. Twenty minutes later they were sitting in their canoe on the casing, ready to be floated off. The submarine proceeded inshore, and at about distance of three-quarters of a mile from the beach the canoe was slipped overboard.

One of the men in the canoe was an officer. The other man was a marine. They paddled gently, exercising great caution as they neared the coast, for voices could be heard and occasional lights observed. Several small craft were seen close inshore, probably local fishing boats. Since the officer knew that the railway ran along the coast, no definite point was made for, but for safety's sake he used a compass-bearing for his run-in. Presently, he sighted a large mass of rock, rising vertically to a height of two or three hundred feet. Since the railway must run either through or round his spur, the officer decided to take advantage of the protection

13

afforded by its shadow. In this he did himself a good turn, for after a short distance, a shingle beach was sighted where the two men were able to land without making too much noise. They hid their canoe from sight among the rocks.

Inland the ground rose steeply. Some distance up the incline, the telegraph poles which marked the railway track could be seen. The two men swung their load over their shoulders and climbed slowly, sweating, for the night was warm, cursing as they slipped on loose stones, making contact with cactus bushes. On reaching the railway they discovered that it entered a tunnel which ran through the spur. Both tunnel and line were unguarded. Some distance away a white light was shining, probably the signal for a train.

Finding no more suitable place, the officer decided to lay his explosive charge in the entrance of the tunnel. The two men knelt down and the work began. They had brought a pick with them, but picks are noisy. They scooped at the stones with their hands and laid their charge between two sleepers, where it nestled conveniently, immediately under the line.

The officer busied himself with the final details. He laid his dual-pressure ignition studs flush with the under-side of the rail. He connected up the main charge. While he was doing this the marine nudged him and pointed. The white light down the line had turned green. A train was approaching.

The officer placed his detonators in positions and the two men slipped away. Voices could still be heard, and in consequence they moved with great care. Two boatloads of fishermen were now lying directly off the beach. The two men hid for some time behind a rock, but their position was uncomfortable, and they were much bothered by gnats and mosquitoes. After a brief consultation they launched their canoe and, unobserved by the fishermen, made off.

Half a mile offshore the officer made a prearranged signal with a torch. He sighted the submarine on his starboard bow. The two men boarded her from the gun-platform. The canoe was passed inboard and dismantled. The submarine got under way.

Some ham sandwiches remained in the ward-room. The canoeists had eaten five or six of these when the officer was called for from the bridge. He mounted the steel ladder in time to see a train entering the far end of the tunnel. Fifty seconds later a large flash was visible. This flash was followed by an explosion.

These events occurred on the night of the 22nd of June 1941, on the western coast of Italy. They represented the first successful attack upon the Italian metropolis and the birth of the Special Boat Service. The men who laid the charge were Lieutenant (R.A.) 'Tug' Wilson and Marine Hughes.

When Dunkirk fell, many things fell with it. General officers retired, pausing on their way to Home Guard duties to buy bowler hats at Lock's. Other officers were promoted, and orders were placed with London tailors for acres of red tabs. To the British public, these changes seemed salutary, but not startling. A disaster had occurred and, no matter how slowly, a disaster would be put right. Meanwhile, the major problem remained how to get to one's office through debris-strewn streets and morning air raids.

But behind the scenes . . . behind the imposing change of nomenclature and command . . . a metamorphosis was taking place in British military thinking. If a cataclysm is required to shake the War Office the reaction of that old-established firm is none the less rapid. In this case, it was also efficient. New personalities appeared with new ideas. The era of the swashbuckling adventurer and the licensed privateer was at hand again, and as the glad tidings spread round, the spiritual descendants of Hawkins, of Peterborough and of Drake swallowed a last double whisky in their messes and took the train for London. They carried with them in their luggage mysterious rope ladders, alpenstocks, home-made bombs and magnetic devices, which they proposed to attach to the sides of enemy ships. England was reeling beneath the nightly assaults of the *Luftwaffe*, but the main concern of these men was to get back in the shortest possible time to the Continent. There was one who had sailed the entire length of the Danube in a rubber boat, and who saw no reason why he should not repeat this exploit on the Seine. There was another who had spent half his life as a Himalayan mountaineer and who offered his experience now for the purposes of cliff-scaling in Normandy. These men were neither deranged nor were they cranks. The gadgets which they invented—from tyre bursters to time incendiaries—their vast experience at sea, in mountains and in many strange countries, were later to form the stock-in-trade of raiding and invasion forces everywhere.

The talent was there; it remained to co-ordinate and direct it. Admiral of the Fleet Sir Roger Keyes, a man universally respected and the hero of Zeebrugge in the First World War, was chosen for this task. Throughout the autumn and winter of 1940 the newly formed Commandos were training for amphibious operations, firstly at Inverary, and later at Largs and in the island of Arran. Looking back, these now seem almost legendary times, comparable only with the foundation of the Roman Empire. Were Romulus and Remus actually suckled by the wolf—who can tell? The historians state the fact blandly, as later they will no doubt observe that even in far-off 'forty, Britain was preparing to strike back. But of the personalities in those early days under Admiral Keyes many are now dead, many dispersed throughout the world, and not a few deep in the respectability of stockbroking and market-gardening. They have done a great deal since Inverary, and they talk, not of training, but of operations. When they came north in that first winter they lacked experience sadly. Each, while willing to learn from others, sought refuge in his own speciality. The men who had crossed the Gobi Desert in rope sandals insisted upon the benefits of marching; the amateur anarchists showed real enthusiasm only during the periods devoted to explosives; officers, who in civvy street had spent much time in night-clubs, issued benzedrine to their sections and expounded upon the benfit of long periods without repose.

There were even advocates of dress reform. George Duncan, a captain, condemned both shorts and battle-dress trousers as useless. 'You must march in breeches,' he would declare, 'trousers chafe the skin ... chafe the skin,' and, suiting the action to his word, he would spend much time with needle and thread. A crony of Duncan's was George Barnes, a Grenadier Guardsman, whose talents lay in another direction. A professional swimmer, Barnes could eat bananas and drink beer below water, accomplishments which stood him in good stead later, when he specialized in the use of the Davis submarine apparatus.

Attached to No. 8 Commando at this period was a small group of highly trained canoeists, whose job was to carry out the reconnaissance for commando landings and to do various small sabotage jobs. This 'Folboat Section', as it was called, was run by Captain Roger Courtney, who had pre-war canoeing experience on the Nile and elsewhere. If Courtney had a permanent residence it was probably in East Africa, where he had spent much of his life hunting big game. Courtney had a persuasive tongue, and he needed it, for the idea, in those days, of canoes as implements of warfare was revolutionary in the extreme. To his flow of golden words Courtney added an ability to drink any two men under a mess table and a propensity for issuing broadsheets to his men. 'Are you TOUGH?' one of them demanded, 'if so, get out. I want ——'s with intelligence.'

Courtney's second-in-command was a lieutenant. His name was 'Tug' Wilson, and with that delightful inconsequence peculiar to the British Army, he had been commissioned in the Royal Artillery, though he was not to touch anything of larger calibre than a tommy-gun for years. Wilson was fanatical in his enthusiasm for canoes. As leader of the first successful raids, by this means, he occupies a position in our hierarchy not unlike that of St. Peter in Holy Mother Church. It was he who, when chivvied by Cairo, was later to say, 'The miserable precautionary methods taken by the Italians to counter our attacks are entirely inadequate and by no means warrant an even temporary cessation of landings'.

Wilson's comrade on operations, his 'mucker' or 'mate' was Marine Hughes. It is useless to ask where Hughes came

17

from. People were not transferred to the then embryonic unit: they *arrived*, following a conversation in a pub or on a railway station. Subsequently, their position was regularized by the ubiquitous Courtney, who could return the soft answer when he so wished. The recruits came, often, from the most unlikely sounding units: for example, James Sherwood, from the R.A.S.C., who did very well in the Middle East before returning to the U.K. and the respectability of a commission. In all, by the end of 1940, about twelve officers and men had been recruited by Courtney, and to each officer his 'half-section' in the shape of a man he filled with buns and tea on all possible occasions.

The atmosphere was far from formal.

The training imposed by Keyes, not only upon the Folboat Section but upon all special service troops in the Island of Arran, had not been without an object. That object, though few realized it at the time, was no less than the invasion of the Italian island of Pantellaria. Wavell was now in Bardia and would soon be skirmishing outside Benghazi. British strategists, fortified by captured dumps of *pecorino* and *chianti*, were beginning to think ambitiously. Only at the last moment was the assault upon Pantellaria cancelled. Speculation as to the likelihood of its success seems to me untimely. It would have been a very bloody operation.

Meanwhile, Wavell had got wind of the formation of these peculiar units in Scotland and, in January 1941, he sent for them. Middle East strategy at that time had two principal objects. The first—the occupation of Cyrenaica—had now been almost achieved. The second was the occupation of Rhodes, for the attack on which island elementary landing-craft and small naval vessels of all kinds were being assembled in Alexandria. On 31st January 1941, the three most highly trained of the new Commandos . . . the 7th, 8th, and 11th Scottish (under Lt.-Col. Dick Pedder) left Arran, arriving in the Middle East by the tiresome Cape route on 11th March. The whole force was under command of Colonel Robert Laycock, from whom it took its name of 'Layforce'. Somewhere in the bowels of one of the smallest ships the still tiny Folboat Section was quartered. The precious canoes themselves had been dismantled and packed in waterproof cases. No replacements would be available in Cairo.

Arrived in Egypt, 'Layforce' settled down to the traditional first tasks of the British 'squaddie' in those parts. They allowed their literal and metaphorical knees to brown. They learnt to wear shorts, learned not to lapse into the symptoms of dementia praecos when pursued all day by swarms of flies. They trained arduously for Rhodes; though, as events turned out, they were to go almost everywhere except there.

For, in late March and early April, unfortunate events were taking place in Greece. Every available landing-craft and small ship was commandeered for the evacuation for the British and Anzac Expeditionary Forces. The attack upon Rhodes was finally and utterly cancelled. In these circumstances, Courtney, who barely knew the purpose for which a chair was intended, let alone being prepared to sit still in it, decided to act upon his own initiative. With a triumphant 'so there!' to his colleagues, he arranged for the transfer of the Folboat Section to H.M.S. *Medway*, where they would work in conjunction with the 1st Submarine Flotilla.

From this moment the Special Boat Section can be said to have been formed, but in spite of the imposing change of nomenclature they were to remain for some time nobody's baby. Parades—when parades took place—revealed that their effectives had jumped to eight officers and approximately thirty men. These parades also revealed the most astonishing variety of headgear ever seen in the Middle East; with a majority inclination towards tam-o'-shanters. The S.B.S. as yet possessed no badge, no motto, none of the personal paraphernalia of a normal unit. There existed, however, a unit stamp. It was neither well made nor easily decipherable. A myopic field cashier, upon seeing it, inquired plaintively as to the nature of this Special *Boot* Section.

Meanwhile, 'Layforce', still bloodthirsty but baulked in all its major plans, was splitting up. In June it was disbanded, but not before 11th Scottish Commando had made its remarkable crossing of the Litani River in the Syrian campaign against some of the stiffest opposition ever met by special service troops. A bleak cemetery beside a lonely road still annotates this now forgotten sacrifice.

Members of 'Layforce' were now offered employment in the newly forced Middle East Commando, the effectives of which were to be made up to strength by the incorporation of the two Commandos which had fought well in East Africa. Many accepted; others passed to the various peculiar organizations, which were now springing up like mushrooms . . . sturdy mushrooms. One of these units, if one accepts its pacific title at its face value, was concerned with transport protection. How it ever got across the desert, killed 120 Italians and captured or destroyed all their transport is a mystery. After this episode the unit name was changed.

This middle and final trimester of 1941 was the raiders' honey-moon. The great David Stirling was already present . . . and could be seen at Shepheard's on occasion . . . but he had not yet thrown his gigantic shadow and his passion for incorporation across the paths of all these little groups. Comfortably installed in the ward-room of H.M.S. *Medway*, Roger Courtney plotted in peace, was affable to the influential, abrupt with the conventionally minded. He got on well with the Navy: the Navy got on well with him. He owed allegiance to nobody and, when he judged the moment ripe for another operation, he would pay a polite call upon Admiral Maund, Director of Combined Operations at G.H.Q.

Admiral Maund was amiability itself . . . indeed, he was more; he was enlightened. His submarines were obliged to carry out their routine patrols. Why not, in the course of them, allow a couple of these queer chaps in tam-o'-shanters ashore with their sacks of gelignite and pressure switches, to do a bit of dirty work into the bargain? Admiral Maund saw no objection, neither did his eminent colleagues. The period, indeed, was propitious for nuisance raids, for there was small comfort elsewhere.

Nor was Admiral Maund the only client: the cloak and

dagger gentlemen, with dingy but sinister headquarters in Cairo, were already sketching predatory tentacles into the more accessible Balkan States. Agents are valuable livestock and must be shielded from the minor irritations of life. The canoes and rubber boats of the Special Boat Section seemed to offer them an insurance against wet feet while landing.

So much for the cargo, the opportunities . . . now let us examine the results.

CHAPTER TWO

One should always, it is said, open one's book with some exciting incident, no matter how boring one is prepared to be afterwards. 'Tug' Wilson's derailment of the Sicilian train, with which I began this history, certainly caused happy palpitations in the Middle East. Hands were rubbed with glee in Groppis, and even in more sacred places. In mid-September 1941, 'Tug' Wilson was instructed to try it again.

Accompanied by Marine Hughes, his 'half-section' and 424 lb. of explosive, he embarked on H.M. Submarine *Utmost* and landed on the west coast of Italy on 22nd September. This time the plan was more sophisticated: the strike was not made blind, for example, but with a tunnel as the definite target. Also, quantities of propaganda leaflets were carried (Hitler *se fregato*, etc.) which Wilson and Hughes patiently scattered among the unattractive scrub. Seven journeys were necessary to carry the very heavy load of explosive from beach to tunnel. This had just been accomplished and the main mine charge laid, when an armed party was observed approaching through the tunnel. Wilson and Hughes crept away and hid behind a bush, hoping that the pile of explosive could remain unobserved. They were unlucky. One of the patrol flashed a torch on it. Wilson leapt up and attempted to make the thing a hold-up job. But Italians are too excitable to be easily taken prisoner in the dark. These ran away down the tunnel and a brisk exchange of shots ensued. The entire neighbourhood was aroused. Lights appeared in private houses not far distant, and a second patrol began to run down the track towards the intruders. Wilson calmed the impetuosity of these citizens with another burst of fire, then retreated to the beach, abandoning the operation.

Wilson and Hughes ate some ham sandwiches, slept, and on the next night tried again, this time on a three-span railway bridge over the River Oliva, in Sicily. Sentries, most of them fortunately carrying lanterns, seem to have been everywhere on this job. There was one on the bridge . . . but he carried no lantern, only a rifle. He challenged with the word 'Duce', to which Wilson gave the mendacious reply, 'Amigo'. The sentry was unconvinced. He snapped back the safety-catch of his rifle. Wilson shot him with a tommy-gun and was rewarded by a hail of fire from some point to the left, probably from a Breda machine-gun. The hail of fire followed the two men all the way to the beach, and in their canoe they were obliged to do some smart zigzagging. Quite unconverted by these two experiences as a figure target, Wilson wrote in his report, 'Bridges and vulnerable points are now well guarded, but long straight stretches of line can still be attacked'.

A statement which he was soon to prove.

Meanwhile, Courtney himself was out in the submarine *Osiris*. Something had gone wrong with the landing of some very important 'bodies' in Albania. Courtney took a look at Scutari and observed parties of workmen, frantically digging fortifications all round the port. The enemy were preparing for a major assault.

At about this same time, Sherwood was landing no less than eight gentlemen in Crete from the submarine *Thunderbolt*, formerly the tragic *Thetis*. This was an operation which fully illustrates the difficulties encountered when persons with one interpretation of military discipline convoy those with quite another. Sherwood and his assistant, Corporal Booth, took their cargo ashore, in a heavy sea, by folboat, instructing each man to wait on the beach until the party was complete. By the third journey, however, all those previously ferried had vanished. Those newly disembarked blamed Sherwood, whose discomfiture

23

was added to by the furtive arrival of four fully armed men. Sherwood held these men up, only to discover that they were Cretans. His experience is far from unique: it was always impossible to land anywhere, in however great secrecy, on that exasperating land, without a dozen of its inhabitants appearing as if by magic.

After debates with Courtney, Wilson decided to try a new area for his next railway job. H.M. Submarine *Truant* was about to patrol the Adriatic. This was a field so far quite untouched and, furthermore, being far from the battle zones, likely to be less well guarded. Wilson and Hughes took passage in *Truant* and landed between Ancona and Senigallia on the Brindisi-Milan main line, on the night of 26th October 1941.

The coast here is low and sandy, with no great depth of water until far out at sea. A fair swell was running. In spite of these handicaps, which involved a long paddle, the operation went well. The line lay some distance from the shore but, when reached, there was no lack of trains. Two passed while Wilson was laying the charge. A minute here or there can sometimes be of great importance. The occupants of those trains probably never knew how narrowly they had escaped death. The third train was not so lucky. It was a passenger with fourteen pullman-type carriages. Wilson and Hughes had just reached the submarine when it crashed. Gangers were still searching in its wreckage the next day.

Agents were now being landed regularly; gentlemen in tight-fitting and often picturesque civilian clothes who clutched their brief-cases with fervour and could not be expected to paddle. On landing, they sometimes complained that they had got their bottoms wet in the cramped confines of the folboat. Poor fellows, they were to endure many worse discomforts than this.

In the middle of November, however, a more interesting operation was planned. For the first time, the co-operation of the Special Boat Section was solicited by an outside force. A small fragment of the 11th Scottish Commando, under Lieutenant-Colonel Keyes, and accompanied by Laycock himself, had been briefed to land by sea and destroy the headquarters of General Rommel, as a preliminary to the Libyan offensive of General Cunningham. The venture was most hazardous. In letters to his family, since published, Keyes has revealed that he did not expect to return from it; an assumption which proved correct. All the world now knows of his gallant death and of Rommel's lucky escape, due to his absence in Rome, where he was attending a birthday party.

Of the twenty-two members of Keyes's force very few were to fight again, but they paid for their lives and liberty with the blood of German staff officers and the disorganization of the enemy command. Keyes is dead, but no one will ever know how many platooons of Germans he caused to be removed from the front line for the protection of eminent brass hats. Laycock, one of the few survivors, was to tramp for over forty days in the desert until he contacted the advancing British forces.

The Special Boat Section role in this operation was arduous, if not spectacular. Two submarines were employed. Folboats were to land, reconnoitre the beach and return, giving the all-clear to the raiding party, whose rubber boats they would then guide in and help to hide. This part of the plan was successful, despite intemperate weather, but when, four days later, the submarines (H.M.S. *Torbay* and *Talisman*) returned for the prearranged pick-up, some very queer things indeed took place.

On the fourth night the agreed signal from the beach was seen, and an attempt was made by Lieutenant Ingles and Corporal Severn to land. This attempt failed, the rubber boat being washed adrift as soon as launched. Meanwhile the report came from the beach that twenty-two survivors of the Keyes's party were present, that they had no idea what had happened to the others, and that the collapsible craft in which they had landed had disappeared. No further boats for massive transportation being available, the submarine commander suggested that they should swim off to him at daybreak. This the survivors, some of whom could not swim at all, declined to do.

Dawn was now very near. The submarine submerged,

departed, and returned on the following night. This time, no signal from the beach was seen. Lieutenant Tommy Langton and a Corporal Feeberry went in to reconnoitre. Together they weighed 28 stones. They capsized in the surf and, after emptying their boat, found the beach deserted. Some distance away was a light—the correct colour, but not giving the correct signals. They walked towards it and were rewarded by a shout and signs of movement inland. On approaching closer, Langton and Feeberry saw nothing further. They returned to the folboat and paddled just outside the breakers towards the light. The glow of cigarette ends could now be seen beside it. This meant Germans, for special service troops, though often careless, do not smoke on enemy beaches when there is an immediate prospect of leave and a hot bath. Langton returned to the submarine in a sinking condition. Next day, through the periscope, he observed groups of enemy soldiers on the beach. They had captured the majority of the twenty-two survivors in their lying-up area on the previous day. Why they did not fire at Langton will always remain a mystery.

At the beginning of December, the formidable Roger Courtney, whose health was not good, returned to England, where he lost no time in forming a Special Boat Section, which proved a lusty infant from the date of its birth. This unit, with headquarters in the Isle of Wight, was destined to spend much time crouching under, and on top of, the cliffs of France. In fact, they specialized in cliff climbing and abseiling—means of descent with the rope secured in a certain way about the body. I well remember taking an inconspicuous part in a demonstration by this group in which some really extraordinary methods of cliff ascension were demonstrated for the first time. They included a harpoon gun with a rope attached, a fireman's ladder and a barrage balloon with a suspended basket. The balloon was most definitely not a success. Later 'English' S.B.S. were to go to the Far East—one of the first special service units to fight in that theatre.

As commanding officer, Courtney was succeeded by Captain Mike Kealy, later to go home and join him. These changes in high places do not seem to have disturbed 'Tug' Wilson overmuch. Somebody had put a veto on his railway attacks in Italy, but he had a new idea now—swimming. In the depth of winter (mid-December) he launched his folboat for the fifth time, and, leaving the comforts of H.M. Submarine *Torbay*, stole into Navarino harbour, Greece, accompanied by Marine Hughes. Enemy destroyers had been reported in the harbour, and Wilson and Hughes paddled twelve miles that night in search of them. No destroyers were located, for they had already moved, but as they paddled about the inner basin, the folboat was seen. Voices were heard discussing their identity, and presently six shots were fired at them at very close range. Wilson and Hughes left hurriedly.

Five nights later they tried again. Periscope observation showed an enemy destroyer lying off Navarino pier. The folboat approached to within 150 yards. Wearing a Mae West and carrying his limpet charges on a buff, Wilson slipped into the water. He proceeded very slowly, partly because of his many encumbrances and partly from fear of stirring up too much phosphorescence. The water was icy. Wilson's teeth began to chatter uncontrollably. He changed his weight-carrying arm in an effort to stave off general numbness. Marine Hughes, who had been peering anxiously into the gloom and paying out the line attached to the buff, now gave the cord a tug. The occasion hardly seemed to him suitable for the death of a perfectly good officer from exposure. The reluctant Wilson was pulled back into the folboat. With teeth still chattering, he wrote: 'I feel certain I would have been successful had I been able to withstand the cold.' This was his last major operation for S.B.S. Later, he found other fields to conquer. I wish I had not got to say good-bye to him.

Cunningham's offensive had been partially successful. Cyrenaica had been almost cleared, and the race-card for the 'Benghazi Handicap'—which was the name given to the annual sprint back to Tobruk—had not yet been issued. Life in forward areas of the desert was in that pleasant state of flux of which Stirling and his Special Air Service were later to take such happy advantage. They hired the S.B.S. now, folboats and all, and transported them in trucks through miles of sand-seas and not a few breakdowns, to attack shipping in the harbour of Buerat. Stirling himself led the party and destroyed his usual phenomenal number of enemy trucks. Captain Duncan with Corporal Barr comprised the S.B.S. contingent. Later, Duncan wrote, a little petulantly perhaps, that 'folboats appear hardly suitable for lengthy overland transport'. He left his damaged canoe on its carrier and, ignoring the harbour, laid, or caused to be laid, bombs on the twenty-three diesel trucks, eight small fuel dumps and a wireless mast and station. The sentry at the entrance to the perimeter was asleep when Duncan arrived. When Duncan left, the sentry was awake and smoking a cigarette. One hour later, when Duncan was three miles away and the explosives began to occur, the sentry was firing Very lights.

Several new men, later to become very prominent, were now joining the gradually expanding unit. One of the best of them, Captain Grant-Wilson, was drowned in an attempt to capture enemy pilots who had been shot down near Gazala. The weather was very rough, and this officer's folboat, containing himself and Jim Sherwood, capsized. Sherwood was finally rescued by Langton, after spending over five hours in the water, during all of which time he had supported the body of his officer in his arms. 'It was not,' wrote Langton, 'until I tried to get him out that I found he still had hold of Grant-Watson. The officer was dead.'

Others now present, though not yet conspicuous, were Corporal Pomford, a former 'Golden Gloves' champion boxer, Corporal Riley, an Irish Guardsman, David Sutherland, a lieutenant from the Black Watch, Captain Ken Allott, Lieutenants Eric Newby and Mike Alexander, and Corporal Booth.

The latter was sent for a busman's holiday in *Torbay* under a new policy of allocating S.B.S. men to submarines as spare machine-gunners in surface shooting matches. *Torbay* was lucky on that trip. A minesweeper and a schooner were attacked and sunk, 'But', complains Corporal Booth, 'owing to the accuracy of the submarine's crew, I myself didn't get a chance to fire'.

A few days later he did. *Torbay* surfaced to engage a supply ship, which opened up with a heavy gun amidships before the submarine's 4-inch could get into action. Corporal Booth cleared the crew of the enemy's heavy gun with his Bren. He then observed a party of men running aft towards another gun. He destroyed this party, too. Finally, he noticed a single figure on the bridge. 'I thought it must be the commander,' he said, 'so I let fly up and removed him immediately.' Corporal Booth received the D.C.M. for this exploit. The crew of the supply ship, which blew up a few minutes later, received harps.

Stirling was busy now. Some hanky-panky was going on in Benghazi, now Axis-held. Later, Stirling, Fitzroy Maclean, Randolph Churchill and others were to wander for hours round its docks, reprimanding Italian sentries for their slackness, casually laying explosives in interesting places, and playing bridge in a garret while the whole town was looking for them. But this present excursion, in which Ken Allott took part, established little more than the already obvious fact that canoes cannot be carried over rugged desert country except in shock-proof containers.

Great interest was being taken by G.H.Q., Cairo, at this time in the stretch of enemy coastline beyond the British-held positions at Gazala. A few weeks later the successful Rommel offensive, which rolled us back to Alamein, was to make this interest seem rather academic. But G.H.Q. who, perhaps, fancied that it was going to be *their* offensive, didn't know this, and Ken Allott, accompanied by Lieutenant Duncan Ritchie, R.N., was sent out to take a *shafti*.

They left Tobruk on 22nd May 1942, in an M.T.B. The same night, they were dropped with their folboat and stores off Cape Ras-el-Tin, well over a hundred miles away. Allott and Ritchie landed and lay up on a low sandhill about fifty yards from the beach. A few of the stunted bushes peculiar to Cyrenaica crowned the sandhill. There was no other cover. During the morning, nothing much happened except that Ritchie made himself thirsty by eating too much chocolate (I was at school with Ritchie and can well believe this), but at noon, a German staff car drove up. Three officers got out and bathed in the sea in front of Allott's position. Had these officers been more observant, they could hardly have failed to notice the marks left by the folboat where it had been dragged across the sand. Allott and Ritchie were having a quiet laugh about this when the sound of singing was heard, and no less than 200 German soldiers arrived at the beach in trucks.

There are times when that pretty tune, the 'Horst Wessel Lied', can sound most sinister. This was one of them. Allott and Ritchie watched the Germans indulgently as they performed strenuous physical training, but the smiles left their faces when the exercises gave place to games . . . and one game in particular: hide and seek. Those Jerries must have hidden and sought each other in every bush except the one behind which Allott and Ritchie were imitating the ostrich. The last party did not leave the beach until nearly six o'clock.

As soon as darkness fell Allott sent a radio signal. This, incidentally, was the first S.B.S. job on which a radio set was used. Allott himself does not seem to have had much time for the new-fangled contraption. That night, with the sea getting up a bit, as they reconnoitred the coast, he threw it overboard to lighten his load. Many have since wished to emulate his example: radios are liable to recall one urgently to base.

The remainder of Allott's trip was uneventful . . . but it was remarkable in this: that in rough seas, at night, and along a hostile coast constantly patrolled by enemy shipping, he covered a greater distance by canoe than has perhaps ever been accomplished in similar circumstances. The distance from Ras-el-Tin headland to Gazala inlet, where he was finally greeted by some astonished South Africans is 150 miles.

Just think that over next time you're paddling at Cannes, will you?

CHAPTER THREE

The month is now June, the year 1942. Rommel has won the Knightsbridge battle and captured Tobruk, with five-and-twenty thousand men in its perimeter. In the good old desert days of thrust and counter-thrust, of almost chivalrous warfare, British tank crews were wont to break off the battle at midday and to prepare their brew-up of tea in full view of the enemy, who, for his part, opened packages of *knackebrot*. But war was chivalrous no longer and, back in Tripoli, Mussolini waited impatiently, recruiting brass bands and striking medals for his entry into Alexandria.

Things looked bad . . . bad indeed. Auchinleck was re-forming on the Alamein line. Meanwhile, the other arm of the German pincers was sweeping down through the Caucasus. It was the enemy's last major offensive throw, though nobody knew this, nobody knew whether the British and Russians would hold; and in G.H.Q. Cairo, mountains of documents were placed in packing-cases. The S.B.S. were briefed for some very confidential work indeed, and David Sutherland, Tommy Langton, and Eric Newby were sent to Syria to reconnoitre beaches in anticipation of an enemy occupation of that country.

The plan was called 'Aluite'. It was very comprehensive. Hundreds of papier mâché rocks, more convincing, more mossy than any slab of limestone, were manufactured in the Middle East and transported to the Lebanon shore, where they were to cover dumps of arms. If the Germans reached Syria, special service troops were to remain in the area and fight as guerillas. The Germans did not reach Syria. Imperceptibly, the flap subsided. Business was about to be resumed as usual.

One man who remained quite unmoved by the German advance was David Stirling. The fantastically extended enemy lines of communication gave his now well-established Special Air Service remarkable opportunities for raiding, pillage, and destruction. His mobile columns, often in collaboration with the Long Range Desert Group, were rip-roaring and rampaging hundreds of miles behind the lines. Nothing was safe from them, be it soft transport, aeroplanes, or armour. The policy so splendidly initiated by Keyes was paying dividends. For every one man in the front line the enemy was obliged to retain two on guard in his base areas. The Afrika Korps was wearing out its boots on sentry duty.

David Stirling was the military Marks and Spencer. Like some vast organization of chain stores his force grew . . . and grew . . . and kept on growing, nourished by success, fortified by prestige and an intriguing aura of mystery. He had by now given it a cap-badge, a blue affair with a white commando dagger and the words 'Who Dares Wins' beneath it. All his men were now parachute-trained (Stirling, with Corporal D'Arcy of the S.B.S. had made the first jump in the Middle East himself), and with the cap-badge went a pair of wings, which officers and men who had done exceptionally well on operations were allowed to wear on their chest. When he considered that he had done well enough, Stirling awarded them to himself. One day, on the steps of Shepheard's, he met General Auchinleck. 'Good heavens, Stirling,' said the General, 'what's that you have on your shirt?' 'Our operational wings, sir,' replied Stirling, saluting smartly.

'Well, well,' observed the General, 'and very nice, too . . . very nice, too.'

The insignia of the Special Air Service had received its official blessing.

Stirling's emporium was full of assorted toys. Jeeps were scarce, but Stirling had them. He had everything, and he worked to get it. Explosives were in short supply, but Stirling had thousands of pounds of plastic and thermite bombs. Naturally, he also had the best Royal Engineer officer in the Middle East: Captain Bill Cumper, a regular soldier with a tongue like the bite of a centipede. I know this to my cost. Once, much later, I stole some explosive from Cumper. He caught me. On a certain occasion, Cumper was clearing mines near Mersa Matruh. A party of officers stood watching him. These officers made the mistake of laughing.

'Mersa,' snorted Cumper contemptuously, 'Mersa . . . I remember this hole in '35.' The officers who had come out for Wavell's first offensive grew pale beneath their tan. They bit their moustaches, patted their corduroy trousers. They slunk away.

At the beginning of June, the S.B.S., still under Mike Kealy, were given the job of destroying petrol and aircraft on three aerodromes in Crete. This contact coincided with a decision by Stirling to destroy petrol and aircraft on a very large scale in Cyrenaica. A conference was called. Stirling saw no reason why all the attacks on the many different targets should not be co-ordinated to take place on the same night. Further, he had been training his own seaborne squadron, under Captain the Earl Jellicoe, for some time, and he considered that it would be a good thing for them to take part in these raids. S.B.S. were not really very pleased about this, but to oppose Stirling was like trying to stop a steam-roller with a banana. Accordingly, they gave in gracefully and Heraklion aeordrome, the most succulent target on the island, was allotted to Jellicoe.

Under Stirling and Major Paddy Mayne, who has quite certainly destroyed more aeroplanes than anybody living, the Special Air Service duly made its attacks in Cyrenaica. Six airfields were honoured by a visit and a total of thirty-four planes and forty German and Italian soldiers removed from further participation in the war; this, quite apart from the odd bomb dumps blown up, trucks riddled with bullets and set on fire, aero-engines in packing-cases mutilated and hangars left looking as if they had been struck by a hurricane.

The purely S.B.S. side of these combined operations went equally well. George Duncan, wearing a pair of his famous

33

breeches and accompanied by Barnes and Corporal Barr, landed near Cape Trikala in Crete, and were met by Captain Tom Dunbabin, of M.O. (4). The target, Kastelli field, was briefly reconnoitred and, no reason being seen for delay, the party went in, to emerge with a bag of eight planes, six trucks, four bomb dumps, seven petrol and two oil dumps. When the bomb dumps exploded, at least seventy Germans are reported to have been killed. The next day all the guards in the area through which the raiding-party had made their entry and exit, were shot for carelessness.

This was a very sweet job indeed.

David Sutherland, with a party including the dour Guardsman John Riley, was not so lucky at Timbaki. Intelligence supplied to him had omitted to mention the fact that this field had now been abandoned. Sutherland spent several pleasant and—in view of the fact that he was to return there the following year—useful days on the island.

At Maleme, Major Kealy, accompanied by Ken Allott and Sergeant Feebery were unable to make their attack at all. 'The 'drome,' he reported, 'was heavily guarded and completely surrounded by wire, with machine-gun posts and searchlights in various positions.' He might have added that the wire was electrified. No one has ever been able to raid Maleme. In its prime there were so many police dogs about that the place sounded like Crufts on show-day. It cost the Germans 10,000 men to capture Maleme, and Germans don't forget such things. Major Kealy brought eight New Zealanders out with him, survivors from the fighting of the previous year. Everybody who went to Crete brought Kiwis away with them.

This leaves us with Jellicoe. A word about this Jellicoe. I once met a man who had met his tutor at Cambridge. That sounds very roundabout, but it is always instructive to glean details of people's private lives before the Army grabbed them ... For all I know, Stirling may have spent his childhood shooting at gamekeepers for amusement. Well, this tutor described Jellicoe as he was in those days; he described a thick-set young man, with an interesting pallor, with studious leanings and an intensity of manner which one feels must have caused many a débutante to rattle her tea-cup and saucer together from nervousness.

How we do change . . . or perhaps how differently we approach the respective problems presented by Plato and Thucydides on the one hand and that of blowing up a Junkers transport aeroplane on the other. Jellicoe, at this stage of his career was about twenty-three years old, brown as a nut, with a nose like the Iron Duke's, and an extensive capacity for irony. He was acting second-in-command to David Stirling, and was one of the few people, apart from Major Paddy Mayne, who could cope with that diverse and volcanic personality.

Never content to plan merely for to-day, Stirling had incorporated Greeks, Frenchmen, and even German interpreters in his motley force. An expansionist by nature, he foresaw the time when these men would come in useful. Jellicoe, who spoke their language reasonably well, had four Frenchmen with him now. They were Commandant Bergé and three other ranks. A Greek guide, Lieutenant Costi, accompanied his party. His target, as I have written, was Heraklion.

The six men embarked in H.M. Submarine *Triton* from Alexandria. Four days later they were in position some miles to the east of Heraklion. Here a periscope reconnaissance was made and a suitable beach was selected. During the remainder of the day, Jellicoe slept, and the French ate melons, of which there were large quantities on board. When they had finished a melon the French threw the rind on the floor, where the crew in due course tripped over it. Some ill feeling was caused.

At ten that evening the party paddled ashore in captured German rubber boats. One of these leaked badly: Jellicoe, always very nattily dressed, sacrificed his best service dress cap as a bailer. When land was reached he weighted the rubber boats, swam out to sea, and sank them.

The party had an extremely long and arduous march, and their tempers were not improved by occasional encounters with Cretan peasants, who insisted on greeting them in English. To forestall this they asked every Cretan whom they met, in German, to produce his identity card. Very few Cretans were deceived.

As always happens in enterprises of this nature, only about half the ground estimated was covered on the first night. At dawn they rested in a cave. The Greek and the three French privates slept. Jellicoe and Commandant Bergé, who had taken too much benzedrine, sat unhappily in the entrance to the cave. They shivered. It can be very cold in the early morning in Crete.

As evening approached, Bergé and Costi put on some natty but quite un-Cretan civilian clothes, and went off to the top of a hill to have a look at the target. They counted nearly sixty-six planes, mostly Ju 88's. They returned and the party moved off, leaving Costi behind at the cave, which they arranged should be their first rendezvous after the attack.

They had intended to attack that night, but the approaches to the field were most awkward and liberally sprinkled with sentry-boxes. Moving through a ravine, they were challenged from one post, lay still, moved on, and were soon challenged from another. It was decided to abandon the attack for that night. The party, who were very sensible about matters of comfort, lay up in a combined orchard and vineyard. Jellicoe and Bergé took more benzedrine. The others ate some grapes and plums and were rewarded by symptoms of colic.

At night, after having secured water from a peasant girl, Jellicoe moved off again. He soon negotiated the outer defences of the field, entering close beside a German barracks, and was about to cut his way through a second belt of double dannert when a German patrol came down on the other side of the wire with a torch.

The leading member of the German patrol did not observe the intruders, but the man following him was more wideawake. He spotted Jellicoe's large and curly head and wished to know what it was doing there. His manner was distinctly old-fashioned. Jellicoe was about to improvise some reply when Corporal Mouhot, a Breton, had an inspiration. He committed a ghastly, lingering, drunken snore. Apparently satisfied—such behaviour being quite normal in those parts—the Germans moved off, murmuring among themselves.

No time could now be lost. As Jellicoe correctly aniticipated, the Germans would return. The party cut their way through the wire and hid themselves in a bomb dump about twenty yards on the farther side. Presently, the same Germans did indeed return, accompanied by others. The gap in the wire was noticed, and a discussion took place concerning it. Jellicoe was doing some quick speculation about prison camps and heaven, when an unhoped-for interruption occurred. A flight of eight Junkers 88's was landing. Behind them came an R.A.F. Blenheim, making the correct signals and zooming over the field to drop its bombs. The bombs missed the airfield, but they caused some very welcome confusion. Profiting by this confusion, the party slipped away into obscurity.

A few minutes later they were roving round the fringes of the runway, laying charges on the aircraft in the bomb-proof shelters. Sixteen aircraft in all were dealt with in this area before the party moved across to the northern dispersal tracks. Here, although delayed by the searchlights which illuminated the runway periodically for returning aircraft, they dealt with a single plane ready to take off and a Fieseler-Storch reconnaissance machine to one side of it. Some trouble had been expected with the mobile sentries who patrolled the field but, in fact, these proved easy to avoid.

The first charges—ninety-minute delays had been used— were now exploding. A bare two hours remained before daylight. Jellicoe and his colleagues approached the main German barracks, where they mingled with the slightly harassed occupants. A dozen or so members of the ground staff were leaving the aerodrome to patrol the road. Jellicoe followed them, and, on the way out, laid the remainder of his charges on sundry lorries.

The whole party escaped successfully from the aerodrome. Almost they escaped entirely but, three days later, Bergé and his French companions were betrayed by a Greek who had invited them to dine with him. The Frenchman resisted arrest and one of their number was killed. The casualties sustained by the Germans in this raid are not known, but it is pleasant to note that the traitor was later liquidated, and his body thrown down a disused well.

Jellicoe and Costi were taken off from the south coast in a small caïque by Lieutenant John Campbell, R.N.R. They had climbed two ranges of mountains and walked 120 miles.

These losses in personnel, severe as they were, left the strength of the S.B.S. untouched. Almost immediately, however, they were followed by others which all but crippled the unit and led to its temporary incorporation in the Special Air Service. In July it was decided to send a party to Malta to attack Sicilian targets. George Duncan led it and was accompanied by Eric Newby, Sergeant Dunbar, Guardsman Duffy, Corporal Booth and others. Duncan wasted little time in Malta and the Germans wasted little time in Sicily, where they captured him with his entire patrol on the night after his landing. Current raids were beginning to sound like the story of the Ten Little Indians; but the worst was yet to come: 'Tug' Wilson, paddling with malice aforethought around Tobruk harbour was seen and captured by a patrol boat. Fortunately, Marine Hughes, too sick to accompany his chief at the time, survived to outlast almost everybody ... but chairs and tables were now being drawn closer in the sergeants' and officers' messes, and lorry-loads of kit were going down to Alex for future transportation to next-of-kin.

Military units react in very much the same way as individual human beings to disaster: they do something quickly. Thus it was that Captain Montgomerie, a new man, but accompanied by Sherwood, Barnes, and Mike Alexander, was briefed to land on the North African coast near Daba and destroy a large store dump about 1½ miles inland. This was extremely tricky work. It must not be imagined that because S.B.S. always seem to land successfully that landings are therefore easy. In this case, Daba, seat of a forward fighter aerodrome and general staging-point, was next to no distance behind the Alamein front line. Tents were pegged down neatly at ten-yard intervals on the sandhills above the beach. To reach their targets the raiders had to pass these tents, and others; to pass a German mobile cinema and a canteen full of happy drunks brandishing bottles of beer brought at great expense from Pilsen. Some of the pairs never reached their objectives at all. These laid their delayed-action bombs on tents, trucks, fuel-oil barrels, even a cook-house furnace. Montgomerie dealt with the dump and some captured British transport, but when he returned to the beach, Mike Alexander and Corporal Gurney were found to be missing. They were not to reappear. Gurney, surprising a German post, had been wounded by machine-gun fire. Alexander had remained behind in the hope of saving him. Both were taken prisoner.

The occupational risks were now becoming clearer. As Andy Lassen, the king of house-to-house fighters, was to say much later, 'You can do it some of the time for quite a while, but you can't do it all the time for very long'.

CHAPTER FOUR

The town of Beirut lies on the last and least-known creek of the vast Mediterranean, of which Alexandretta is the fundament. The French did not build Beirut but they modernized it, planting rich and stately avenues, installing comparatively noiseless tramways and building many hotels, two among which are incomparably the best in the Middle East. Beirut has few flies and is not noticeably malarial. The harbour is excellent and was used throughout the German war as a base for naval coastal forces and for submarines. You can eat civilized French food in Beirut, and people do not pester you . . . as in Palestine . . . to sell them guns. The Lebanese are a pleasant, industrious people who wash both themselves and their clothes. Beirut is the Levantine Toulon, a city which, indeed, it closely resembles. Behind Beirut rise the glorious mountains of the Lebanon . . . in winter you can ski down from the cedars almost to the city itself . . . in summer, if you have antiquarian tastes (Jellicoe had them) the ruins of Heliopolis are not far away.

Towards the end of August 1942 a small party of S.B.S. assembled in Beirut. They were led by Ken Allott and David Sutherland, supported by Sergeant Moss, Corporal McKenzie and Marines Duggan, Barrow, and Harris; and completed by a Greek officer and two Greek guides. Greeks, from now on, were to form a customary component of most S.B.S. operations.

A greater contrast than that presented by Allott and Sutherland it would be impossible to imagine. The nicknames by which British squaddies call their officers are often revealing, sometimes embarrassingly so. Allott was known everywhere as 'Tramp' Allott, by reason of his utter disregard for the conventions of dress. A razor blade, to Allott, was something with which you picked at a rope before splicing it. He could sometimes be coaxed into Service dress, but only with great difficulty and the promise of beer; Sutherland, on the other hand, was known as 'Dinky' Sutherland. He could sleep for three nights in the hold of a caïque and emerge neat, well groomed, cheerful, having used his last mug of tea to wash and save himself. Sutherland was a regular officer; he had served in France, been through the Commando mill in Arran, and come abroad with 'Layforce'. He was slight, sandy-haired, with a serious, freckled face. He spoke only when he had something to say.

The objective of these licensed brigands was Rhodes. Elements of Middle East Commando had carried out a costly raid upon the satellite island of Castelrosso in the previous October, but the capital of the Dodecanese had yet to feel any shock more severe than that of an occasional light bombing. Rhodes contained two large airfields. The first, Marizza, lay in the north; the second, Calato, somewhat to the south-east. From these airfields, German Junker and Italian Savoia-Marchetti bombers were annoying our Mediterranean convoys; every machine accounted for meant a quieter run for merchant seamen.

The party left Beirut in the Greek submarine *Papanikolis* on the last day of August 1942. The voyage of four days was passed in cramped boredom and in language difficulties. On 4th September a periscope reconnaissance was made, the landing-beach verified, and that same night the patrol put ashore in conditions of flat calm from three Carley floats and a folboat.

The usual under-estimate of time taken to cover distance now made themselves felt. When looking at a map in conditions of comfort at base, wishful thinking, however sternly abjured, is inevitable. A fifty-pound pack, a dark night, a mountain with a razor edge, which was but a contour until two hours ago, make up the difference.

Hercules himself would lag behind his schedule.

On the first night the party covered only three miles, on the second five, and on the third, five again. They did, however, reach a cave which they considered a suitable rendezvous before splitting up; Allott being about to continue north to Marizza, Sutherland moving down to Calato. One reason for this slow progress was the incompetence of the guides, who at first maintained that they knew the way, but later openly confessed that they were ignorant of their surroundings. 'One can hardly blame them,' wrote Sutherland, 'since they volunteered to come on the operation at great risk to themselves. No guide, however, is better than a bad one.'

On the night of 7th September Allott's party moved off towards Marizza. Sergeant Moss, normally David Sutherland's 'mucker' and strong-arm man, accompanied them, since only he knew sufficient Italian to converse with the guide. Sutherland himself moved off a little later. He had time to spare: the attacks were not due to take place until 12th September, the rendezvous with Allott was not due until the 16th. Two days later, he was lying-up on the mountainside, overlooking the aerodrome and the entire valley in which it lay. Water was now the main problem, and the carriage of it involved contact with the civilian population. The guide, however, was reassuring: he could barely tell a goat-track from a secondary road, but he seemed either to know or to be related to everyone in the area. Much useful information about the enemy defences was forthcoming, and meals of fruit, cheese, and bread were provided. At night the party, who numbered six, slept in groups of three. The position of 'centre' man was much coveted, for it was very cold.

On the target night the party was further split up, Marines Barrow and Harris being allocated to Lieutenant Calambakidis, the Greek officer, and Marine Duggan accompanying David Sutherland. The guide was instructed to withdraw to the rendezvous with all spare stores. The two sections separated on the dry bed of a river, close to the aerodrome. 'From that moment,' wrote Sutherland, 'I never saw any of 'B' party again.'

It was now very dark, with pelting rain: ideal for concealment, if not for comfort. Sutherland had thoroughly pin-pointed his targets from the mountain-side, and now had only to approach them. By the side of the first, a Savoia-Marchetti bomber, a sentry was standing. Sutherland waited. At midnight the sentry obligingly moved off, and Sutherland laid bombs on this aircraft and on two other bombers alongside of it. Crossing some wire and an anti-tank ditch, he walked down a path between buildings and the main landing-ground. A sentry stepped forward, challenging and shouting. Duggan nudged Sutherland and they withdrew into the obscurity. To be discovered at this early stage might compromise the other party.

Investigating cautiously, Sutherland found a petrol dump. He adorned it with bombs, adding some more to the aircraft which he had already attacked, and withdrew. By the time he was back in the river-bed three bombs were exploding, followed shortly afterwards by those of the other party. From this moment onwards explosions were frequent. A red glow spread over the rainy sky and fifteen separate fires were visible. These fires spread. Ammunition, bombs, and material of all kinds in the vicinity of the planes caught alight. From the runway the wailing of enraged Italians could be plainly heard. Searchlights swept the bay and the foothills. Panic-stricken though they were, the enemy seemed to realize that this had been a ground attack. The very considerable garrison spread out in all directions. At about three in the morning Sutherland heard the sound of automatic fire from the north-west, to which a Thompson gun was replying.

'B' party were in the bag—or dead.

Sutherland's guide now began to give trouble. The searchlight beams were worrying him and he would not move. Since the man could easily pass as a civilian, Sutherland decided to leave him. Sutherland made his way back to the rendezvous. Here he contacted Captain Tsoucas, the second of the Greek officers. Together, at first light, they observed the damage done to the airfield. The wreckage of burnt-out aircraft and fuel dumps lay everywhere. At 0900 hours, a large aeroplane landed, and was immediately surrounded by ground staff running from all sides of the field. A general had arrived to tot up his losses.

Sutherland now moved to a position above the beach selected for re-embarkation. He had seen signs of intense enemy activity in the plain, and wished to head off Ken Allott before he ran into the danger zone. Allott, however, was not to arrive: he had penetrated the very stiff defences of Marizza and done his job, but was to be captured with all his men as they reached the beach. Early in the afternoon of the following day, Marine Duggan spotted twenty-four soldiers advancing in the direction of the lying-up area. They were accompanied by civilians. The three men seized what kit they could carry and ran over the crest of their hill, eventually arriving on a small sloping ledge fairly high up the mountain, with a well behind it. They had not even had time to conceal themselves here before a number of small parties appeared round the foot of the mountain.

The second arm of the pincers had arrived and was closing in.

Sutherland lay with his two comrades in the open, not daring to move. It was now obvious that one at least of the guides had been captured and forced to reveal the point of landing and embarkation. This was afterwards verified. The information was obtained by torture. The Italian search-parties moved slowly, combining the bare slope. One group passed not more than ten or fifteen feet below the crouching fugitives. The enthusiasm of the enemy was evident, but their reasoning was at fault. Unaware of the height which a man with liberty at stake can climb in five minutes, they presently resumed their fruitless patrolling of the lower slopes.

An hour or two later, Sutherland observed a boat coming down the coast from the direction of Lindos. He identified her as a motor torpedo-boat of the Baglietto class. On the fo'c'sle a small group of soldiers were standing, evidently a landing-party. Disappearing behind a cliff, the M.T.B. cut off her engines. Presently, she emerged towing three black objects which were only too easily recognizable as the British party's Carley floats.

Sutherland and Duggan were now in a dreadful position.

They were, and had been for three days, without food. They were without any means of re-embarkation and, with the beach compromised and the hunt at its hottest, it would be very difficult for the submarine to put in for them at all. Sutherland decided that his only chance was to go down to the beach, where some Mae Wests and signalling torches had been hidden in a cave.

Tsoucas was left with the haversacks by the well. At nightfall Sutherland and Duggan moved off. They succeeded in slipping past the enemy sentries, recovered a torch and lifebelts from the cave and made their way back. Meanwhile a very large enemy party had moved into position between themselves and Tsoucas, with the evident intention of waylaying Ken Allott and his party when they should attempt to reach the sea.

The area in which Sutherland and Duggan could move freely was now small indeed. They crouched under an overhanging rock, and at dawn observed about fifty enemy soldiers not far away, who were talking and shaking out their greatcoats preparatory to moving off. These men again searched the whole neighbourhood, and one sat for five minutes on the rock under which Sutherland was lying. The sun was now very hot, and both men were enduring agonies from thirst and from the cramped nature of their hiding-places. Shortly after midday, they heard the sound of shots from the direction of the cave. Much shouting followed, and all the troops in the area seemed to converge towards the beach. Sutherland and Duggan lay low until dusk, when they moved on promptly with the intention of reaching the shore before the night patrol took up its position.

They were successful: no enemy were to be seen, but Tsoucas, who should have joined them, did not arrive and had obviously been captured. At 2130 hours, Sutherland sent out his first group of recognition signals. Duggan said that he thought that he had seen a faint reply, but could not be sure of this . . . actually the reply had been flashed through the persicope of the submarine, which was still submerged. At 2200 hours Sutherland at last received a positive acknowledgement and replied with the words: 'Swimming

45

. . . come in.'

The pair inflated the Mae Wests, entered the water and swam for about an hour in the direction of the signals, Duggan occasionally replying to them with his own torch. The sea was very calm, 'But,' wrote Sutherland, 'our physical condition for such a swim was hardly adequate'—a statement which is scarcely surprising when one considers that neither man had eaten for five days nor drunk any water for two.

They swam one and a half miles. Eventually they heard the sound of engines, but when these died away they were very near to abandoning all hope. 'However,' wrote Sutherland, 'we encouraged each other to continue, for we would not, in any case, have had the strength to return.' Numb, haggard, starved, and utterly exhausted, they were discovered by the submarine about five minutes later and helped on board. They were taken below and the submarine submerged, to be immediately depth-charged severely by the Italian destroyer which was hovering in the vicinity and the source of the 'engine noise' which the swimmers had heard.

Next morning they reached Beirut, where Sutherland was found to be dangerously ill. It had not been my intention to intersperse this book with gratuitous comment, but of this operation I can only say that it is a privilege to write it. Further, the devotion to duty shown by all ranks in H.M. Submarine *Traveller* in standing by for over two hours in dangerous waters cannot be too highly praised.

Ken Allott, Moss, the two Greek officers, Marines Barrow and Harris and others paid with their liberty, but the price which they exacted for it was heavy. Marizza and Calato airfields, in Rhodes, were in the hands of the repair gangs for two weeks.

CHAPTER FIVE

Weakened by these losses in personnel and without any really valid case for separate existence, the S.B.S. was now swallowed temporarily by the Stirling octopus . . . a vigorous and amphibious creature which was stretching its tentacles in almost every direction. For some time both organizations had been living and training at Kabrit, in Egypt, and the amalgamation was merely a matter of form. Stirling's Special Air Service, in which every man was parachute-trained, now consisted of four squadrons—'A', under the redoubtable Paddy Mayne; 'B', under Peter Oldfield, who was later captured, with Vivian Street deputizing; 'C', under Richard Lea; and 'D', under Tommy Langton. This last squadron, with George Jellicoe, was to form the new seaborne element. All available members of S.B.S. were drafted to it together with a troop from the Greek Sacred Squadron (Colonel Tsigantis), which had recently come under Stirling's sphere of influence. As soon as he was fit enough, David Sutherland took this last motley collection of bodies up to Syria, where they underwent a course of training: a course which was later to become standardized.

Meanwhile, General Maitland-Wilson, commanding 'Paiforce' in Persia, had sent a request to General Alexander for a Special Air Service unit to be placed at his disposal, capable of operating on skis in the Caucasus. The general idea was to place a group of specialists at the disposal of the Russians should the Germans threaten the Armenian passes. General Alexander passed on this request to Colonel Stirling, who sent one of his officers, Captain Fitzroy Maclean, to Baghdad, with instructions to recruit and train men. Maclean, who was a Member of Parliament, had done well on Stirling's most ambitious Benghazi raid. He possessed a fair knowledge of languages and was later—as Brigadier Maclean—to become something of a British legend in Yugoslavia.

We shall hear more of this group later.

Tommy Langton, with that fragment of S.B.S. not in Syria under Sutherland, was now called upon to take part in the great autumn raid of 1942 upon Tobruk harbour. This was a very ambitious operation indeed, involving the offshore co-operation of the destroyers *Sikh* and *Zulu* and the landing of parties from motor torpedo-boats at various points.

On 22nd August 1942, a squadron of the Special Air Service left Cairo in seven three-ton lorries for Kufra Oasis. They were accompanied by detachments of Royal Engineers, Coastal Defence, Signals, and anti-aircraft units, and were later joined by a patrol of the Long Range Desert Group under Captain Lloyd Owen. The intention was to drive into Tobruk in three of these lorries, disguised as British prisoners-of-war, with a guard made up from members of the party dressed in German uniforms.

The lorries were intended to drive along the south side of Tobruk harbour, then to halt in a secluded *wadi*, where the troops would de-bus and divide in two parties ... Lieutenant-Colonel Haselden (commanding the group) was then to attack positions on the west side of the bay; Major Campbell, his aide, to capture the positions on the east. Meanwhile, Langton was responsible for signalling in the M.T.Bs. and meeting the landing-parties as they came ashore.

The entrance went smoothly. No check posts were encountered. After de-bussing and sorting their stores, the German uniforms were hidden and the two parties set out. Langton, with a section under a Lieutenant Roberts, had not gone far before a rifle shot was heard, evidently a warning. Roberts took his section round the back of the hill and discovered a number of Germans about to man a machine-gun. He killed them. At the same time, the success signal, a Very light, was fired by Lieutenant-Colonel Haselden's party. Langton and his men now became intrigued by a small building which they judged, correctly, to be a wireless station. This was destroyed and the personnel inside it dispatched, again largely by Lieutenant Roberts.

Langton now went down to the beach alone and began to signal to the M.T.Bs. There was no definite reply. While thus occupied, he had left his haversack and tommy-gun upon a rock and, on returning, found them missing. A moment later he almost walked into two well-armed Germans. 'I hit them,' he said, 'with my revolver.' The Germans ran away.

Farther down the coast Langton found two M.T.Bs. which had succeeded in getting ashore. They were already unloading. He borrowed another tommy-gun and resumed his signalling. The alarm, however, had now been given, and searchlights were sweeping not only the harbour, but also the shore. Langton found the lingering inquisitive beams definitely unpleasant, but he was in a happier position than the M.T.Bs. still at sea. 'I could see the tracer positively *bouncing* off them,' he said.

Dawn was now breaking. In the growing light, in this devastated town 800 miles behind the front line, Langton spotted one of the M.T.Bs. ashore some distance away. He hailed her but received no reply. Thinking it time to contact the main party he made his way up the hillside. A platoon of Germans lay blocking his retreat some three hundred yards away. Prudently, Langton returned to the M.T.B. and boarded her. The ship was deserted. Langton filled his water-bottle and made a breakfast of bully and biscuits. While he was munching, Lieutenants Russell and Sillito and Private Hillman and Watler came on board. A conference was held, and it was decided to put the ship's guns to some practical use. Accordingly, Lieutenant Russell opened up with the twin Lewis-guns forrard against the now more aggressive Germans on top of the hill. The Germans disappeared.

Private Watler, a mechanic, now made an attempt to start the ship's engines, but this was quickly seen to be a hopeless task. By no means discouraged, the five men embarked in one

49

of the assault craft lying alongside the ship and paddled sedately round the bay pursued by heavy but inaccurate small-arms fire from the astonished enemy. Parties both of Germans and British could be seen playing hide-and-seek in the rocks and caves of the harbour. From one point the smoke of heavy explosions was rising. Far out at sea, H.M.S. *Zulu*, with H.M.S. *Sikh* in tow, was limping home under shell-fire. The position was confusing.

After he had put what seemed to be a reasonable distance between himself and the enemy, Langton beached his assault craft and, leading his party, crossed a couple of minefields and discovered about twenty survivors of the raid in a deep *wadi*. From there he was able to obtain some idea of the sequence of events: the action led by Lieutenant-Colonel Haselden had gone remarkably well. A number of strong-points had been captured and the enemy manning them exterminated, with the unfortunate exception of four Italians, who had run off towards the town shouting the alarm.

Germans are always reluctant to move by night, but at dawn they had effectively counter-attacked with a force of not less than a battalion. Lieutenant-Colonel Haselden's party had taken to their trucks and attempted to escape, but were ambushed and halted, with the exception of Lieutenant Barlow, who drove straight through the road-block, dismounted and brought his two Lewis guns into play from the flank with terrible effect. Many men were now wounded or dead. Lieutenant-Colonel Haselden, therefore, shouted to those who were left to charge the enemy. He led the charge himself and was killed by a grenade a few yards from a party of screaming Italians, who did not live to boast of their exploit. Lieutenant Barlow rallied the now tiny force and withdrew with them under heavy enemy fire. Farther to the left, Lieutenant Roberts and his section had been left behind to deal with some concrete gun-emplacements. That they dealt with them there can be no doubt; no man was to return to base from this detachment, but in one night's work they had accomplished more than many people in the entire course of the war.

The survivors in the *wadi* now split up in the interests of safety. They made for the Tobruk perimeter. Twenty-five strong when they set out on their march, only three men were to reach safety. These three were Langton and Privates Watler and Hillman. For the first few days they followed the desert road, dodging German camps, being fired upon frequently by patrols, sleeping at night in caves. Finally, desperate from hunger and thirst, they reached an Arab village, where they were hospitably received, fed, and given water.

The next stage in their journey was less arduous. The Arabs passed them from village to village, informed them in good time of the approach of enemy patrols and reconnoited the ground ahead. One night, when they were lying up close to the sea, a boat put in, and a voice shouted, 'Any British here?' Langton and his companions, who had already observed a large *carabinieri* post close to this point, were not deceived.

After three weeks, Sergeant Evans, who had accompanied the party and marched gallantly despite acute dysentery, became too ill to go any further. He was carried to the road at night and left to be picked up by the enemy in the morning. One of the two Fusiliers Leslie, who were twins, suffered the same fate a night or two later; his brother elected to go with him into captivity. That left only Langton, Hillman, and Watler who, with ten water-bottles, some bully-beef and some goat meat, started on the last long lap on 26th October.

Three nights later they crossed the frontier wire between Cyrenaica and Egypt. On 13th November they were picked up at Himeimat, 400 miles to the west of Tobruk. They had been marching for seventy-eight days, the greater part of the time with bare feet. The only comment made by Langton when congratulated upon his great feat was that he wished he had been better supplied with world news. Had he known that Montgomery was about to break through at El Alamein he would have attended the Eighth Army in comfort among the Arabs. A party was held in his honour, at Kabrit, towards the end of which Major Mayne drove a jeep through the mess. Casualties were slight.

Now to Persia: while Langton was marching, Sutherland and Jellicoe training, and Stirling heralding the advance of the Eighth Army by raids far in advance of their forward elements, Maclean was slowly gathering about himself an extraordinary force in the heat and stench of Baghdad.

Maclean arrived in Baghdad in 1st November 1942. His first, and most important, acquisition was Lieutenant J. S. F. (Stewart) Macbeth, who obtained release from his duties as A.D.C. to General Anderson in order to join the new unit. Macbeth was a young man of a type so far unknown and very badly needed in the S.B.S., whose officers, although admirably forthright, were too prone to call a spade a bloody shovel in quarters where it was best referred to as an agricultural implement. Macbeth was tactful, possessed considerable charm of manner and, if never quite able to prove black white, could always be relied upon to make a creditable attempt. From now on, he was to become the unit's professional diplomatist, smoother of ruffled feathers and envoy extraordinary. The congenial relations which have always existed between the S.B.S. and its various employers can very largely be attributed to this officer.

Various other officers were recruited, but the majority were recalled by their units before leaving any definite mark. The interest lies rather in the men, the first large such batch to be enrolled which had not come out from England already trained for special service duties. They were drawn on a volunteer basis from the adequate regiments then stationed in Persia. Scotsmen and Irishmen predominated, as Scotsmen and Irishmen will always predominate in any raiding-force drawn from natives of the United Kingdom. I do not know why this is so, but it is a universal truth. Jocks are deadly in drink and can smash café tables more quickly than any other troops, but they can also carry greater loads and carry them farther. Micks are incurably sentimental, obstinate as bedamned, but, well-officered, will go anywhere. At no time have these two nationalities formed less than sixty per cent of the S.B.S. fighting effective. Most of the Irishmen, incidentally, have always come from the south.

For their training, Maclean took his men into the

mountains. Here they were joined by Captain Bill Cumper, whom Stirling had sent over to teach them the use of explosives. Cumper, who never travelled anywhere unless accompanied by at least ten hard-bitten assistants and several tons of stores, arrived in state like some Oriental panjandrum. It was a good many years since Cumper had been in any climate more equable than that of the Libyan desert. The mountains met with his disapproval.

'Damned cold here,' he remarked.

The following morning he watched the first efforts of some novices attempting to ski. Cumper's expression was sceptical. He delivered his course of lectures and as soon as decently possible returned to the warmth of Egypt.

All training and, indeed, all planning was suddenly cut short by the loss of David Stirling in Tunisia. Leaguering for the night with his column, he had been betrayed, and surrounded by the enemy. Not until many days later did the Germans discover that they had in their hands the officer whom, beyond any other, they had desired to capture.

CHAPTER SIX

We are now at the end of what must be called the 'Legendary' period. Documents, of course, have survived from that golden age—dog-eared, yellowing operational reports and instructions, crumpled scraps of paper covered with scribbles from Tom to Harry and Harry to Dick, an occasional sketch-map, but for much of my interpretation of those early, buccaneering days I have relied upon unit folk-lore and upon the interrogation of survivors. The S.B.S. was now to become, at least outwardly, respectable: it began to keep a war diary.

With the capture of Stirling chaos ensued. That is not too strong a word for it. A great and powerful organization had been built up, but it had been an organization controlled and directed by a single man. Stirling alone knew where everybody was, what they were doing, and what he subsequently intended them to do. When he disappeared, his Adjutant, Captain Bill Blyth, Scots Guards, spent nearly two months clearing up outstanding business. A consignment of jeeps would arrive: Stirling had ordered them and had obviously earmarked them for somebody, but nobody now knew for whom. The squabbles over the precious transport would become bitter, to be interrupted for a moment by a party reporting from Sousse or Tabarca or the Fezzan and demanding further instructions. No one except David Stirling and their commander was absolutely sure what they had been doing there in the first place.

These were not the results of inefficiency, but of control by a powerful personality with a hundred different irons in a very cramped fire. Stirling, alone, had known the whole story. His capture was catastrophic.

This difficult situation was dealt with in a sensible way. It was recognized at once that the organization could not carry on as formerly constituted. To replace it, and to continue its work, the majority of Stirling's men were formed into a new unit: the Special Raiding Squadron, under the command of Major Mayne, D.S.O. Simultaneously the S.B.S., regaining its separate identity, was glorified by the title of 'Squadron' in place of 'Section', and was commanded from this time onwards by Major the Earl Jellicoe, D.S.O. Both units now moved up to Palestine, where they established their headquarters at Azzib, north of Haifa. Both retained the cap-badges, the curious beige beret and the wings adopted by Stirling, and both owed allegiance to the all-over direction of Raiding Forces: Commanding Officer, Colonel H. J. Cator.

With the subsequent history of Major Mayne's group we need concern ourselves but briefly. In the summer of this year (1943) they did excellent work behind the lines, first in Sicily, then in Italy. In the autumn, they returned to England, to repeat these exploits in France, Germany, and, finally, Norway.

George Jellicoe began his long tenure of office by the selection of a camp, coupled with administrative reforms. The camp chosen lay at Athlit, south of Haifa, where a long stretch of golden sand terminated at the foot of a Crusader's Castle. Here the S.B.S. moved on All Fool's Day 1943, and here it was reconstituted into three Detachments—'L', under Tommy Langton, from Kabrit; 'M', under Fitzroy Maclean, from Persia; and 'S', under David Sutherland, from Syria. Each detachment henceforth consisted of five patrols, ten strong, increased by two signallers and commanded by an officer. In addition, the leader of each detachment retained a headquarter patrol for his own use. Total fighting strength, therefore, was in the neighbourhood of 230 men, to which must be added the numerous administrative personnel, referred to unkindly sometimes as 'base barnacles', but without whose work no squadron would ever have been able to take the field at all.

Inter-detachment rivalry was from now on very keen, but seldom bitter. It was seldom bitter because the many subdivisions of the unit made rivalry difficult and finally ridiculous. Two young gentlemen, sitting before their beer in the canteen, would vociferously proclaim the supremacy of their particularly detachment, but no sooner had they established their unanimity on this point than they would begin to argue about the merits of their respective patrols. Actually, all three detachments were very much alike, and their records reflect rather the opportunities which they were given than any merit peculiar to themselves. When they first came to Athlit, however, Maclean's detachment was regarded—and perhaps regarded themselves—rather as being apart. They used blanco extensively, wore a shoulder-flash, and shined their brass. Blanco was always viewed with healthy suspicion in S.B.S. As for shoulder-flashes and other insignia common in England, these were felt to be the height of ostentation, and were liable to call forth remarks about Christmas trees. When I, myself, came from Italy I was still wearing the badges of my previous unit. They were numerous, they were garish, they were large. I made the mistake of walking into Bill Cumper's office.

'My God, look out ... the commandos are here,' he shouted, and diving for his Lüger, attempted to shoot out the lights.

Jellicoe's former contacts with 'Layforce' and his personal prestige in Cairo and London were soon to be of value. Laycock, after his adventures on the Rommel raid, had gone home and was now commanding the 1st Special Service Brigade in England, with the rank of brigadier. He had not, however, forgotten his desert days, and in April 1943 he made S.B.S. a present of two officers from 62 Commando, then being disbanded.

One of these officers was to kill or capture more Germans in the Eastern Mediterranean than any other man and finally to exert a direct and personal influence upon the re-deployment of enemy garrisons.

His name was Anders Lassen. By birth he was a Dane and

at the outbreak of the war had been a cadet in his country's merchant service. Stranded in England, he joined the British Army, where he was discovered by Marsh Phillips, who was at that time recruiting for a rather peculiar piece of business in French West Africa. Three German merchantmen, of respectable tonnage, were lying under Vichy-French protection in waters not far from Dakar. The party moved down to Nigeria, sunk two of the ships with limpets and made off with the third. On the voyage home it was observed that, while all the other members of the band were officers, Lassen was only a lance-corporal.

'I think we'd better have you commissioned, Andy,' said Phillips gruffly.

In this way Lassen gained his first pip.

He had not been back in England very long before somebody saddled him with about fifty of his compatriots, including his brother, with instructions to take them up to Achnacarry, the Commando depot in Scotland, and to train them.

'Well . . . *did* you train them?' I once asked him.

'Yes, of course. But I got bored with them. I told them to go home.'

As a matter of fact the Danes took his advice; they ultimately did excellent work for the underground movement in their own country. Lassen himself returned to Marsh Phillips and followed him upon many of the very successful and daring raids which 62 Commando were then making upon the French coast. It was Lassen and his fellow recruit to S.B.S., Phillip Pinckney, who were responsible for the celebrated attack on the Island of Sark, which resulted indirectly in the chaining of British prisoners-of-war.

'It is not tro-o-oo that we stuffed the mo-o-thes of the prisoners with mud,' Lassen used to declare indignantly. 'We stuffed their mo-o-thes with gra-a-ass.'

In the spring of 1943 Phillips and nearly all the veterans of 62 Commando lost their lives in a *coup de main* near Boulogne. They had been taken prisoner and were killed 'while attempting to escape'. Unfortunately for many Germans then lying snugly in their bed, Lassen was not in this raid. He was to live to cause much discomfort.

Pinckney, Lassen's fellow-passenger from England, was not, unfortunately, destined to stay long in S.B.S. In the summer he was sent for by 2nd Special Air Service in Tunisia, worked with them in Sicily, and in the autumn dropped by parachute on the Brenner Pass, where he blew a railway tunnel, but was later captured by the enemy and shot in direct violation of International Law. His death was not established until long afterwards. Not a few S.B.S. men have disappeared in this manner, and in some cases their fate remains obscure. This, when dealing with a ruthless enemy who used the word 'sabotage' to suit his own convenience, came to be regarded as an occupational risk. I have never heard anybody complain about it: rather it was said that since front-line infantry were under fire for much longer periods at a time, it was but right that the 'private armies' should face this additional hazard.

Philip Pinckney's stay, though brief, left its mark. He was a food specialist, and would spend hours in the fields collecting snails, slugs, grasshoppers and other apparently inedible faunae. These he would mix with dandelion salads, shallots, and nettle leaves, and eat to the accompaniment of draughts of rose water. Sometimes he would oblige his patrol to share these delicacies, and in consequence, they lived in terror of him.

'You must learn to live on the land, Sergeant,' boomed Pinckney, seizing the wretched man and forcing a slug down his throat.

Some of his other ideas about food were less unorthodox. It was Pinckney who experimented with elements of Arctic and composite rations and worked out a satisfactory diet for various eventualities. This, although suffering perpetual modifications, was finally adopted as the standard for operations—despite a certain amount of grumbling from David Sutherland, who had a fixed, and I am sure, erroneous, belief in the value of oatmeal and raisins.

The S.B.S. in its final and modern form was slowly emerging. Officers and men were being recruited and actually *staying*; not returning to their units for one reason or another after a few weeks. Stirling had instituted a thoroughly democratic but somewhat disruptive system in which the value of officers, in particular, was assessed, not so much by their own protestations and apparent achievements, but by what their men thought of them. After a given operation under a new officer, Stirling would drink a glass of beer with the wretch and then stroll over, Judas-like, towards his sergeant:

'Well, Sergeant X, and how did it go?'

If Stirling found any cause for dissatisfaction, the officer—and sometimes the sergeant too—were very rapidly seeking fresh fields for their talents. This system worked, but you had to be damned good to know where you were with it. When I began to write this book I asked not to portray anybody as leaving the unit under a cloud. That was a reasonable request but, in my opinion, an unnecessary one. You either are or you are not suited for raiding work. The number of medals won by ex-members of the S.B.S. is in no way smaller than those gained by men who stayed in it.

One officer who joined S.B.S. at this time deserves special mention. He was Captain Milner-Barry of the somewhat flamboyantly named Transjordan Frontier Force. Milner-Barry was unusual in that his age was considerably above that of the normal officer, who had in many cases leapt into the Army almost from the cradle. For this reason, Milner-Barry was universally and libellously known as 'Papa'. In private life he was an official of the Shell-Mex Company, and Palestine, that dreary breeding-ground of Jews and Arabs, was for him a second home. Milner-Barry was exceeded in tact and diplomatic experience only by Macbeth. Jellicoe, who had a dislike of Personal Appearances, believing quite rightly that the good wine should be kept until last, frequently used the pair of them as his envoys. Their departure or arrival anywhere, together, was to launch many a rumour.

Towards the middle of July, Maclean left the unit and embarked upon a gilded Balkan future. Jellicoe chose as his successor Captain J. Neilson Lapraik, M.C., an officer in the tradition of Roger Courtney, who had served in Abyssinia with distinction (he had received the ribbon of the Lion of Judah from the Emperor himself), and who had recently been in Malta training a small force of Commando troops. Lapraik brought with him Lieutenant Dion, 'Stud' Stellin (why he was called 'Stud' I leave to your imagination) a tall, wiry New Zealander, who possessed the curious distinction of having served in all three fighting services. Stellin and Lassen are probably the luckiest acquisitions which Jellicoe ever made.

Those days, those quiet, sunlit days in the spring of 1943, were some of the most pleasant which the unit ever spent. Training never became a fetish under Jellicoe: its object being solely to keep the soldier fit and to equip him for battle as an individual.

We shall see the results of that training. Up to this moment the Germans across the narrow sea have felt only occasional pinpricks. From now on they are subjected to continuous pressure and to a war of nerves, which their frantic reshuffling of garrisons is to increase rather than to diminish.

CHAPTER SEVEN

The first fixture of that season was a perennial affair. Crete had been raided in 1942, was to be raided again now, and again in the following year—always at approximately the same season. When, finally, the German occupation of the island collapsed and the garrison retreated into the northeast corner, elements of S.B.S. were, appropriately enough, present to invest and harass him.

It had now become fashionable, even in the Middle East, to give operations a code name. This one was called 'Albumen', and the execution of it was entrusted to David Sutherland's detachment. As in the previous year, the objective was the enemy aerodromes—Kastelli, Heraklion—from which bombers harassed our Malta-bound food convoys.

On June 22nd David Sutherland landed near Cape Kochinoxos on the south side of the island. He was accompanied by a dump party and two patrols under Lassen and Lieutenant Kenneth Lamonby. Five nights later, reconnaissances having been made and information collected, a third patrol was infiltrated under the command of Lieutenant Ronnie Rowe, Scots Guards. This was the famous 'Irish' patrol, containing such deadly customers as Corporal Henderson and Guardsmen D'Arcy and Conby, all three veterans of 'Layforce'.

This operation being somewhat diffuse, I shall follow Lassen, who, leaving the dump on 23rd June, set off for Kastelli aerodrome with Sergeant Nicholson, Corporal

61

Greaves, and Gunner Jones among his party. Very little of interest took place during his approach march (very little ever *does* take place during approach marches: they are merely boring). All attacks were to be co-ordinated in terms of time, and on D-minus-one Lassen was duly lying-up and observing his target.

He saw eight Stukas, five Ju 88's, a few fighters and some old reconnaissance planes. The Stukas were obviously main target, but the local inhabitants, who were friendly, pronounced them impossible to attack. Each plane, they said, had three guards sleeping in shifts, and, as evidence of this, they pointed to the guard-tents situated among the planes. They further declare that since the attack in the previous year a ring of sentries had been posted round the runway. 'This', said Lassen, 'I considered to be a stupid exaggeration.'

Nevertheless, he modified his plan, determining now to send Nicholson and Greaves to attack from the east while himself and Jones created a diversion from the west. 'Diversion' is what Lassen called it: actually he was to offer something approaching a full-scale battle.

At 2230 hours on the following night he cut his way through the perimeter and, followed by Jones, walked along the taxi-track, which made a half-circle round the Stuka shelters. At intervals he halted and observed. About seventy yards away he could see a fire with a group of Italians sitting round it: the Italians were singing. Lassen left the taxi-truck and was immediately challenged by a sentry, whom he bluffed by pretending to be a German officer. A second sentry then approached him, with whom he employed the same ruse.

Lassen passed three sentries in this manner and was passing the fourth when a shot was fired by one of the men whom he had duped. The last sentry immediately came to the 'on guard' position. 'I distracted his attention by pointing to the fire,' said Lassen, 'and shot him twice at close range, in the stomach, with my automatic.'

The fat was now properly in the fire. At least twenty men were firing in Lassen's direction. He withdrew towards the perimeter. Half an hour later he was back again. 'I had noticed,' he said, 'an area where everything seemed to be quiet.'

The area was not quiet. A ring of men surrounded the pair and subjected them to a considerable amount of chivvying. Lassen replied with a grenade or two, then slipped away: 'I had seen another area which seemed to be quiet,' he said.

He entered it and was at once challenged. 'I went up to the man,' said Lassen, 'and disposed of him.' Very lights were now being sent up and, as Lassen had foreseen, reinforcements began to arrive from the eastern side of the airfield. His work was now over. He withdrew as he had come—with deliberation—pausing to lay some bombs on a large caterpillar tractor and pursued by heavy but inaccurate small-arms fire. Next day, while resting, he was betrayed by some villagers and chased into the mountains by a German patrol. Here he lay up for eighty hours without food.

Meanwhile, Sergeant Nicholson and Corporal Greaves, who had already cut their way through the wire, heard the shooting on the far side of the field and guessed that Lassen was at work. Unobserved, they lay bombs on a two-seater observation plane but, on approaching its neighbour, found three sentries in conference. Creeping cautiously they dealt with Junkers 88 about twenty yards away. The firing in the distance was now very heavy. Very lights were rising. Nicholson and Greaves lay low for ten minutes, then advanced and placed a bomb on a Stuka. A sentry saw them and fired. Nicholson and Greaves ran into some trees. Here they discovered a petrol dump, which they garlanded with more bombs. Several bombs remained so Nicholson walked out and succeeded in laying one on the Stuka guarded by three sentries. As he retreated, a truck drove up, disgorging a party of Germans who scattered in all directions, shouting. This was very stupid of the Germans for it left the remaining Stuka unguarded. Nicholson laid a bomb on it, found Corporal Greaves and began to withdraw. Searchlights were now covering the perimeter wire, but the two men succeeded in getting through it unobserved. Three days later they were back at David Sutherland's base after a pursuit which, at times, had been very close indeed.

Rowe, at Timbaki, found—as had the party in the previous year—that there were no planes and nothing to attack. He returned disconsolately to base. Lamonby, at Heraklion, seeing no planes worthy of attack on the field decided to devote his bombs to a large petrol dump in the vicinity.

This was not an easy target, for the sentries were numerous and accompanied by dogs. Lamonby, with Lance-Corporal Holmes, laid bombs on pits containing 200,000 litres of petrol. He was undetected, withdrew successfully and later joined Lassen in the mountains.

The enemy, however, had learnt much from his experiences in the previous summer. On this occasion he did not, as then, waste time and men in a futile combing of the hills and valleys close to the targets. Instead, he rushed large and mobile forces to the south coast, where he felt reasonably sure that the raiders would attempt to re-embark. He was undeceived by glaring headlines in the Cairo newspapers and by radio reports to the effect that the various parties had been successfully withdrawn on the night following the attacks. These reports, though no doubt well meant, succeeded only in causing the Germans to redouble their vigilance.

On 10th July, when all expeditions had returned to the dump, Sutherland was informed of considerable enemy activity in the area. His situation was precarious and was complicated by the presence of a large number of vociferous and undisciplined Cretans, who had attached themselves to his forces. Leaving Lamonby's patrol to keep these people quiet, he spread out the others in preparation for the inevitable clash.

Presently, two Germans were seen approaching along the *wadi*. Conby and D'Arcy stood up and the two men were captured without bloodshed. While they were being searched, however, the Cretans observed two more Germans some distance away and, as Sutherland put it, 'being for once in their lives upon more or less equal terms, could no longer restrain their exuberance'. The Cretans blazed away with their ancient weapons while the two Germans, quite unmoved, retreated towards the sea, making skilful use of cover.

With re-embarkation imminent, the noise occasioned by this skirmish was extremely distasteful to Sutherland. Accordingly, he dispatched Lamonby with four men to stop the firing, if necessary by force, and to prevent the escape of the two Germans. In the first part of this task Lamonby succeeded: the Cretans withdrew reluctantly, sulky that their fun had been spoiled, but obedient. Lamonby then sent his men back to the shore and began a private stalking match with the two Germans.

Up and down the scrub-covered rocks the three men moved. At last Lamonby saw one of his opponents. He fired, killing the man. Simultaneously the second German, who had been well concealed, fired, killing Lamonby. These facts were unknown by Sutherland, who sent out search-parties and spent a considerable time in an attempt to locate the missing officer.

The boat (H.M. Motor Launch 361, Lieutenant R. Young, R.N.V.R.) arrived that same evening. The return voyage to Egypt was without incident. At Groppi's, Sutherland and Lassen, who were on their way to report, stopped off for an ice-cream soda. The German prisoners were present and, not wishing to leave the two men in the truck unguarded, Sutherland took them inside.

So many curious uniforms are to be seen in Groppi's that nobody noticed anything strange.

Towards the middle of August 1943 it became obvious to all that Italy, if not yet actually out of the war, was tottering and must soon capitulate. An operation was therefore immediately planned and mounted with the very exiguous forces at the disposal of G.H.Q., the intention being to obtain rapid and effective possession of the key island of Rhodes. This operation was known as 'Accolade', and involved the infiltration of the entire strength of S.B.S., reinforced by elements of Long Range Desert Group and Mayne's Special Raiding Squadron. These forces were to capture and hold various strong-points, whereupon the 8th Indian Division would be landed and assume control of the island. With Rhodes and its airfields in our hands, the remainder of the Dodecanese, chain-garrisoned almost exclusively by Italians, would not, it was felt, offer serious resistance.

There remained one imponderable: the degree of co-operation, or failing co-operation, resistance likely to be offered by the Italians when the news of the armistice and its terms became known to them. Admiral Campioni, Governor of Rhodes, was known to be a weak personality: vain, vacillating, easily (as things turned out, *too* easily) influenced. If Campioni could be persuaded to surrender his island peacefully, much time, and much blood, might be saved. It was decided that the attempt was worth making. A small mission was hastily assembled, and Jellicoe and two other officers instructed to drop by parachute in Rhodes and begin immediate negotiations. Colonel Turnbull, officer in charge of the mission, was to follow with the remaining members of it, as soon as the initial negotiations had commenced.

Meanwhile, as a welcome sign of some positive action after a great deal of discussion, Sutherland and his detachment moved up to Castelrosso, easternmost of the Dodecanese, and occupied that island without opposition on the morrow of the armistice.

After a delay of one day caused by bad weather, Jellicoe dropped near Marizza airfield in Rhodes from a Halifax bomber, on the night of 9th September 1943. He was accompanied by Major Dolbey, official Italian interpreter at G.H.Q., and by Sergeant Kesterton, a signaller.

The events of the following hour were exceedingly unpleasant. A stiff breeze was blowing and the three men fell widely apart. Dolbey, who was no youngster and who had never made a parachute descent before, was unlucky enough to land on the metalled surface of a main road. He broke a leg. Jellicoe and Kesterson received only a severe shaking, but were subjected to very heavy fire from the ground as they floated down. The Italians had received no warning of the arrival of the mission and, indeed, believed them to be Germans.

Dolbey, immobile, and in great pain, was discovered by an Italian search-party to whom he explained the position. A second search-party was sent out to look for Jellicoe. He was found suffering from acute thirst and nausea. Believing himself surrounded by a hostile patrol, he had eaten, and somehow succeeded in swallowing, General Maitland-Wilson's personal letter to Admiral Campioni.

Once convinced of their initial mistake, the Italians proved charming and accepted the strange situation with composure. Dolbey was immediately sent off to hospital. Jellicoe and Kesterson were hospitably entertained in a near-by officers' mess until transport arrived to take them to the Governor's palace, where they were immediately introduced into the presence of Admiral Campioni.

The interview which now took place—at two o'clock in the morning—must surely be one of the strangest of the war. Dolbey, who was carried in on a stretcher, interpreted Campioni, who received the party somewhat coldly at first (he had, after all, just got out of bed) and explained that the announcement of the armistice had come as a complete surprise to him—indeed the first news of it which he had received had been through the wife of a German officer who had heard it on the radio. He seemed, on the whole, willing to resist, but pointed out that his troops, numbering 35,000 were widely dispersed and short of transport. The 10,000 Germans, on the other hand, were concentrated in the neighbourhood of Rhodes town. On the night of the armistice a German from the staff of General Klemann had sought an interview with Campioni and an agreement had been reached whereby troops of both armies were to remain in their respective positions. The Germans, of course, had at once dishonoured this pledge, throwing out mobile columns in all directions and occupying the landing-grounds of Calato, Cattavia, and Marizza. According to Campioni, an order to resist these attempts at infiltration had been issued, and fighting was even now going on in several areas. He demanded to know from Jellicoe what assistance was likely to be forthcoming from the British.

Jellicoe, who well knew that here lay the crux of the problem, did his best to put some heart into the old gentleman. Sugaring the pill in every possible way, he explained that while small bodies of parachutists and special service troops could arrive very soon, no substantial reinforcements of British troops could be expected in under six days.

On receiving this news, Campioni, as might be expected, became glum and petulant. He readily gave permission for the naval wireless station to be used to contact Cairo, placed a room, a bed, and a doctor at the disposal of Major Dolbey, but begged Jellicoe not to show himself more than absolutely necessary about the castle, not to leave it, and to don civilian clothes immediately.

It was apparent, in fact, that while the admiral—and some members of his staff in particular—were willing to resist, they had hoped to obtain some better guarantee of eventual success than that which Jellicoe was able to offer. These men were, after all, no heroes. Their lives were at stake, and upon their actions in the next few days depended their prospects of survival. They had vegetated very comfortably for three years in a pleasant and moderately secure island. They were neither the first nor the last to be found wanting in decision when the press of great events swept them beyond matters of petty routine.

Thus, the admiral vacillated, willing and anxious to play the British card (he asked for an immediate bombardment of Marizza and Calato airfields), but until that card was presented with a greater show of force to back it, obliged to continue his negotiations with the Germans, whose emissaries were now becoming more pressing. In his journeys about the place, Jellicoe had great difficulty in avoiding them and, during an air-raid alert, Sergeant Kesterson narrowly escaped sharing a shelter with a high German staff officer.

Radio contact with Cairo was now established and plans laid for the arrival of Colonel Turnbull and his party: they were to be flown to the neighbouring island of Simi by seaplane, and come on from there in an Italian M.A.S. boat. Meanwhile, intermittent shell-fire had been heard all day. Jellicoe had at first been favourably impressed by this, assuming it as evidence that the Italians were attacking the German positions. He was therefore seriously disquietened when one of the orderlies attached to him remarked casually that he could not understand what all the noise was about, as every shell was being fired out to sea.

Seeing that nothing further could be done for the moment, Jellicoe attempted to snatch a little sleep. He was awakened shortly after five o'clock in the evening by the Governor himself. Campioni stated that the situation had now seriously deteriorated. The Germans had confronted him with an ultimatum and were about to attack Rhodes town. In these circumstances he had given orders for Colonel Turnbull not to proceed beyond Simi. He reiterated his desire to resist, but said that, for their own safety, Jellicoe and his party must leave the island, remaining handy at Simi, or Castelrosso, until conditions should have improved.

Jellicoe, who realized that his continued presence upon Rhodes might well be embarrassing if the Governor were genuine—and pointless if he were not—agreed to go, but suggested with his customary wiliness that all available intelligence concerning minefields in the Aegean generally, and of the defences of Rhodes in particular, be placed at his disposition. This, Campioni could not very well refuse, and as additional evidence of his good faith, he promised to send Colonel Fanetza, his chief of staff, with Jellicoe, in order to inform Turnbull at first hand of the situation.

Shortly after dark a peculiar little party left the Governor's palace, dressed in civilian overcoats too big for them, carrying a wireless set, several bottles of Rhodes wine and a picnic-basket. They embarked by M.A.S. boat for Castelrosso, which was reached the following morning.

Here, after an arrival marred by an undiplomatic tumble taken by Colonel Fanetza into the slimy waters of the harbour, Jellicoe greeted Sutherland who, with his detachment, had just completed the occupation of the island, and learnt that Colonel Turnbull had left an hour or two previously for Simi. He breakfasted and set off for Simi accompanied by Fanetza, in the same M.A.S. boat.

This Fanetza, however, was a less amiable man than he had hitherto taken good care to appear. History is sometimes decided by small incidents, and in this case a brief immersion in the water was decisive, for Fanetza had not forgotten the involuntary smile with which Jellicoe had greeted his appearance, dripping and viscous, as he emerged from the harbour. While Jellicoe slept Fanetza instructed the captain of the M.A.S. boat to put about and return to Castlerosso, explaining his sly move later—when Jellicoe discovered it— by talk of a radio message received from Campioni.

No sooner had Jellicoe returned to Castelrosso than he received the news of the formal capitulation of Rhodes to the German Commander, Von Klemann. The main island had now, therefore, been lost, but there remained the others, hardly less important. Quick action might yet succeed in saving them from German occupation. The forces available—one detachment of S.B.S. and a few naval motor launches—were contemptibly small but, on the morning of 11th September 1943 Jellicoe, acting under orders from Colonel Turnbull, proceeded with sublime impudence to take over the Dodecanese.

CHAPTER EIGHT

Before I become further involved with the intricacies of the first Aegean campaign, I must go back some two months to another theatre and another climate. Events do not, unfortunately, always take place to the convenience of historians. To write the story of S.B.S. in something approaching chronological order is like with one of those tiresome naval splices: you tuck one strand of the rope away, another immediately wrestles free.

About the middle of June, Jellicoe, to whom distance was never any impediment—it was habitual to him to dine in Cairo one night and breakfast in Palestine the following morning, having driven some reluctant batch of victims across the Sinai desert all night—took a run across by sea to Tripoli, where the 2nd Special Air Service were training for some pre-invasional pranks in Sicily and the toe of Italy.

Those were stirring and somewhat equivocal days. Having driven the enemy from Tunisia, the Allies were endeavouring, by widely dispersed bombing raids, to cause the maximum amount of uncertainty as to their next objective. This, of course, was Sicily itself, but not a few arm-chair strategists in both camps were inclined to favour Sardinia, a belief which G.H.Q. were prepared to encourage with the diversionary forces at their disposal.

Accordingly, it was arranged that Langton's squadron— less Langton himself who was ill—should be dispatched to that infertile and malodorous island by the twin means of air and submarine. They would land shortly before the Sicilian invasion took place, attack the now familiar airfield targets and endeavour to cause confusion. Arrangements for their landing were excellent, those for their evacuation somewhat less so. In extensive operations, where men become necessarily expendable, detailed plans cannot always be laid for the re-embarkation of forty or fifty individuals.

Meanwhile, since the total strength of the squadron was not required for this operation, Jellicoe arranged for the remainder of it to be dropped by parachute with elements of 2nd Special Air Service, to disrupt enemy lines of communication in Sicily. I shall deal with the adventures of these men later.

In the absence of Langton, 'L' Squadron was commanded by Captain John Verney. Two parties were organized: the first under Verney himself with Captain Imbert-Terry as second-in-command, to drop by parachute north of Lake Tirso on 7th July; the second, under Captain Brinkworth, to land by sea a week earlier. Both these parties were introduced into the island successfully.

Verney and his party dropped from about 800 feet. On landing they marched east on a compass course and laid up before dawn in the hills above their target. The airfield lay in two halves, separated by a main road. Enemy patrol activity was negligible. That night the attack was made; Verney, accompanied by Lance-Sergeant Scott and Private Rogers going to one side of the field; Captain Imbert-Terry with Lance-Corporal Brown and Private Hand to the other. No sentries and no opposition were encountered. Bombs were laid in a number of planes and petrol dumps, and telephone wires were cut. The raiders had withdrawn and were almost in open country, when they were challenged by a German sentry. Verney walked up to this man and spoke to him. The German was left, muttering darkly, but apparently reassured.

The bombs were now exploding. The whole countryside seemed to be illuminated by the flames of burning petrol. Verney marched his party east, towards the coast. He would have liked to return to his original rendezvous, where he had left his heavier kit, but intense enemy patrol activity made this impossible. Instead, he calmly walked into a village where he bought eggs, cheese, and bread. As he sat eating them outside the local café, two young men came up and asked him if he wanted wine. Verney confessed that the thought of wine was very tempting to him. He followed the two young men, who took him to a house. From this house, *carabinieri*, heavily armed and to the number of twelve, suddenly emerged and surrounded him. 'What is the meaning of this?' demanded Verney indignantly. 'I am a German officer.'

'We do not believe that you are a German officer,' declared the *Maresciallo*.

'I am a German officer,' repeated Verney, 'and as for you, you can that and this and this and that and the other yourself,' and calling to his men he marched off, leaving the *carabinieri* arguing heatedly among themselves and quite unable to decide what to do.

Something rather similar was happening that day to Captain Brinkworth and his party. Their aerodrome had turned out to be as deserted as the traditionally deserted Timbaki, but Brinkworth was compensating himself for this disappointment by marching about the main roads in defiance of all training principles, watched by open-mouthed peasantry, who whispered '*Inglesi*' with awe, but made no attempt to obstruct him.

Brinkworth was just leaving one village after a hearty meal when he was approached by the commandant of the police, revolver in hand. To even things up, Brinkworth took out his own revolver and held it in his hand. He then began to speak German, which the policemen did not understand. Finally, they compromised on French. The policeman was just about to make a spectacular arrest when Brinkworth shook him warmly by the hand and walked off.

You can go a very long way indeed if you possess sufficient impudence. The adventures of both Verney and Brinkworth are due in a large measure to their inability to take the Italians seriously.

Three or four days later Brinkworth was halted by another and larger party of Italians. He approached them

73

courteously and spoke at some length in German. The Italians listened respectfully, shook hands all round and, as a sign of their trust, loaded the entire British party with figs. Brinkworth and his men marched off, munching figs and singing *Lili Marlene*. The Italians, however, appear to have been unconvinced. Presently, they ran after Brinkworth and begged him politely to come to the nearest village for the purpose of identifying himself. Brinkworth was furious: 'How dare you talk to a German officer in that way?' he shouted. He walked on. Greatly daring, the Italians fired a shot over his head. Brinkworth ignored this military solecism and presently was lost to view around a bend of the road.

Meanwhile, Verney and his men, tired of tramping, had secured a lift in a horse-drawn vehicle forming part of an Italian convoy. Whatever his hosts may or may not have thought concerning his identity, they were evidently unwilling to oppose their ancient carbines to the automatic power of his Thompson guns.

These adventures, obviously, could not continue indefinitely. The whole of northern Sardinia was now in an uproar. Reports spread, mysteriously, but like wild-fire, that the Allies had landed and captured several of the larger towns. Anguished police officials spent the greater part of every day answering telephone calls from frightened citizens who had seen large bodies of 'parachutists' wandering in the neighbourhood of their homes. Verney and Brinkworth were becoming something of a legend.

They remained at large, the former for eleven, the latter for seventeen days. Rather more than half the garrison of the island were diverted from their normal duties in order to search for them and, when found, very large bodies of men were needed to surround and pin them down.

When arrested, both parties were taken to the transit prisoner-of-war camp at Villagrandi. They were not well treated. The food given to them was abominable, their living quarters insanitary in the extreme, the attempts made to persuade them to reveal information most despicable and— worst of all— three men who were suffering from malaria were allowed to die of this disease for lack of proper treatment.

On 22nd August the whole party was transferred to Cagliari and embarked upon the Italian cruiser *Arditi*, destination Naples. From Naples they were taken by train to Chieti where, most unfortunately, the officers were separated from the men. Poor Brinkworth and Verney . . . if ever men deserved to escape it was surely these two. The enemy, however, were taking no chances with them. Within a week the pair were in Germany.

Not so the remainder of the expedition: their arrival at Campo 59, Servigliano, coincided with the announcement of the Italian armistice. After a certain amount of trouble with the guards, whose weapons had to be removed as they persisted in firing them, the whole party, less one or two sick men, made good their escape, and splitting up into small groups, marched south towards the allied lines.

Lance-Sergeant Scott, who had been with Verney on the airfield raid, marched the fastest. On arriving near Pescara, he was surprised to meet an old friend, Lieutenant McGregor of 2nd Special Air Service, who was present in this area, a hundred or so miles behind the front line, on urgent business connected with the evacuation of ex-prisoners of war.

Time hanging heavily on McGregor's hands, he suggested to Lance-Sergeant Scott and his companions that they might profitably join him in the shooting-up of enemy columns and transport until their evacuation could be arranged. Scott, who was accompanied by Privates McMillan, Rogers, and Johnston, agreed with alacrity. 'We had trouble with the Germans, killing four,' he writes. He does not, however, seem to have been unduly disturbed by this, and the incident provided his party with weapons.

McGregor, together with Captains Lee and Bailey, also of 2nd Special Air Service, was living with his men on the summit of a mountain, from which base they moved out almost nightly, destroying *carabinieri* posts and terrorizing the enemy garrisons across a wide stretch of countryside.

Eventually, towards the end of October, Scott and his companions were evacuated to Termoli, but hardly had this extraordinary N.C.O. reached the safety of his own lines, than he volunteered to return to enemy territory and assist in the evacuation of other ex-prisoners. There is an old Army maxim to the effect that one should do one's duty, but not stick one's neck out. Lance-Sergeant Scott very nearly proved this to be true. On his second excursion into German-held Italy, he became separated from his companions and, finally, made a perilous exit in a rowing-boat. He—and indeed all the survivors of Langton's squadron—then returned to England; the rule being that men who had once been taken prisoner in a given theatre of operations could not again serve in it.

The loss to the S.B.S. was very great: Langton's squadron had to be virtually re-formed.

Meanwhile, that fraction of it which had been detached to operate with 2nd Special Air Service in Sicily, on 12th July, had been victims of a bizarre but not unamusing accident. Owing to some mechanical defect, the green light (the signal to jump) appeared nearly ten minutes before the aircraft was over the dropping zone. A sergeant-major, coming aft in the Albemarle to dispatch the men, was startled to find the compartment empty.

On the ground the small S.B.S. contingent, led by Corporal R. A. (Safari) Summers, collected their equipment and set forth on an odyssey which was to last more than four weeks. Summers was a Cockney and possessed in an astonishing degree the Londoner's wit, stamina, and resilience of temperament. He was called 'Safari' because of the long stories of epic marches and feats of endurance which he was fond of recounting. Curiously enough, all these stories were true: very few men could out-march Summers, and nothing had ever been known to surprise him.

It was possibly this last quality, above all others, which preserved Summers and his companions from capture during over-long periods. 'We found a nice spot to lie up that night,' he writes. 'Looking on my map I saw that it was called Dell Inferno. This was a good name for it, too.' A few nights later, after laying booby-traps on various roads, he discovered an Italian lorry lying under camouflage in a country lane. 'We were a bit hungry, so we opened the boxes and pockets inside and had a look at the contents. In the front compartment we found some cigarettes.' Three Italians who had been sleeping near the truck, now woke up and demanded to know what was going on. 'I answered,' said Summers, 'with an old English expression.' The party walked away some little distance and examined their haul. 'It was very disappointing,' said Summers disgustedly, 'a pair of officer's breeches, a mess tin, and two *gas masks*.' In the kitbag he found two onions.

They now began to cut telephone wires. They cut a great many. Their relations with the Italian peasantry appear to have been cordial . . . 'He then cut up half a sheep for us,' or 'The vino we received at this place wasn't half bad.' Summers, in brief, was as much at home in central Sicily as he would have been on Southend sands. Methodically, he broke into deserted houses, removing the necessities of life with a thoroughness that Genghis Khan himself might well have envied.

Towards the end of the month, their stock of explosive exhausted, the party began to thread their way through the front lines. They passed groups of demoralized Italian soldiers, from whom they did not even attempt to hide. 'Some of them,' said Summers, 'kissed us . . .'

But the Germans were still resisting strongly, and the last stages of the journey were not without danger. On several occasions they were sniped. There was constant difficulty in negotiating minefields.

At last, nearing a wood, they saw the first British troops. Summers put his beret on his carbine, waved it and announced that he, too, was English. The soldiers—a platoon of the 2nd Seaforth Highlanders—were unimpressed. They obliged Summers and his companions to keep their hands above their heads for quite a long time.

'Nark it, mate,' complained Summers bitterly. 'Nark it.' When he was led before an officer for identification he was most indignant.

CHAPTER NINE

We must now return to George Jellicoe who, on the night of 12th September 1943 was sailing north into the Aegean in command of a miniature armada of assorted shipping and some fifty-five fighting men. Strange indeed was this week of compromise, treachery, and counter-treachery, furtive capitulation. It will always remain a matter for surmise as to which of the three parties most directly concerned—the German Balkan Command in Salonika, the British G.H.Q. in Cairo, and the Italian local garrisons—was the most unprepared when Badoglio and Umberto caused the hearts of a thousand brass-hats to flutter by their signature of a piece of paper.

For the Italians themselves it is difficult not to feel a certain sympathy. Let us take a hypothetical example: Captain Santini, commanding a company of Arditi in the remote island of Levitha might well, remembering his oath of allegiance to his King, wish to observe the terms of the armistice, surrender his troops and place himself at the disposal of the British authorities. But the problem confronting Captain Santini was unfortunately not so simple as this. Under his orders were two or three subordinate officers.

Of the views and political allegiances of these officers, Captain Santini was completely ignorant. For twenty years both he and they had paid lip-service to the doctrine of Fascism. Santini had new to decide, and to decide at once, how many of them he dared to take into his confidence.

Captain Santini was luckier than some other local commanders, in as much as there were no German troops on the spot to complicate the struggle of his conscience. Ten miles away, however, in another island, Ober-Leutnant Küchler, with forty men of the Brandenburg Regiment at his disposal, was watching the manoeuvres of Captain Santini with considerable interest. Ober-Leutnant Küchler even went so far as to pay a visit to Levitha in his motor launch. He drank a bottle of the embarrassed Italian's excellent Samos wine and explained to him gently but unmistakably, in terms laced with threats, that considerations of military necessity dictated a certain course of action. This course of action involved Captain Santini sitting tight, making no move which could be construed as hostile by his allies, and awaiting the arrival of German reinforcements.

Ober-Leutnant Küchler was, of course, both bluffing and playing for time, but behind his bold words he did at least possess the certainty that the power of the *Wehrmacht* would presently be brought to bear. Meanwhile he was damned if he was going to be betrayed by any scented and overdressed Italian. Captain Santini, for his part, possessed no such certainty in respect of imminent aid from his newly acquired British friends. Unpleasant stories, too, were beginning to reach his ears concerning the removal to another world of Italian officers in Rhodes, who had declared their sympathies too hastily. His inclination, prompted by thoughts of his wife at home in German-occupied Milan, was to do as Ober-Leutnant Küchler suggested. Captain Santini did not like Ober-Leutnant Küchler, whose neck resembled a dartboard, but he was very fond of Signora Santini.

And so it happened . . . islands in the Dodecanese where a German garrison was present, even in a small minority, were taken over without bloodshed from their former rulers. Rhodes, where Admiral Campioni was merely another more hesitant, more pusillanimous Santini, is a case in point. Other islands—fortunately more numerous—where no German garrison existed, fell, also without a shot being fired, under British influence. This was due in no small measure to the excellent work of Jellicoe and of Colonel Turnbull's

Dodecanese mission. Simi and Castelrosso had been occupied on the very day of the armistice. Forces were not immediately available to garrison other islands of strategic importance, such as Leros and Cos, but their commanders were canvassed at once and persuaded without much difficulty to throw in their lot with the Allies.

The stage was being hurriedly set, the alignment of forces was becoming more plain, but the struggle for the eventual possession of the Dodecanese chain had yet to be fought . . . and in that struggle the Germans were now to possess throughout the key airfields of Marizza and Calato in Rhodes.

Dawn of 14th September found Jellicoe and his armed fishing-fleet off the southern coast of Cos. The night had been uneventful, the Germans being too busy consolidating their position in Rhodes to patrol the channel between it and the Turkish mainland. Cos, which from a distance seems austere and forbidding, is in reality a beautiful and well-cultivated island. Behind the port, the roofs of the houses glittered that morning in the strengthening sun. A vast crowd collected on the quay to welcome the new arrivals, and as David Sutherland and his detachment stepped ashore, flowers were thrown and much *vino bianco* distributed and consumed.

Jellicoe himself remained only long enough in Cos to verify the peaceful intentions of the local commander. After breakfasting, he continued the voyage towards Leros in an Italian M.A.S. boat. He was soon to wish that he had not eaten. The breeze, light at first, freshened considerably. The little ship began to labour in the mounting seas, and conservation of the bridge became limited to occasional gloomy exclamations by the captain of:

'*C'est grave.*'

Jellicoe, who had never been in a craft of this kind, and who possessed, in any case, a sense of personal destiny unconnected with a watery grave, was not alarmed. Presently, however, it became clear that the M.A.S. was in serious difficulties. This was confirmed by the captain's final unredeeming cry of:

'*C'est pire.*'

Not until they reached the calmer water under the lee of Leros did Jellicoe feel completely reassured.

He landed in front of the Governor's palace and was escorted to see that dignitary. Jellicoe's ancestry made it fitting that he should specialize in admirals, and here was yet another. Admiral Mascheroa seemed friendly and co-operative, but Jellicoe was displeased to find the saturnine and ubiquitous Colonel Fanetza already at the Governor's elbow.

'I was very doubtful about this man's attitude,' he said, 'and anyway found him a disagreeable and odious character.'

Having sent off brief signals to Cairo and to Colonel Turnbull, Jellicoe accompanied the admiral on a tour of the island, and selected a dropping zone for parachutists and supplies. Returning to Leros town, he was guest at a banquet, during which speeches were made and toasts drunk with an assiduity which can only be described as Russian.

Comatose from food, wine and an utter lack of sleep, Jellicoe was flown back to Castelrosso by seaplane. His mission of five days' duration involving a parachute descent and incessant journeys by road, sea, and aeroplane was now at an end.

'I reported,' he said, 'the not unsatisfactory state of affairs in Cos and Leros, then slept very soundly for fourteen hours.'

To Sutherland's tiny advance guard presently transferred from Cos to Samos and later established in Leros, reinforcements of all kinds were now being added. In Cos, a general officer was actually about to arrive and battalions of the Royal West Kent Regiment and the Buffs, both formerly garrison troops in Malta, were sailing to serve under his command. Other troops were standing by, and it became apparent that the British intention was to hold Cos and Leros in force.

Meanwhile, a second mixed detachment of S.B.S under Major Jock Lapraik had already left Haifa on 12th September and after calls at Castelrosso and Cos were diverted southwards to Simi. Lapraik arrived off that island on the evening of 17th September, and sent Lassen ashore in a folboat to contact the Italian authorities. These latter, somewhat uneasy at the approach of strange shipping at nightfall, opened fire with two 20-millimetre guns. They were calmed by Lassen with a flow of four-letter words and later, more diplomatically, by Lapraik himself.

Lapraik, who was a lawyer in civilian life, was admirably fitted for this task. In brief interviews with the Italian military and civil commanders he issued his orders and a number of suitably worded edicts. He became, in effect, King of Simi, an island which he was either to rule himself or make uninhabitable for the enemy for the next three months.

Lapraik immediately directed S.B.S. to take up positions and, on the following morning, made a tour of the island. The Italian garrison, he discovered, consisted of about 140 all ranks. Their defence dispositions were quite sound, but somewhat ornate. Lapraik indicated improvements which might be made to them, and returned to Simi town to receive a deputation of the local inhabitants, nearly all of whom—as is the case throughout the Dodecanese—were Greeks by blood.

That a very lively hatred of the Italians existed among these unfortunate people was only too obvious. 'I let them know,' declares Lapraik in his Hansardesque manner, 'that wrongs would be righted in due course, that there would be equity for all, but that, for the moment, the efficient progress of the war rose above other considerations.'

Considerable friction, indeed, existed between the Greek inhabitants and the Italians, the latter threatening all manner of reprisals if the S.B.S. should leave the island. The trouble threatened to become serious when the Italians attacked a man for neglecting to salute the lowering of their flag at sunset. 'I sent for the Italian commandant,' declared Lapraik. 'I told this man, among other things, that his soldiers would not act in a way repugnant to British law and order. I said that a greater measure of respect would be paid to British officers.'

Meanwhile, to pacify the Greeks, he aranged to raise and

lower the British flag at the same time as the other. The population were asked to observe the joint ceremony, and did so, despite some surreptitious expectoration at the sight of the Fascist symbol. Lapraik was quite impartial: when a certain officer (*not* from S.B.S.) created a disturbance in a café by shooting at a portrait of King Victor Emmanuel, he had the culprit confined aboard a caïque and forbidden the future use of the port.

But Lapraik had not come to Simi to devote his entire time to civil administration. Towards the end of the month, he succeeded in handing over these duties to another officer. His intention throughout had been to make the island a base for raiding and reconnaissance parties; a role for which its proximity of Rhodes made it particularly suitable.

Lapraik wasted no time. His instructions were to discover what was taking place in Rhodes and, on 21st September he put 'Stud' Stellin and one man ashore through a narrow gap in the minefields near Villanova, with orders to carry out a reconnaissance. Five days later 'Stud' returned: his presence on the island had become known to the enemy, and he had been chivvied and harried from mountain to mountain, being exceedingly lucky to avoid capture. At the end of the month, Lapraik sent him in again and this time 'Stud' remained in Rhodes nearly three weeks. He collected some very valuable information and, once again, was very nearly made prisoner. A German patrol had surrounded the house in which he was staying. Fortunately a wedding had just taken place, and the guests were dispersing. 'Stud', his long legs concealed by masses of evil-smelling straw, was dumped with his three companions in a cart and removed under the very noses of the enemy.

Lapraik now had no less than six caïques at his disposition, manned partly by S.B.S. personnel and partly by Greeks, who were not afraid to enter enemy waters. He sent Lieutenant Bimrose and his patrol to Scarpanto to pick up the crew of a British bomber, who were reported to be stranded there. To Lassen he assigned the task of strengthening the defences of Calchi, an island lying only a few miles off the coast of Rhodes.

Lassen found Calchi garrisoned by only twelve *carabinieri*. He landed stores and ammunition for them, built barbed-wire barricades and machine-gun emplacements and, to tone up their muscles, made every Italian undergo an assault course. He concluded his visit with a brief lecture on tactics and a stern warning: 'When the Germans come here, as they will,' he told them, 'you will resist them. If I hear that you have not resisted, I shall return with my men and deal with you severely.' The *carabinieri* were so frightened by Lassen that when the Germans did actually come, a few days later, they resisted most strenuously and caused many casualties.

Each side was now building up its forces for the coming struggle. Outwardly, at least, the Aegean campaign was still anybody's battle, for if the British lacked men, the Germans lacked transport. Much, it seemed, would depend upon the will to resist the enemy of Italian garrisons in the British-held islands.

Meanwhile, at elephantine cadence, reinforcements began to arrive, on the one hand in Rhodes, on the other in Cos and Leros.

Towards the end of September, David Sutherland and his detachment were relieved on Samos by a battalion of the Royal West Kent Regiment. They proceeded to Calino, which island it was hoped would also become a base for raiding operations throughout the winter. Vain illusion! For months S.B.S. had been attacking Germans and could conceive for itself no other role. In the miserable and humiliating weeks which followed, the unit was to be employed largely on a ferrying force, expending its energy and the lives of some of its best men in nocturnal trips to Turkey, and in the successful defence of islands which it was later ordered to abandon. 'I have always felt of these operations,' said an officer who was in an excellent position to know, 'that the small risks such as the initial occupation of Castelrosso, Cos, Leros, and Samos by eighty men and two motor launches were gaily accepted, while the big, worth-while risk of scrambling for Rhodes was shirked.'

That statement is true and the judgement of posterity will prove it so. The British Army can afford to be frank about its reverses. It should be frank about this one. In the Aegean, the Germans—who never expected to win—won because having gained an initial advantage, they exploited it with a boldness and a sense of purpose which was conspicuously lacking in their opponents.

On 22nd October, the Germans invaded Cos. Fighting was fierce, brief, and bloody. Making full use of their local air superiority the enemy drove us from Cos town and occupied Antimachia airfield, the only remaining British fighter strip in the islands. David Sutherland, watching the struggle from Calino, four miles away, sent in Walter Milner-Barry and his patrol, who had just returned from a reconnaissance of Chios, to retard the advance of the enemy by demolitions. If resistance ended, Milner-Barry was to embark as many members of the garrison as possible.

Milner-Barry, on landing, discovered that resistance everywhere was indeed crumbling. But Walter had not been an official of the Shell-Mex Company for nothing: within a couple of hours of his arrival he had set in motion a system through which no less than 105 persons were evacuated. On eight successive nights his tiny caïques returned, dodging the vigilant German patrols, and embarking the small parties of men which he had collected. To provide more room on these boats for his final, weary passengers, Milner-Barry and some of his men decided to make the return journey by raft. The raft became water-logged. It sank. Milner-Barry and his patrol, fortunately wearing Mae Wests, spent most of the night swimming among the porpoises in the none too warm Aegean. They were removed from Cos on the following evening by more conventional means.

Meanwhile, Private Watler, who will be remembered for his long march with Langton from Tobruk, had succeeded in getting himself lost again. Placed on sentry duty, he spotted a group of Germans coming towards him. Not wishing to indicate by his own presence that of his comrades, Watler hid: when he emerged from hiding, both his patrol officer and the Germans had gone.

To a man who had already wandered about in enemy territory for eighty days, these facts were not necessarily depressing. Watler, who was thirsty, decided that his first requirement was water. Unfortunately, the wells were guarded and Watler was captured. He immediately pretended to be suffering from malaria, with the symptoms of which disease he was well acquainted, and was gratified to see that the ruse delayed his evacuation from the island with the main body prisoners.

Private Watler, who was confirmed in Cos Castle, was now tired of captivity. Using a length of electric wire which he had somehow procured, he slipped over the wall. Five hours later he was recaptured and put back in the castle. The same night the British navy shelled the town and Private Watler observed that no less than seven of the bastards (his captors) were killed and eighteen wounded by a projectile which landed in the courtyard.

Forty-eight hours later Private Watler escaped again, and by the same means. He went directly to the seashore and swam a couple of miles down the coast. Some Greek civilians provided him with a lodging for this and the following nights. While awaiting evacuation Private Watler employed his time in driving nails into German petrol barrels, and in this way emptying them.

As a result of this, and of his previous escapade, Watler became known to his annoyance as the 'man the Germans couldn't hold'. Satirical. Other ranks, posing as newspapermen, were continually asking him to give interviews, and locks from his hair were demanded—and taken—as mementoes.

CHAPTER TEN

Gratified by their success in Cos, the Germans immediately attempted to capture the apparently far more vulnerable island of Simi. Lapraik, however, was ready for them. At first light on 7th October, a caïque was observed attempting a landing in Pedi Bay. This caïque was immediately engaged and put out of action by Lapraik's Bren guns on School Hill.

Reports now began to flow in from other beaches. The Germans had landed in force and succeeded in occupying the southern ridge of the island. By 0600 hours, the Italians were falling back before them, cautiously pursued by Fascists wth megaphones who called upon their compatriots to surrender and lay down their arms.

In this emergency, Lapraik sent Lassen and the Irish patrol to rectify matters. Lassen began the day's work by capturing a veteran German sergeant who had served in the desert and at Sevastopol. Two privates who were following behind this man also fell into Lassen's hands. Simultaneously the Irishmen disposed of three other Germans who were advancing nonchalantly a little way off.

So heartened were the Italians by this example that they began to resist with new vigour. They were aided by what is euphemistically described as the 'advice and backing' of Lassen's patrol. In point of fact, Lassen stood behind the Italians with his gun and permitted no further withdrawal.

By 0800 hours the enemy were held in the upper part of Simi town. Lapraik now decided to establish a Bren position on the southern ridge itself, but while attempting to do this, one man was killed and another wounded. It was here, too, that Lieutenant Charles Bimrose received the first of the long series of flesh wounds which were to mark his whole career in S.B.S.

Lapraik now sent Captain Clynes, his second-in-command, down to observe and direct frontal fire on the enemy positions, while Stewart Macbeth hurried off to Panormiti village with instructions to put in a flank attack with the Italians in reserve there. At 1300 hours these Italians, with a leavening of S.B.S. leading, began to advance along the lower slopes of the town. Despite a raid by three Stukas who dive-bombed School Hill and the British positions, the enemy withdrew rapidly and in some disorder. By 1500 hours he was evacuating his wounded and attempting to extricate his main force to the beaches.

Lapraik at once ordered an armed caïque to put out and intercept the most important German landing-craft, a large schooner. The caïque was too slow to do this, but succeeded in forcing the schooner to change course to within range of the Brens on School Hill. The Brens then raked her crowded decks for several minutes.

The attempted invasion of Simi was over. The final extent of the German casualties will never be known for the majority undoubtedly occurred on board the schooner as it fled. On land, sixteen Germans were killed, six captured intact, and thirty wounded. Several more Germans escaped to the hills where they were shot or decapitated by the Greeks. S.B.S. lost one killed and two wounded, the Italians ten wounded. Lapraik had some reason to feel pleased with himself.

On the following day, S.B.S. positions were dive-bombed by Stukas at intervals of two hours from dawn to dusk. Leaflets were also dropped urging the Italians to join with the Fascist brothers against the perfidious English. As evidence of his sentiments the Italian Commander, Corradini, who had comported himself with great courage on the previous day, assembled troops and went publicly into the closet with one of these pamphlets. Two Stukas were shot down by the indefatigable Brens, but one S.B.S. man and over twenty civilians were killed in the course of the raids.

In one of the last of them Lapraik's headquarters received a direct hit. Two men, Corporal Greeves and Private Bishop, were trapped beneath tons of debris, the former with a great weight on his stomach. The situation was tragic in the extreme since any attempt to extricate Greeves intact involved allowing a mass of wreckage to fall on Bishop.

This was explained to Bishop, who agreed to the amputation of his foot in an attempt to save his comrade's life. With the severed foot still in place among the ruins, Greeves would be safe for the moment. At dawn on 9th October, Private Porter Jarrell began the amputation under dreadful conditions and with very inadequate equipment. Bishop was extricated alive but died almost immediately from shock and pain. He died in vain, for his companion, when removed, was also dead. It is difficult to imagine whether Bishop, who had to confront this situation, or Jarrell, who had to explain it to him and to perform the operation, are deserving of the higher praise. Jarrell, an American citizen, had served in the desert with the volunteer ambulance unit, and had asked to be transferred to S.B.S.

On 10th October, Simi was again heavily dive-bombed. Lapraik received orders to withdraw to the mainland and prepare a base from which to carry out future raids. At the last moment the order was countermanded, but on 12th October it was repeated and the withdrawal took place. All military stores and equipment were either transported or destroyed. A week later Lassen returned to Simi with the intention of attacking any German who might have landed there. The island was unoccupied. The Germans were cautious about Simi and when Lapraik resumed operations, after reporting to Cairo, they were to be more cautious still.

With the fall of Cos, the enemy inevitably transferred his entire attention to Leros. This island, a naval base with an almost land-locked harbour, now constituted the only remaining British bastion in the Northern Aegean. True, Samos was still in our hands but if Leros fell Samos would fall—for Samos, large, comparatively flat, with a coastline of many scores of miles was indefensible. To the south, Calino, barren and traversed by deep, rocky valleys, had also proved indefensible. Outflanked by German-held Cos, Calino had been abandoned without a struggle. Upon its northern peninsula German patrols now looked across two thousand yards of salt water at the beach defences of Leros. Occasionally, when other amusement was lacking, the two sides would machine-gun each other.

Would Leros hold? In Cairo, those most directly concerned displayed their conviction that it would by the dispatch of reinforcements to the island throughout the whole month of October. Air cover they could not provide, for the nearest British bases were in Cyprus. The reinforcements themselves were of good quality and equipment, but they suffered from one great psychological handicap. Many of them, as I have already stated, had formed part of the garrison of Malta. There they had endured for months on end some of the worst bombing of the war. But in Malta there were deep shelters were a bomb explosion was a dull thud and a shuddering of concrete. In Leros, where there were no shelters at all, one had to take one's bombing in the open air, and like it. There is a limit to every man's enjoyment of Stukas.

The situation was now far too serious for any independent action by the S.B.S. to be envisaged. Useful reconnaissances of neighbouring islands had been carried out but, in the main, David Sutherland's detachment—the only one available—was concentrated in Leros and given the definite task of countering any attempt to airborne invasion. The regular garrison now consisted of three battalions of British infantry, one battery of light anti-aircraft, together with numerous and relatively well-organized Italians.

During the first week of November, Leros was bombed continually, the main deliveries of high explosive occurring in the early morning and evening. There was not a great deal of room in Leros. If you moved, you were as likely to move near a falling bomb as if you remained in your carefully dug slit-trench. Men did not move. They played cards and waited, for it was common knowledge, miraculously circulated, that a German parachute battalion diverted from the Russian front, had arrived in Athens. To give his men some action, David Sutherland sent a small party to reconnoitre the tip of Calino and there annoy the enemy. The enemy expressed his annoyance by rapid and well directed small-arms fire. Evidently, in Calino, he was vigilant . . .

At least the invasion, when it came, came as no surprise. At dusk on Armistice Day 1943, Jellicoe, who had been on the island for some time, returned from a conference at Brigade Headquarters with the news that a landing was expected the following morning.

That night, S.B.S. moved out to take up their positions covering the only area in the island where it was possible to land by parachute.

At dawn, the seaborne assault on the island was launched. The enemy landing-craft, intent upon other matters, failed to observe that a small caïque had swelled their numbers. This caïque contained Lieutenant Keith Balsillie of S.B.S., and his patrol, who had been carrying out a reconnaissance of Patmos and Archi Islands. Balsallie knew nothing of the invasion and was surprised to find himself surrounded by so many Germans. Since, however, they made no attempt to molest him, he landed in their wake and making off across country, regained his unit position.

In these initial landings—those from the sea—S.B.S. were not involved, but by 0900 hours it became clear that the situation was serious. The enemy had gained a footing in the village of Clidi, where the Brigade reserve company had been ordered to counter-attack. S.B.S. placed their machine-guns in readiness and waited. They were not to wait long. At precisely midday, after a fifteen-minute air lull, the sky to the north of their positions was filled with Junkers 52 transports flying in close formation, which proceeded to disgorge some six hundred parachutists. Simultaneously, Messerschmitts, diving and strafing, attempted to divert fire from the descending men.

Jellicoe immediately ordered all patrols out to engage the enemy and, if possible, to prevent them reaching their parachute containers. This latter object was achieved. Sniping continued throughout the afternoon and every attempt by the parachutists to reach their vital stores of food and ammunition was met with a hail of fire. Discomforted and hungry the parachutists retreated to the summit of a mountain. At night they came down to salvage their containers but by this time the S.B.S. had already looted most of these.

If things were going well in our area, they seemed to be going still better elsewhere. The Germans had failed to establish themselves. No British position had been taken and the issue remained in doubt. Confronted with a stalemate it was expected that the enemy would attempt to land reinforcements. This expectation proved correct. During the early hours of the following morning, schooner-load after schooner-load of the Brandenburg Regiment approached the coast and succeeded in gaining a footing. At dawn a further shower of parachutists was released over the S.B.S. positions.

Weather conditions now, though, were by no means those of the previous day. A forty-mile-an-hour gale was blowing. Four of the transports, with their valuable human load, were shot down as they manoeuvred to gain height. Of over 200 men who actually left the aircraft not more than a dozen ever went into action. Some, whose parachutes were evidently damp or packed in a hurry, fell to their death with a roman-candle of silk streaming tautly above them . . . some reached the ground alive, only to be dragged over rocks and four-foot walls, unable to twist the release-catch of their harness. . . . Some fell in the sea and there drowned, their bodies floating for hours with the canopy of a parachute for winding sheet.

From the packs of the dead on the ground, S.B.S. removed the concentrated food, the safety-razors, the chocolate: German parachute rations are exceptionally well packed. The remainder of that day was spent resting. Intensive and continuous air activity made movement very difficult.

At dusk, Jellicoe ordered two patrols to reconnoitre the ground in the vicinity of Navy House at the head of Alinda Bay. These patrols, under Captain H. W. Blyth, returned at dawn in two jeeps. They had found the jeeps abandoned and loaded them with stores and ammunition. No enemy had been encountered. On their hill, the German parachutists were drinking their last drops of water in splendid, but uncomfortable, isolation.

The next day, the third since the invasion, was the decisive one. S.B.S. patrol activity was continued and much sniping carried out, but in other parts of the island things were going badly. The enemy were making a supreme effort. Their ground troops did little, but throughout the entire day squadrons of Stukas from Rhodes, from the Greek mainland, from Crete . . . from every field with a few unemployed aircraft, some ammunition and a bomb dump . . . flew over the battle area, strafing, diving, endeavouring to break the morale of the defenders. Reports began to come in of dwindling resistance in the harbour area. By mid-afternoon, Jellicoe, who had then been out of communication with Brigade Headquarters for over twelve hours, determined to penetrate the enemy lines by jeep and to discover what was happening.

He took with him Sergeant Workman and Corporal Dryden. He arrived at his destination to find an Anglo-German peace conference in progress.

This, of course, was quite unknown to S.B.S. and other special service troops in the hinterland of the island. They had destroyed numbers of parachutists, suppressed with zeal a score of professional snipers and driven the remainder of the invaders in their area to the peak of a waterless hill, there to remain with docility ever since.

When, therefore, Jellicoe returned in the early hours of the following morning to announce that Leros had surrendered unconditionally and that all resistance had ended, the news was greeted with surprise and horror. To many it seemed, despite the total absence of air cover, despite the apparently inexhaustible flow of German reinforcements, despite the incessant harrying by Stukas and Messerschmitts, that the island could have held. It is only fair to add, however, that S.B.S. took little part in the grim street-fighting and indeed, suffered only seven casualties. They retained their optimism as to the final result, because they were never thrown into the blood-bath at Portolago. The extent of the carnage on both sides in this five-day battle can only be described as Thermopylaean. When the island was recaptured, eighteen months later, 1,000 German graves were counted, 400 British. Not one house, no hut, no wall remained intact.

Things might have gone very badly for S.B.S. had the Germans themselves been less exhausted, had they been able to devote more time to the rounding up of stragglers. As it was, the entire detachment, with their weapons and stores, escaped by caïque during the course of that night. They lay up unobserved in the neighbouring island of Lisso during the following day. Finally they proceeded to Turkey. Keith Balsillie, who had been left behind with severe dysentery, absconded with a German rowing-boat a few days later, and pulled across to the mainland to join the main party.

Relief attempts, on the lines of those used on Cos, were now made with the intention of evacuating any British soldiers who might still be at large in Leros. On four successive nights motor launches were sent in, and parties landed by folboat to contact stragglers on shore. No opposition was encountered from the Germans. A number of men were successfully re-embarked.

So ends the first, the almost unrelievedly gloomy period of the long Aegean struggle. The fall of Leros ensured that of Samos. The garrison was withdrawn from the latter island almost immediately. Excluding Castelrosso, no fragment of the Dodecanese now remained in British or in independent Italian hands. The Germans stood, apparently supreme, their forces deployed from the Sporades to the territorial waters of Turkey. They had scored their first success in any theatre of operations since Stalingrad and—in terms of territorial acquisition—their last. We shall analyse how real, how unchallenged that supremacy was to remain. Since all islands were now hostile territory, all were fair game for raids. The S.B.S. could revert from garrison duty to its natural, its traditional role. The generals had departed—some to German prison camps, some, sadder and wiser men, to Cairo. The extent, the nature, and motive power behind future pinpricks became the concern of raiding forces once again.

Colonel Turnbull, who had served so well on the Rhodes mission, was to command them.

CHAPTER ELEVEN

The patrols crept forward, each upon their separate route. The island had already been reconnoitred. The dispositions of Germans and Fascists alike were known. From these reconnaissances and from information received, the position in Simi appeared to be the following: the garrison consisted of one German major, two Italian captains, sixty Fascist militia with ten attached personnel, the original *carabinieri* and eighteen Germans. Strong positions were held at the Governor's house in Castello, at Molo, and at Panormiti. The patrols crept forward.

The moon was at the full. Visibility was excellent, but progress was slow, due to the broken glass from earlier German bombings, which littered the alleyways of the town. Lieutenant Bob Bury led this particular patrol. 'We arrived finally,' he said, 'at the southern end of the Governor's house. A large open window gave access to the first floor. We entered. A Stuka bomb had landed near this part of the house and caused great damage inside. I saw no sign of human life, but our progress being slow, it was impossible to avoid making a noise. Presently, voices were heard on the ground floor. I reconnoitred and discovered what appeared to be a German light machine-gun billet. I threw a Mills grenade inside it, and heard groaning.' Voices were then heard upon the quayside, apparently discussing this disturbance. 'I went down,' said Sergeant Geary. 'I saw seven Germans in conference. I emptied a Schmeisser magazine into them at thirty yards' range. Three men fell down, and a fourth began to crawl towards the house. I dealt with him and with the remainder of the Germans, who were standing as if uncertain what to do. I think I killed them all.'

Meanwhile, Bob Bury had become interested in a window. Behind this window another man was shouting. Bob Bury propped himself upon the sill and shot this man with his carbine. He then detonated a twenty-five pound charge of explosive on the ground floor of the house next door. This house collapsed. Part of the Governor's house collapsed with it. Bob Bury and his patrol retired, leaving a ten-pound pack of explosive on the street behind them. The pursuing Italian Fascists were incautious enough to pick this pack up and to attempt to neutralize it. They were transformed into raspberry jam.

Lapraik, elsewhere, was active. With three men he visited another enemy billet. A decoy bomb was thrown, and the enemy reinforcements shot as they ran out. Lapraik spent the remainder of the time at his disposal in setting fire to the caïque yard, and in destroying a large food dump. A little to his left, Sergeant Whittle, with two, was attempting to enter the power-station. Six Germans and two Italians made the mistake of opposing him in the open. They were killed, and the power-station was blown up. Sergeant Whittle, who suffered from no shortage of ammunition, now engaged the Italian machine-gun positions in the port with his Bren gun. These positions were silenced.

Lapraik, who had been intended to reinforce Leros and only diverted to Simi because the former island was falling, now proceeded north with his men in two caïques. Under Bimrose, he put a patrol ashore in Nisiros on 22nd November. Bimrose blew up the telegraph station, the air landing-strip and all caïques under German charter in the harbour of this island. He removed a schoolmaster who was suspected of Fascist sympathies, and the mayor who, it was felt, could feather his nest just as well in Cairo. On the following day, Lapraik visited Piscopi, destroyed the telegraph station and disarmed the *carabinieri*, whom he forced to perform various antics for the amusement of the Greek population.

Dick Harden

Against a Turkish background

Macris, a great Greek

Govier at Megara

Guerrillas—Samos

Turkish friend

M. and V.

Sutherland and friend

Lassen's Sergeant Nicholson

Trooper Crouch (*killed in action*)

Base

Manhunting in Jugoslavia

Waiting for a cupper

Folboats away

Leros

Greek conference

Base

Hide-out

Lying up

On the way

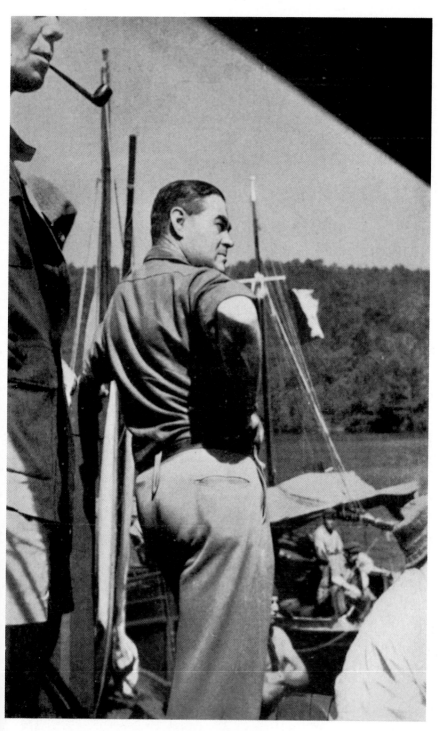

Brigadier Turnbull

Jellicoe and friend

Rough passage

Sean O'Reilly

Trophy

A rare shave

Ski interlude

Jellicoe

Lassen and Casulli

Captured craft

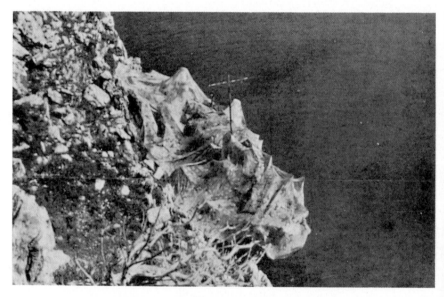

Find the ship—*Fairmiles* under camouflage

Homeward bound

Port Deremen

Leros gets it

The stores come in

On 25th November, Lapraik was back at Simi, where he landed three patrols, one of which he led himself. Lapraik possessed friends in Simi. He contacted them. An abbot of the Greek Orthodox Church, in particular, was most helpful. The new enemy dispositions were a puzzle no longer.

The abbot was no mere theorist: he consented to act as guide to Bob Bury's patrol in their attack upon the enemy. Quite without fear, he led the raiders towards a machine-gun post situated beneath a large plane-tree. This machine-gun post opened fire. The abbot, tucking his skirts above his head, ducked and lay low until it had been neutralized. He was not a young man, and his beard was considerably ruffled by this precipitate fall. Some Italians now most stupidly stood up, silhouetted by the moon. Bury shot these men and simultaneously discovered that the machine-gun post was not under the tree, as stated, but in a kind of sewer let into the wall, with its opening towards the harbour. The wall was about four feet high and, possessing no apertures, prevented the defenders of the post from firing. They were obliged to content themselves with lobbing Italian red devil grenades at intervals. These grenades are useless, and will never kill a man unless they hit him on the chest. Mills grenades are quite a different matter. Bury and his men slung several into the Italian emplacement. There was no further sound from it.

While withdrawing, Bury's other sergeant, Cameron, was molested by a search-party of the enemy. He gave these individuals a burst from his carbine and had the satisfaction of seeing several of them fall. Neither Cameron nor Bury, who both embarked successfully, were further annoyed. On the day following this second S.B.S. raid, fifteen Italians, accompanied by four Germans, deserted from the island by rowing across to Turkey. Their garrison duties, it seemed, no longer appealed to them. These men were the first of the few. Of Lapraik it will always be remembered that he was the first to hit back.

There are operations which, at the first reading, do not appear at all exciting. No blood is spilt in these operations, and few enemy are even encountered. None the less, the previously mentioned occupational risks apply. That canoe which you were paddling at Southend, at Brighton, or at Wimereux last summer: try landing in it upon a hostile beach, try walking along the beach and shouting in the hope of contacting lost comrades. That is what Corporal Flavell, accompanied by a Greek civilian interpreter, was obliged to do upon four nights following the surrender of Leros, never certain for one moment that the motor launch which had landed him would not be driven off by hostile shipping, never certain for one moment that a German patrol would not spring out from behind this—or the next—gorse-bush.

Corporal Flavell and his friend rescued twenty-two men, and they had to work hard in order to find them.

Lieutenant Stefan M. Casulli, of the Greek Army, was doing very similar work at this time. An extraordinary man, this Stefan, with his classical nose and solemn eyes, his prematurely grey hair and his sensitive lips so seldom lit by a smile. Stefan was under no obligation to join the army . . . *any* army. He was not even a real, a Continental Greek. The Casulli family owned one of the oldest, the most respected businesses in Alexandria. Stefan had been reared in that city, but while his brothers, when the guns boomed, had sought respectable employment, Stefan, inexplicably, had chosen the S.B.S. Their loss, our gain: until his death in action, Stefan was to set a standard ever afterwards to remain the criterion for foreign officers attached to our unit. Stefan had a wife and one small child. He was very fond of them. Some people said that Stefan was so fond of them that he was not really interested in fighting; but that was not true as Stefan was to prove the hard way when he was shot through the chest in a doorway through not possessing Lassen's instinct for danger. I once overheard Stefan's wife talking to Jellicoe at a dull cocktail party: 'How I like you all, George,' she said, 'and how I *loathe* you.'

I do not suppose that any wife could have expressed better the sentiments of all wives. It has fallen to my lot to censor the letters home of men in that unit. 'Dear Mother,' I would often read, 'I am having a fine time. Everything goes on as usual.' The mother of that man believed that he was stationed in an ack-ack battery somewhere in Palestine.

98

Special Boat Service, she thought—and some people do still think—was an organization designed to provide brief trips at sea for men on leave. The standard of security among other ranks in the S.B.S. was extraordinarily high . . . always much higher than that maintained among officers. I remember a sergeant who—he wrote to his wife every day—explained his occasional silences by a reference to recurrent bouts of malaria. When decorated, to his secret horror, with the Military Medal, he rose to the occasion unperturbed. An enemy bomb, he declared, had fallen in the vicinity of his coast-watching post. The bomb had not exploded. He had neutralized it, by this means obtaining the above-mentioned decoration. I censored that letter, God help me, and franked it with my signature.

Sometimes I wonder if the security maintained was not excessive. After all, the enemy, even if he had no idea where the next blow would fall, knew at least something of our methods, knew our cap-badge, the names of some of our more prominent personalities, the situation of our bases and the composition of and delays employed in our explosives. I mention this because towards the end of the war one noticed that an increasing number of wives were leaving or having trouble with their husbands in the unit. The case of Mrs. Ball seems relevant in this connexion. After the landing in Normandy, Mrs. Ball wrote to her husband, Gunner Ball, to the effect that her neighbours were causing much trouble because Gunner Ball (who had been abroad for three years) was squatting in the Middle East instead of doing his duty in France. In point of fact, Gunner Ball, when he received his wife's letter, was squatting in Crete, where he had just assisted in blowing up a petrol dump, for the second year in succession. Gunner Ball was rather annoyed by this letter, and replied to it in a harsh manner. The pair separated, and were only reunited by the exercise of much tact on the part of Stewart Macbeth.

Winter, with its complement of gales and other navigational difficulties was now at hand. Winter, in itself, was no impediment to carefully planned operations, and Jellicoe did not intend that it should be so. Before raiding could be resumed, however, it was essential that the unit be regrouped. Lapraik's and Sutherland's detachments had lost valuable men, and these must be replaced. At Athlit, in Palestine, an extra new detachment was being trained to replace that which had been lost or dispersed in Sardinia. Langton, its original leader, had now gone home for reasons of health. A new leader had to be found, and Jellicoe, typically enough, had discovered him in the bar of the officers' club in Cos, during a ten-minute break for vermouth.

Major Ian Patterson, second-in-command of the 11th Parachute Battalion, was in Cos as much for the holiday as for purposes of serious work. His unit was presently to go home, and he had no intention of going with it. He was rather intrigued by the S.B.S., and he made the mistake of saying so.

'You can join it if you like,' said Jellicoe, who again, typically, had found out everything about Patterson before even appearing in the bar. They had also met at Kitzbühel before the war.

'Well, I don't know,' said Patterson cautiously. 'Have you a vacancy?'

'I have a vacancy for a detachment commander,' said Jellicoe nonchalantly.

'I'm not sure that that would suit me,' said Patterson. 'I'm rather fond of having my own way, you know.'

'You can have it as much as you like,' said Jellicoe. 'If I don't like you, you'll go.'

Patterson had his own way. He returned to Athlit and fired four or five officers and fifty of the men who were training there. He became wildly unpopular. Officers came, paid their mess bills, and left for an unknown destination with monotonous regularity. I remember once coming into the mess and inquiring for a certain gentleman. This gentleman owed me two pounds. Unfortunately, he had left the previous evening. I have said that Patterson was unpopular: that was so. Later, when he saw action with his detachment, I do not think I have ever seen a commander to whom his men were more deeply devoted. When he was killed, much, much later, more than half of the members of his detachment put pen to paper in order to write to his mother. It is not at all usual for the British soldier to do this.

Patterson, with his insistence upon efficiency, was aided by the Germans, to whose snipers in the Aegean so many had fallen. The unit was seriously under strength and, as was customary in such emergencies, a recruiting tour was arranged. Those chosen to conduct it were David Sutherland, bemedalled, obviously sincere, obviously experienced, and Stewart Macbeth, who was diplomatic, who was prepared to deal with cases of conscience, and more especially with those who had languished—doing nothing— since the transport had landed them at Suez.

The scene is an Infantry Reinforcement Training Depot in the Middle East. Here, men have lain idle for weeks, some for months. One day a notice is posted upon the board: recruits are required for a special service unit. It is preferable that they should possess some knowledge of boats and a liking for the sea. A lot of young gentlemen, who possessed definite private information that this involves supervisory service upon Royal Army Service Corps schooners, duly sign their names on the list. They are, in consequence, somewhat appalled by the first question posed to them:

'Are you willing to parachute?'

These young gentlemen withdraw their names from the lists very rapidly. Those who remain now constitute a solid core: at least they are willing to parachute. They are interrogated separately and very fully. About one-quarter of their total number are accepted, and these by no means always those who have been in action before. Often, the young soldier who had spent half his Service life on an anti-aircraft site in Cyprus is taken in preference to the guardsman who has been through Knightsbridge and the rearguard action at Matruh. The officers who interrogate are accompanied by an experienced other ranks—sometimes Marine Hughes, sometimes Sergeant Nicholson, sometimes Cameron, of Lapraik's detachment. Often, the final affirmative, the final negative, rests with these men.

It is because of their sure choice that so few men are returned to their units while training.

CHAPTER TWELVE

Left to themselves for a few weeks—though they were by no means certain on this point—the Germans employed the unexpected lull in an inspection of their newly acquired territories and the consolidation of their garrisons therein. Eleven islands of the Dodecanese now formed their south-eastern front line, and behind these islands lay many others in the Cyclades and Sporades, which had been taken over peaceably from the Italians.

The Germans were gratified at their unexpected success. It had always been a pleasure for them to outwit the British in campaigns involving seaborne communication lines. On the occasion of their hard-won success in Crete, nearly three years earlier, every global strategist, every military commentator and purveyor of eulogies who was in possession of a pen, had been let loose in the columns of *Signal* and the *Hamburger Fredenblatt* to point out that *now* no island could continue to feel safe.

That sinister jest, aimed at the morale of hated England, was apposite no longer. As the year 1944 dawned with disaster after disaster on the Russian front, the German people well knew that the invasion of the United Kingdom was a chance of victory which had been for ever allowed to slip by. The propagandists who now celebrated the elimination of the British from the Aegean made no mention of it. Instead, they dwelt long and significantly upon the genius of a Balkan staff which had surmounted the dreadful problems of extended communications, upon the courage and fortitude of the German soldier before the twin obstacles of treachery and shortage of supplies.

Shortage of supplies: there, indeed, was the problem, and General von Klemann, in his castle overlooking Rhodes harbour, General Brauer, in the white and well-appointed villa at Cnossos, in Crete, were neither of them the happiest of men. As the old year drew to its close, these two officers had many consultations together. A common policy was decided upon, and representations and demands were made to their superior, Field-Marshal von List, at Salonika; and to their inferior, the Admiral commanding Athens and Piraeus. The representations concerned reinforcements; the demands an organized fleet of vessels with which to take these reinforcements to the islands and there maintain them.

Von List, a very astute commander, was amenability itself. He drafted for the immediate use of Klemann an entire fresh brigade of excellent mountain troops and one poor quality division, the 999th Infantry, which was composed mostly of ex-political detainees. At the same time, he greatly increased the fleet of Junkers transport planes which were maintaining the daily liaison between Athens, Maleme and Marizza airfields. From the west, where they were no longer serving any purpose, he obtained a number of these same aircraft of floats. Meanwhile, down the Danube and through the Black Sea and the Bosphorus, came convoys of flat-bottomed ships—'L' and 'S' Lighters from the shipyards, 'Magda'-type barges from the Ems Canal.

Brauer, who had been long established in Crete and who, personally, was contemptuous of any British attempt to land there in force, was well satisfied with these conveniences. Klemann, who was not so sure on this question of British invasion, thanked List warmly for his aid, and immediately set about redeploying his mixed forces.

His first move was to disarm Italian troops and to send all those who refused to take the new oath of allegiance to the Führer to concentration camps, or internment pens; there to await transportation to Greece. Italian civilian administration he permitted to continue, but only under the closest supervision. Klemann's treatment of the Greek subjects of his domain was, in fact, infinitely more liberal than anything which these much persecuted people had known previously. He allowed them, for example, to reopen their schools and—unprecedented concession—to teach there in Greek if they chose. This piece of legislation was no doubt aimed at the Italians, whom it infuriated, but on the whole, Klemann was a just man. British agents and those who had aided British raiding-parties, he shot when they fell into his hands; but this is conduct which can be justified under International Law. Of the excesses of one German General, whose private pastime was public defaecation, preferably in front of his soldiers, and who massacred whole villages of Cretans upon the slightest pretext, von Klemann was, on several occasions, most outspoken. He ruled and behaved like the good soldier that he was. Unfortunately, the same cannot always be said of his men.

Klemann now had troops to play with and he distributed them wisely and well. In Rhodes he retained a garrison, the numbers of which fluctuated—but never to a point below divisional strength. To Scarpanto, the long barren island to the south-west, with its satellites, Casos and Saria, he sent 800 men, stationing them for the most part in the southern extremity for the defence of one of the most important radar station in the islands. Leros and Cos, next in importance, received 4,000 and 2,000 men respectively; Stampalia, 200, Simi and Piscopi, 150 apiece.

With the remaining islands under his command Klemann was undecided what course to pursue. He began by giving them small token garrisons, but soon discovered that this replaced a heavy strain upon his sea-transport service. He then regrouped these scattered companies and employed them to garrison single islands for short periods at a time.

He was still experimenting with this latter system when the resumption of raids by S.B.S. took the initiative in the matter of garrison deployment out of German hands.

General Klemann's manoeuvres had not passed unnoticed in Cairo and Beirut. Particularly in Beirut, where a naval gentleman with the euphonious title of Flag Officer, Levant and Eastern Mediterranean, was very, very interested.

Folem, as this officer was skittishly called, was interested because under his command lay a sizeable fleet of coastal motor launches of various denominations, and another of small, untidy, disreputable-looking caïques, which a closer inspection revealed to be well armed and converted with great care for the task of carrying small parties deep into enemy waters. A pool of officers, all very experienced in raiding work, were available to direct these two fleets—two names stand out among them: those of Commander R. E. Courage, who commanded the coastal forces, and of Lieutenant-Commander Adrian Seligman, a well-known amateur yachtsman in peace-time, for whom no craft had ever been too small, and no command too unimportant if the assignment offered prospect of tricky navigation and contact with the enemy.

Towards the end of December 1943, while Brauer and Klemann were conferring, a very different conference was taking place in the Middle East. It was decided that, with the New Year, detachments of S.B.S. working in rotation would resume operations, and simultaneously landing and re-embarking troops and nightly patrolling on their own account, the narrow waters of the Dodecanese. Nor did these decisions stand alone: squadrons of R.A.F. Beaufighters, stationed in Cyprus, were instructed to intensify their attacks upon German shipping in the area, and H.M. submarines of the gallant 'U' Class, who had already been so closely associated with S.B.S., began to establish a virtual blockade of the ports of Piraeus, Heraklion, and Portolago.

These decisions were not mere measures of retaliation, of employment of surplus men and shipping. Britain has never possessed any surplus men, and her shipping situation was as precarious then as it had been two years earlier. No—a definite Aegean strategy was at last emerging, a strategy in three movements, which was to make the German occupation an uncomfortable and precarious tenancy of short rations and sleepless nights.

In the first movement, all attacks, whether by the Navy, S.B.S., or from the air, were to concentrate on shipping. The Germans possessed many caïques and, as has been seen,

105

reinforcements of other categories were now arriving. But with their innumerable and widely dispersed garrisons, the total of available tonnage would always be inadequate. That total was now to be whittled down to a point where the Germans—though still able to reinforce—*could no longer evacuate* their garrisons. Here, the role of S.B.S. was most important: for, for every ship which they themselves could destroy in enemy harbours, the course and position of a dozen others could be signalled to the vigilant patrols of the Navy and Air Force. So much for the first phase . . . a phase which was intended to leave the equivalent of six enemy infantry divisions immobile and virtual prisoners, when the great blow fell in the west.

The second phase was an extension of the first. S.B.S. attacks would now be switched to outlying garrisons, thus obliging the enemy to employ more shipping for the purposes of investigation, evacuation of his wounded, and reinforcement. For these adjustments the Navy and the Beaufighters would lie in waiting. Bluff would play no small part in the S.B.S. tactics here: for example, an attack would be made and installations destroyed on an island of insignificant military value with the object of luring a large enemy garrison there. This garrison, having weakened other garrisons, would subsequently be difficult to evacuate themselves.

The third phase, from the S.B.S. point of view, was pure banditry: the *nervenkrieg*, with the tables turned. Every island would now have been raided, every island would be waiting for our next visit. Short of food, and short of mail, with leave at home a distant memory, with horizons bounded by a few square miles of rock and scrub, the disgruntled garrisons would toil up nightly from their comfortable billets to the trenches which they had dug on bleak hillsides, there to keep vigil.

This was to be the phase of desertions and mass surrender.

A great statesman, when asked from what base his planes had raided Tokyo, declared that they had come from an imaginary country described in a famous novel. I do not intend to employ such a subterfuge here. To begin with, it would be doing a disservice to our loyal and often misjudged ally, Turkey, whose assistance to us has been gravely under-estimated. Nor, I think, would anybody be deceived if I were to suggest that S.B.S. operated direct from Beirut, or even from Castelrosso. A glance at the map would prove me a liar.

S.B.S. operated from Turkish waters. They had been operating from Turkish waters since the dark days of the Cos evacuation, when bases on that sparsely populated coastline had been reconnoitred and dumps established. The Turks had raised no objections, either then or later. True, their country was neutral, at peace with all belligerents, but neutrality is an attitude easy to strike but most awkward to maintain. Everyone is familiar with the chequered history of the Turkish chrome deliveries. The manoeuvres and counter-manoeuvres, the ponderous Foreign Office notes, the faint reproaches, the sniggers and snarls of the Wilhelmstrasse. Equally, much fuss was made about the passage of German shipping from the Black Sea to the Aegean, but the Turks were within their International rights in permitting such movement . . . and, as they somewhat whimsically pointed out at the time, they were equally willing to permit Allied shipping to pass from the Aegean into the Black Sea if it so desired.

This—for obvious reasons—Allied naval craft did not desire. The Turks were, in consequence, quite willing to allow us another and more convenient favour, and one which was not without risk to themselves. The S.B.S., the Greek squadron, the Navy, moved into and stayed in Turkish territorial waters.

The Germans knew of this from the start. They were very angry. If a move of this nature had taken place a couple of years earlier there would have been immediate reprisals. Smyrna and Ankara would have been bombed to rubble, and a punitive expedition dispatched to destroy the intruders in their lairs. Such action was now quite out of the question. The Germans did not want Turkey to come into the war . . . indeed, they now prized this particular neutrality even above that of Sweden. They contented themselves with sending occasional reconnaissance aircraft from Rhodes. These aircraft took pictures of S.B.S. and naval craft, lying under camouflage netting in remote creeks. The pictures were dispatched to Ankara, where von Papen, the German Ambassador, would lose another night's sleep in studying them. On the following morning he would call at the Turkish Foreign Office.

'I have here,' he would say, brandishing the prints, 'indisputable evidence of the presence of British shipping in your coastal waters. These photographs were taken from a Junkers 88 observation plane over Yedi Atala Bay, the day before yesterday. See . . . observe this picture, my dear sir . . . the ship in the lower right-hand corner is quite certainly a British motor launch!'

The Turkish Porte-Parole would purse his lips and place his finger-tips together. 'My dear Ambassador,' he would reply, 'I am most grateful for this information. If what you say is true—and I will have it investigated immediately at our Admiralty—a most deplorable breach of our neutrality has indeed occurred. But, as you know, the British sold us some of their motor launches several years ago, and this may well be one of our own ships. Incidentally, if I may ask, what was this German plane you mention doing over our territory, my dear Ambassador? . . .'

And von Papen would retire discomforted.

Sometimes, since the conventions must be observed, the Turkish Porte-Parole would make a call at the British Embassy:

'Tch! Tch!' the official who received him would observe when the prints were laid upon his desk, 'Tch! Tch! Well, of course, I cannot deny myself off-hand that this *is* one of our motor launches. I will have the matter investigated immediately.'

And investigated it was, sure enough. The motor launch usually *did* turn out to be British. It had come into Yedi Atala, under its belligerent right to stay there forty-eight hours, in order to repair some engine defect. Of the caïques photographed lying in its vicinity, nobody, of course, knew anything: they were obviously Turkish fishing craft.

Despite the near-certainty that the Germans would never

commit the folly of attacking us, precautions were always taken by both Navy and S.B.S. when lying-up in Turkish waters. A plan of defence was the first requirement when moving into a new anchorage. Depot ships were scattered and concealed by either natural or net camouflage. In deference to our Turkish hosts, landings on shore were restricted to the fulfilment of the natural needs. Excursions into the interior were absolutely forbidden. Not many people live along that lovely wooded coastline and the attitude of the local military posts appeared to be one of tactful ignorance of our presence. Sometimes, when curiosity concerning us became too great, or official business required transaction, a trim little motor launch flying the Star and Crescent would draw alongside, and an officer wearing the peculiar grey woollen uniform of the Republic would clamber up the gangway. A jar of special raki, conserved for these occasions, would be opened. The proceedings usually ended in a pig hunt and shooting competitions. Conversation was conducted in French. I had always thought the simple, unadorned English accent in that language the final philological monstrosity—but the Turkish accent is worse.

Some forty anchorages had been reconnoitred between Castelrosso and the tip of Samos. Many of these were used as staging-posts, others only for fast surface craft who were patrolling some particular channel. The main base of all raiding operations was always at some point in the sixty-mile deep Cox channel.

It was for this that Ian Patterson and his detachment, accompanied by Lieutenant-Commander Seligman as naval officer in charge, sailed from Beirut on 20th January 1944, in various motor launches and the 180-ton Levant schooner *Tewfik*, a cumbersome and ugly old tub with temperamental engines and a sea-roll like the swing of a pendulum.

Four thousand, seven hundred pounds of explosive was the main cargo, and not much of it was to be wasted.

CHAPTER THIRTEEN

Lassen, who was accompanied by his inseparable companion, Guardsman Sean O'Reilly, had not forgotten his visit to Calchi in the previous autumn. He had heard of the resistance opposed by the Calchian *carabinieri* to the German invasion, and he was curious to see what had become of the magnificent defences which he had erected for their benefit. Jellicoe, who had accompanied Patterson to Castelrosso, raised no objection. Lassen had the honour of being chosen for the first operation of the new series.

He landed on the last day of January from H.D.M.L. 1083 (Lieutenant Wilson). His party consisted of four men and a Greek officer interpreter, Lieutenant Katsikas. The mayor of the town was contacted, and declared that the island garrison now consisted of only six Fascists.

'This,' said Lassen, 'hardly seemed to me to be worth the voyage, but I proceeded to the police station and ordered those inside to open the doors. They refused, so I broke the doors down. I took the Italians prisoner, and with them, one typewriter, one shot-gun, six rifles, a wireless receiver, two Beretta machine carbines and a telephone. I could not find any money, but I noticed a safe. I was about to blow open this safe when I heard the sound of a motor-boat engine . . .'

Lassen was in luck. 'A launch of respectable tonnage', belonging to the German flotilla at Rhodes, was entering the harbour. The German habit of staying at islands, without orders and *à l'improviste*, to obtain a meal or to indulge in the mania for taking photographs was now as on so many

110

occasions later to prove disastrous. Lassen concealed his men and opened fire at close range. Two Germans of the six on board were wounded. The remainder surrendered immediately. The motor boat with its load of stores and four live pigs was added to Lassen's booty and towed back in triumph to Turkey. Lassen himself was the only British casualty. Moving with his usual indifference to danger about the scene of the action, he was slightly wounded in the foot by the cross-fire provided by O'Reilly.

This Irishman, who had packed about as much turblence into his forty-two years as any man living, was not afraid of many things . . . but he was afraid of Lassen. During the entire voyage home, he skulked in the forepeak of the motor launch, not daring to show his face. Eventually, Lassen approached him: 'It's all right, Sean,' he said, 'it's all right.' 'Oh, sir,' said O'Reilly brokenly, 'oh, sir . . . I *shot* you.'

His tone was sepulchral. Lassen soothed him with rum. The scene was really most pathetic.

At base the prisoners were handed over to the Intelligence sergeant, Priestley, for interrogation. This Priestley was a South African. I do not in any way wish to libel South Africans, but they are not conspicuous for those qualities of mercy popularly associated with Englishmen. Priestley, though never physically brutal, insisted upon the truth. He was not fond of Germans. At the head of all his prisoner interrogation summaries was a sentence which expressed his intentions very clearly. That sentence read, 'I will say all I can and all I know.' These particular Germans knew a great deal. Cajoled by Priestley, they told it.

Meanwhile, Jellicoe had dispatched a second patrol to Stampalia with priority orders to attack shipping there. Stampalia—although a recognized Italian naval base—is an island which has not yet achieved any prominence in this story. The reason lies in its position as westernmost of the Dodecanese, and in consequence, as the most inaccessible of the group. During the fighting of the previous autumn, the British had left its defence to the Italians. The inevitable had occurred: 150 determined German parachutists had captured over 800 Italians without the necessity of having to

111

fire a shot.

The patrol now chosen was that commanded by Captain M. E. Anderson, another South African and, like George Barnes, a champion swimmer. Anderson, at base, was a menace, perpetually attempting to drown himself and others with endless adaptations of the Davis apparatus for under-water exploration. He was to come near to drowning himself now.

Anderson left Castelrosso on 27th January in H.D.M.L. 1238. The weather was appalling with force-six gales, and the short, choppy seas so characteristic of that area in winter. Stampalia, and particularly the strength of its garrison being still something of an unknown quantity, the party proceeded cautiously. The shape of Stampalia is that of a wasp; two oviforms with a thin neck between them. The garrison lived in the thin neck. In bad weather Anderson's patrol landed in a sandy bay on the lower of the two oviforms, and lay up for the night in a cramped but comfortable cave.

They had with them as interpreters Signaller Stephenson and Private Manoli Kanakakis, two inseparables, who had first met in Crete. Of these two it was hard to decide which spoke the better Greek. Stephenson, who had been left behind in the British evacuation of Crete over two years earlier, had remained on the island, hiding in the mountains with young Manoli, and helping to evacuate hundreds of his fellow fugitives. The pair were devoted to each other.

Emboldened by the presence of interpreters, a veritable procession of notables arrived at the patrol's hide-out during the course of the following day. They included a priest and a doctor, both very frightened and very tired as a result of their long journey by mule. Much useful information was obtained from them and, as a result of this, Anderson was able to determine his plan of attack.

He himself embarked that night with Lance-Corporal Nixon, with the intention of coasting round the island to the main harbour, and there attacking shipping and fuel dumps. At the same time, he sent the remainder of the patrol overland under Corporal Asbery with instructions to destroy a seaplane and five caïques, which were known to be at anchor in a certain bay. All attacks were to take place at midnight on the following night.

Anderson was prevented from reaching his objective by bad weather. Asbery succeeded. In bright moonlight his party made their way through the barbed wire entanglements and mines at the bottle-neck of the island to lay bombs on a Junkers 52 seaplane at anchor. The Germans were quite unaware of Asbery's approach, but there is an ineradicable tradition in S.B.S. that the withdrawal is unimportant. The footsteps of Asbery's party were heard, and a well-nourished fire from all types of naval artillery opened on the peninsula. Asbery, however, was clear of the danger zone by this time. He proceeded calmly to the beach. The five caïques lay moored in line. Some discussion now took place: everybody was anxious to destroy the caïques, but few fancied a twenty-minute dip in the icy sea. Such a discussion, of course, could only take place among British soldiers. The enemy were already searching the neighbourhood in strength for the intruders . . . meanwhile these same intruders dipped their big toes in the sea and argued.

At last, four men, including Asbery himself, swam out and laid their remaining charges impeccably in the engine-room of three caïques. One of the charges was deliberately designed not to explode. This particular ship belonged to a friendly Greek. The swimmers now returned, grumbling and shivering. The patrol withdrew. In due course two caïques blew up and sank, and the Germans, who had wasted a fair amount of ammunition on the peninsula, wasted a good deal more here.

Anderson, who had so far accomplished nothing himself, observed these interesting events from a small island on which he lay concealed. He was fired with the idea of emulating his corporal. On the following night he reconnoitred and discovered the two enemy caïques, which were still floating. He laid bombs inside them, and in due course was rewarded with explosions. No enemy shipping remained in Stampalia.

Ian Patterson now sent his youngest officer, Lieutenant

David Clark, to Simi. Not long before, David Clark had been working for the cloak-and-dagger gentlemen in the Middle East. He complained, with some reason, that he had seen the cloak but not the dagger. Growing tired of acting as conducting officer to various swarthy agents leaving for the Balkans by air from Derna, he had joined S.B.S.

In appearance, David Clark was fair and juvenile. His attitude was casual in the extreme, and many people who were deceived by his appearance were plunged deeper in their deception by his apparent vagueness.

For David Clark was, indeed, vague. He never wrote an operational report unless ordered to do so, and, normally, the most that could be dragged from his was that it had all been most awfully unpleasant, that such and such a number of Germans had been killed, and that there had been some trouble or other at a telegraph station. 'We blew it up in the end, didn't we, Sergeant Miller?' 'Yes, sir. You laid the charges yourself, if you remember.'

The interrogator would be puzzled. From other members of the patrol he had received definite information that they had been ambushed after finishing the job. He would mention this fact.

'Oh, you mean those stray *shots* . . . ' David Clark would say. 'A couple of Germans tried to knock off Mr. Clark,' supplemented Miller, 'we killed them.'

Something of this kind occurred in Simi. David Clark found his way to a German billet, and pushed the door open gently with his foot. The Germans were playing cards. David Clark spoke their language.

'It would all be so much *easier* if you would just raise your hands,' he said.

The Germans do not appear to have agreed with him. An *unter-offizier* put *his* hand in his pocket and pulled out a Lüger. First he shot out the lights, then he shot at David Clark. This bullet struck David's carbine, wrecking it. David and Miller withdrew and threw grenades through the window into the room until all noise had ceased. There were about ten men in the room. 'Such a *tiring* walk back,' was David's comment. 'People *would* keep on firing at us.'

This raid, following so soon after Lapraik's succession of return matches on the island, broke the nerve of Simi's garrison completely. From this time onwards, they wore their tin helmets day and night. They never moved about in groups of less than six.

The islands of Patmos—despite its connexion with the evangelist—of Lisso and of Archi, are not of the first importance even in the Dodecanese. In consequence, little was expected by way of results when Captain Bruce Mitford was sent out with a small party and a minute caïque with instructions to entice shipping, liquidate the small garrisons and cut cable communications.

Mitford, a serious-minded man, whose report makes some of the most amusing reading in all the S.B.S. files, was favoured with good fortune from the start. The first sight which met his eyes when sailing boldly into Archi Harbour was that of two large caïques under German charter. Mitford sank the first by gunfire. Then, realizing that such an opportunity for practical experiment would not easily recur, he laid a complicated charge inside the second caïque, and retired to watch the result. The caïque blew up and sank in two minutes, with her back broken.

To the crews assembled on the quay, Mitford read a lecture on the inadvisability of and economic risk involved in working for the enemy.

Mitford's next move on Archi was to contact two R.A.F. airmen whose plane had been shot down in the sea, and who had been stranded on the island for over a week. This done, he destroyed the cable station and all overhead telephone wires. The Italian garrison, who presumably were intended to prevent such outrages, had taken to the hills the moment that Mitford landed.

Mitford had just sat down to a well-earned dinner in the house of a friendly doctor, when he was informed that a third and still larger caïque was entering the harbour. She was the *Eugenia* of Piræus, a single-master, bound for Leros with a cargo of stationery and officers' 'comforts'. Mitford moved on board and explained to the Greek crew that they were under arrest. The Greeks appeared delighted, and willingly showed the British patrol their cargo, which consisted of six cases of Chandon et Moet champagne; ten cases of genuine Pilsener beer; thirty kegs of Samos wine; twenty-five radio sets; eleven typewriters and innumerable rolls of mauve and perfumed toilet-paper.

After removing a case of Pilsener for consumption during his subsequent operations, Mitford sent the *Eugenia* off to base with a prize crew of one man, Marine Smith, who had instructions to sink her with explosive, rather than allow her to be recaptured by the enemy. The *Eugenia* arrived safely at Yedi Atala.

Mitford, with four, set sail for Patmos.

Very rough weather was experienced on this trip, and the motor dory, which was being towed for use on subsidiary expeditions, broke loose and was lost. Mitford landed successfully, but the caïque, unable to contain a hold with her kedge in the exposed anchorage, was compelled to cruise round it for two whole days like a soul in torment.

Had the garrison been more wideawake, Mitford would quite certainly have lost his ship. In point of fact two *carabinieri* did actually hail her, inquiring her nationality. On receiving a certain answer in broad Scots they ran away. Mitford, who had no desire for them to make trouble, pursued the two Italians to the police station. A brief pitched battle took place, in which one German was killed and a second wounded. Six Italians, who were found hiding under their beds, were taken prisoner.

The sight of his ship circling round the harbour began to irritate Mitford. Hailing her, he gave orders that she proceed to Lisso, destroy all installations on that island and return to re-embark his party. The caïque, under Corporal Miller, accomplished this mission satisfactorily. The cable station of Lisso was wrecked, and one small ship flying the German flag, sunk. In addition, Miller took prisoner all an Italian coast-watching post of four men, but, on hearing that they were spoken well of by the islanders, contented himself with disarming them and removing their lower garments.

In Patmos, Mitford was deeply involved in matter of ecclesiastical politics and theological dogma at the famous monastery of St. John. The abbot, a venerable old gentleman, Mitford found charming but timid. 'I had twenty tons of food on board my ship,' said Mitford, 'and wished to land it for the relief of the islanders. The abbot, however, insisted that any such distribution must be done legally and through the Red Cross. This, with an average of three persons dying from starvation every day, seemed to me needless hairsplitting. Accordingly, I landed the food and distributed it myself, thereby irrevocably antagonizing the powerful religious interest . . .'

The philanthropic activities of the two monasteries were, indeed, far from obvious. As the greatest landowners on the island, they enjoyed a considerable revenue in money and in kind, but apart from the maintenance of casual orphans, they offered little in return except spiritual consolation. Each monastery housed about twenty monks . . . 'as ignorant and dirty,' wrote Mitford, 'as they were inoffensive.'

Of the charitable activities of nuns in the convent of Evangelismos he speaks more warmly. The Reverend Mother here was only too pleased to assist in Mitford's food distribution.

The schoolmaster, an Italian, had fled on Mitford's arrival. Mitford had him brought back and interrogated the man. He seemed inoffensive, and was released. But the poor fellow was not to remain in peace for long. A month or two later another S.B.S. raiding-party discovered a Fascist party card in his bedroom. He was removed from the island.

Mitford's remarks in his report concerning personalities encountered are amusing. Thus:

'Orlando-Retrosi	Prisoner, Maresciallo, notorious bully and Fascist.
Traza	Prisoner, corporal, bully and Fascist.
Ioannes Stratas	Wealthy merchant, according to some, head of Axis espionage. Others say no more than a rogue, trimmer and black marketeer.
Parthenios	Young monk, a fine leader and patriot.
Phengaros	Would make good fighting man. Game for anything.

117

| Vesti Maria | Wealthy and educated widow. Influential and trustworthy. Made eyes at all of us.' |

Mitford attended the opening of the school under new management. Some eighty pupils were present. Before lessons began, the British and Greek national anthems were sung. A distribution of chocolate and bully-beef earlier that morning may not have been unconnected with this charming scene.

On 13th February the caïque arrived from Lisso, and the whole party re-embarked for the return to base. As Mitford had suspected, heavy inroads were found to have been made upon his stocks of champagne.

CHAPTER FOURTEEN

The two German privates were rather doubtful about the value of the whole business, but the commanding officer on Piscopi was convinced that he was being exceedingly clever. For some weeks now his store and petrol dumps had been sabotaged with a depressing regularity. The commanding officer suspected that a British patrol was lurking somewhere on the island. He dressed the two privates in battle-dress, and told them to go out and look for it.

'But how do we find them, Herr Hauptmann?'

'Just ask the Greeks to direct you to your British friends,' said the *Inselkommandant* genially. 'See . . . here are two pipes . . . smoke them.'

'And when we do find their hiding-place, Herr Hauptmann?'

'Just come back and tell me,' said the *Inselkommandant*, and he went off quickly for his dinner was getting cold.

In due course the two privates set out. It was a dark night and, understandably enough, they were somewhat nervous. They were not very hopeful about the success of the venture. They were even less hopeful when the first two islanders whom they greeted replied to their questions in German.

'I think we have come far enough for one night, Hellmut,' said one private.

'I agree with you, Hans. Let us sit down and smoke these pipes.'

While the two privates were enjoying their smoke, four vast shadows suddenly leapt over the wall just behind them.

Hans was so terrified that his sphincter valve gave way. There was little that he could do about it, however, for a revolver muzzle had been rammed down his throat.

Having discovered the password for that evening, Anderson handed the prisoners over to his signallers and proceeded with his main party towards the outlying German billets. Two sentries were patrolling outside these billets, meeting occasionally for a chat and a surreptitious smoke. Anderson waited until the sentries had been joined by two other men—probably their relief. He then ordered his patrol to open fire. The Germans were killed.

A single German now ran out courageously from one of the billets with a Schmeisser. This man was at once incapacitated by a phosphorous grenade. Two police dogs, which might have caused serious trouble, were shot down as they charged. The patrol, led by Sergeant Summers (our Sicilian acquaintance), now moved from house to house with their incendiaries. The buildings were soon well ablaze.

German mortar-fire was opened upon the entire area. Their work finished, the raiders withdrew. On their way back they contacted Lieutenant Dick Harden, whose patrol, stationed between the billets and the town, had been shooting the fleeing Germans as they ran past. They had shot nine.

On this same night David Clark and Lance-Corporal Crotty penetrated into the centre of Calino town, and laid bombs on a large caïque under construction in the stockyards. A store of fuel oil was also set on fire. The German sentries patrolling the area were executed a few days later for neglect of duty.

Elsewhere in Calino, David Clark's Sergeant Miller, with Corporal Chambers and Private Bentley, was attacking a German observation post. The German on guard was made prisoner by Miller, who placed his hand over the man's mouth and frog-marched him towards the door of the building. The wretched German, who was still aggressive, bit Miller's hand. 'I was just about to knife the bastard,' said Miller, 'when Chambers threw a grenade. I was unhurt but the sentry caught most of the burst in his stomach.'

The Germans inside the building now awakened and began firing wildly. Almost fifteen minutes were employed in silencing them. Two were killed and four seriously wounded. Miller made an attempt to evacuate the man most likely to live, half-dragging him, half-supporting him over the rocks. The German, who spoke English, begged him to desist.

'I shall die, anyway. Let me die here.'

Miller gave the man a swig of rum and left him.

During all this time and throughout these operations, Ian Patterson had been sitting enviously and impatiently in Turkish waters—a reluctant spider weaving an increasingly cloying web. Patterson had made several attempts to get out himself, but on each occasion he had either been defeated by bad weather or reminded by Jellicoe that this was not the role of a commander, whose duty was, rather, to plan.

Jellicoe, however, had now departed to Syria, where he was pursuing a lightning courtship. His attention, therefore, was temporarily distracted from S.B.S. affairs, and Patterson, never really at his best in a subordinate role, was able to plot with freedom.

At the beginning of March a reconnaissance party on Piscopi reported that two 'P' lighters, laden with food, wine, and reinforcements, were due to stage at Nisiros *en route* for Cos. This was the opportunity for which Patterson had been waiting. He hurriedly recruited a scratch patrol under Dick Harden, and set sail for Nisiros with seven men. Lieutenant-Commander Ramsaur of the United States Navy, who was attached to S.B.S. as an observer, accompanied the party.

Nisiros, almost completely circular in shape, and of volcanic origin, was one of those islands which the Germans garrisoned only periodically. At this period it was unoccupied. Patterson and his party landed in comfort and billeted themselves in the pretty little town of Mandracchio in expectation of events. Harden, with two men, proceeded to the island's second port, Palo, with instructions to send back a note by runner should enemy shipping appear there.

At about eight o'clock on the following morning, Harden's note was delivered. The two 'P' lighters had kept their appointment, and their crews were even now unloading sacks of flour on Palo quay. Patterson observed them from the crest of the hill, for some time. He noticed that very few of the enemy remained in the lighters themselves. This pleased him, for their armament of two 20-millimetre and machine-guns was not inconsiderable. Patterson estimated the total enemy strength at about thirty men. He was wrong. There were twenty-four.

Signaller Stephenson—that same who had spent so long a period in Crete—now volunteered to go down to the docks in civilian clothes and discover the enemy intentions. Patterson sent Stephenson off with a Greek, having arranged to meet him later. He was preparing a plan to attack the two ships when he was dismayed to see them weigh anchor and set sail. Raving and cursing, Patterson ran over the hill, expecting his prey to disappear from sight at any moment. To his inexpressible relief he realized that the lighters were only coasting: presently they entered Mandracchio harbour and moored to the east side of the jetty there with their kedge anchors out.

Information was now brought to Patterson by the Mother Superior of an orphanage that the Germans bore orders from Rhodes that all the children in her charge were to be removed to that island. This good lady, who had no desire to lose her occupation, wept copiously. Patterson, on hearing that a party of Germans would call for the children at three o'clock in the afternoon, realised that by this division of forces the enemy were playing into his hands.

'Would you,' he asked the Mother Superior, 'be prepared to let me use your orphanage in order to capture the Germans?'

'Anything,' sobbed the Mother Superior. 'Anything so long as I can keep my children.'

'Then take your brood up to the top of the mountain,' said Patterson, 'and stay there until the fighting is over. The children's luggage you can leave with me, and I will lay it outside the house as a decoy.'

Mother Superior, nuns, and infants of all ages, trudged solemnly up the slope, sucking chocolate and sweets from

British twenty-four hour rations. They were to have a grandstand view of all that followed.

Stephenson returned presently to say that an opportunity had been missed, for while these negotiations were being carried out, no less than eighteen of the enemy had been sauntering round the town, leaving only a few men and a very attenuated guard on the ships. Patterson, who was determined to make the capture one way or the other, was not particularly interested. He was wondering whether the Germans would come for the children in the lighters or on foot. He rather thought that they would come in the lighters.

He arranged for his men to be posted at various strategic points in the orphanage itself and—a stroke of genius this— dressed up as a friendly Italian in priest's attire.

The bogus priest would welcome the Germans, invite them all in to the building, as if for a snack or a speech of welcome. The shooting would then begin.

At three o'clock to the minute Patterson observed a party of men starting off along the road which led to the orphanage. Realizing that none must be allowed to escape, he sent a message to Dick Harden to this effect. He himself doubled round behind the men in order to cut off the retreat of the enemy.

The bogus priest, whose self-possession was beyond all praise, met the visitors and led them along a narrow passage which terminated in the orphanage refectory. Harden and Patterson followed and were manoeuvring for position when somebody, whose nerves could stand the strain no longer, shouted, 'Hände Hoch'. The Germans turned round. They saw Harden and Patterson standing about ten yards away. They opened fire.

Fortunately the S.B.S. had undergone training in a battle-school, whereas the Germans had not. Their shooting was wild. A terrific battle at close quarters was now engaged in the several rooms of the orphanage in which Lieutenant-Commander Ramsaur, the American, who had scarcely fired a pistol before, distinguished himself. At one stage, Patterson, whose gun had misfired, was seized by a German. Running from behind, Ramsaur blew the man's brains out

123

(he almost blew Patterson's out as well). No German escaped from this imbrogolio. Two or three who had leapt through windows in an attempt to take to the hills were captured by the sentries outside.

When the final count was made two enemy were found to be dead, three were unhurt but prisoner, and seven were more or less severely wounded and prisoner, including an officer. S.B.S. had suffered no casualties whatsoever. No time could now be wasted. The Germans still on board the lighters would grow suspicious if the return of their comrades seemed delayed. Leaving the prisoners in charge of his medical sergeant, Kingsbury, and a few more than willing Greeks, Patterson set off with the remainder of his men at the double. The patrol carried a Bren gun, five magazines, Lewis bombs, and indeed everything necessary to bring the engagement to a successful conclusion. Working their way unobserved up a hill about 300 yards from the ships, they put the Bren into position. On board, the Germans were seen to be lounging about the decks. Some were sleeping. It was evident that they had not heard the fracas in the orphanage.

Patterson was only just in time. Barely had he climbed the hill when two Germans who had been sent from the lighters to investigate the delay were spotted entering the orphanage. One of them must have seen the blood spattered on its walls. He came out shouting and ran back towards the lighters. Patterson opened up with the Bren, killed this man and then sprayed the contents of two magazines over the target area.

Harden, with Corporal Long and Lance-Corporal Clark, both marines, was now only about 150 yards from the quayside. Covered by the Bren, they ran forward and engaged the enemy at short range with carbines and grenades. The Germans, who throughout both engagements fought bravely, succeeded in getting one machine-gun and a Schmeisser into action. But this retaliation was neutralized by Patterson, who held a commanding position and frustrated all attempts to get heavier metal to bear by deadly automatic raking shots. Harden, who had run out of grenades, began to throw one-pound primed charges of plastic explosive into the boats.

124

This was too much for the Germans. A white flag was raised, and the few of them who could walk came out meekly with their hands in the correct position. Two more Germans were killed in this second engagement. Of the remaining eight men, six were found to be wounded.

Almost the entire population of Mandracchio had watched the battle, and at its conclusion their exultation knew no bounds. The Germans, who were mostly special service engineers, accepted their defeat with good grace, with the exception of the officer, who was surly and unco-operative. His defeat by numerically smaller forces he attributed wholly to 'the black treachery of the Greeks'. 'I shall be back in Nisiros within six months,' he declared, an intention which he later tried to implement by breaking out of a prison camp in Egypt. He was captured after covering only five of the five hundred miles to the Aegean.

Patterson now made preparations for departure. The lighters were started without difficulty and anchor was weighed. Five of the Germans wounded in the orphanage brawl were too ill for immediate removal, and had already been put to bed by the kind-hearted nun. Patterson left Stephenson behind with instructions to embark these men on the motor launch when she returned that evening. Then, having received the congratulations of the mayor and other notabilities, he set course for Turkey, where he arrived safely the following morning.

Apart from the total of five Germans killed and seventeen taken prisoner, nearly 40 tons of foodstuffs destined for the garrsion of Cos were discovered in these lighters, together with four live pigs and much wine and brandy.

Stephenson's adventures were not yet over. At midnight the motor launch arrived and he embarked his prisoners. The return voyage was almost half over, and the ship well within territorial waters, when the naval commander (Sub-Lieutenant Hickford, R.N.V.R.) sighted two lighters ahead, apparently in difficulties. Judging these to be the ships already captured, he closed with one of them and had already secured himself at her side when he discovered that she was crammed with Germans. A third lighter now put in an appearance, supported by a heavily armed caïque.

In this emergency, Stephenson, with two sailors, seized tommy-guns and leapt over the taffrail as a self-appointed boarding-party. Moving among the closely packed Germans, who had no means of distinguishing friend from foe, they caused terrible havoc. Those few whom they did not injure, shot each other with their own weapons.

The identity of the British motor launch had now been discovered. Fire was directed at her from all sides as she sheered off. A direct hit from the 3-inch gun on board the caïque knocked out her forr'ard Oerlikon, killing its crew of two men. A second shell exploded in a small compartment after used for storing flares. The resultant blaze must have convinced the enemy that the launch was sinking. They ceased fire for some minutes and, profiting by this lull, Hickford got his craft away. It was not until almost an hour later that he discovered that Stephenson and two of his crew were missing.

Stephenson, seeing the launch disappear, was undismayed. He had worked his way up behind one of the twin Bredas by this time, and was sending fusillade after fusillade down the crowded decks. When the ammunition was exhausted, he shouted to the sailors. The three men dived overboard. They swam to the Turkish coast, which lay about a mile away. Next day, still wet, but otherwise none the worse for their adventures, they returned to S.B.S. base by mule. From prisoners taken later by himself, the total of German casualties on that lighter was established as twenty-six.

With this operation the tour of duty of Patterson's detachment came to an end. They were succeeded by Sutherland's men. Patterson himself, with Ramsaur, was sent by caïque to Izmir, there to proceed for an interview with the British military attaché in Istanbul.

Von Klemann, who had once protested that the Dodecanese were not a fighting command, was being given his money's worth. His subordinates, who were quite frankly nervous, were now inclined to leave their *Kasinos* in groups of not less than three on dark evenings.

CHAPTER FIFTEEN

There has always been a certain similarity between the life in the S.B.S. and that led by actors—brief 'engagements' followed by periods spent 'resting'. Not until much later was there sufficient work for more than two squadrons simultaneously. The unemployed third squadron infallibly became the victims of Jellicoe's fertile fancy.

Thus, while Patterson was amusing himself in the Aegean, the remainder of us were climbing mountains at the Middle East ski school.

'But *why* ski-ing?' somebody had demanded.

'It is a pleasant sport,' Jellicoe had replied.

'But will we ever be *used* as ski-troops?'

'You ask too many questions,' said Jellicoe. 'Get fit and don't bother me.' Jellicoe could never suffer fools gladly.

In the Army there exist certain quaint and pleasant backwaters, exclusive retreats in which cranks, inadequately disguised by khaki, continue to practise those accomplishments which distinguished them in civilian life. Burglars give lock-picking courses for the benefit of commando troops and agents; poachers, with sergeants' rank, tell bored recruits how to live off the land; artists become camouflage experts; photographers gain experience in the examination of other people's obliques and mosaics. All these people enjoy themselves immensely and are paid for their trouble.

The Middle East ski school was no exception to this rule. Within its central-heated walls were gathered together more heroes of St. Moritz and Kitzbühel than could be cross-checked against the legs of a centipede. To do these people justice, they did honestly believe in the likelihood of ski-warfare developing, and the course which they gave to prepare troops for it was well planned, strenuous, and comprehensive. Sympathetic relations did not, however, always exist between pupils and instructors, and for this the blame must undoubtedly be laid upon the S.B.S. rank and file. The S.B.S. rank and file did not like ski-ing. They did not see what it had to do with Germans and attacks upon German-held islands. With the illimitable scepticism of the other rank they derided snow and everything connected with snow, particularly the somewhat abstruse theories of mountain warfare to which they were continually required to listen. There was irritation upon both sides and, in his report, the commanding officer of the school was bitter.

'I do not,' he wrote, 'see how this unit can ever be put into action against the enemy.'

Some reports of actions in which S.B.S. had already contacted the enemy were placed in this officer's hands.

The incidents closed. I mention them because it must not be imagined that S.B.S. were universally popular. Their discipline was that born of mutual respect, and of this kind of discipline there is little conventional outward evidence and no heel-clicking. The clothes worn by S.B.S. were somewhat odd, the manner of wearing them even more so. Many is the correctly attired officer with a Sam Browne and Africa Star who has looked down his nose at Lassen, who did not often wear his Military Cross and two bars. Many are the military policemen who have learned that it is not wise to annoy Guardsmen Conby, D'Arcy, and O'Reilly when this inseparable trio were returning home tranquilly in the early hours of the morning.

But if the approbation of the vulgar multitude was not always forthcoming, that of G.H.Q. in Cairo, was given unreservedly.

'After all, it takes all sorts to make a war,' murmured a certain general, rather equivocally.

Captain Eberhart Wiebelitz, of the German Auxiliary

Merchant Navy, was really a most unfortunate man. He had spent Christmas with his wife and family in Strettin, and had only been in the Aegean a few weeks when my patrol took him prisoner in Stampalia.

If Wiebelitz had followed the advice given to the young lady who was warned never to accept dinner invitations from strange men, his service career might have been greatly prolonged. Instead, on the very day of his arrival in Stampalia, he agreed to take dinner with Ober-Leutnant Wilhelm Beurath, the naval commander of the island. News of the dinner-party reached me while I was lying-up in the cave previously used by Anderson's expedition. Both men were captured without difficulty. They proved docile and talkative prisoners. Simultaneously, my patrol shot up a German post containing twelve marines, eight of whom were wounded. The panic-stricken Germans ran out of their billet in all directions. They were wearing ankle-length night-shirts and were therefore easy targets. A folboat which we sent round to the harbour under Trooper Rodney Hancock to attack Wiebelitz's convoy was not so fortunate. It was a very dark night. The convoy was dispersed all over the wide bay as a precaution against submarines. Hancock paddled for hours within a few feet of the German posts, but was unable to find the ships. Next day he was almost caught. Lying-up under camouflage on a small island, he was considerably shaken to see a large party of the enemy approach and begin rifle practice over his head. They did not leave until the evening.

At about this same time Lieutenant Kingsley E. Gordon Clarke, whose breath-taking moniker was normally reduced to Nobby, was repeating Bruce Mitford's grand tour of Patmos, Lisso, and Archi. Nobby's patrol, which was exceptionally strong, containing such old hands as Pomford, Holmes, and a deadly Hebridean named McAulay, found these islands dull. To enliven the outing they marched to Scala, in Patmos, with the intention of attacking the Italian garrison of ten men.

'But they refused to fight,' wrote Nobby disgustedly, 'and I was forced to take them prisoner.'

Nobby returned to base with his unwelcome cargo. Italian prisoners, somehow, were never very well thought of—David Sutherland, in particular, being inclined to turn up his nose at them—but since Italians always surrendered at the first opportunity, the only alternative was to kill them.

S.B.S., of course, never did anything like *that* . . .

Keith Balsillie, who was fortunate enough to number Marine Hughes among his patrol, had got away to a flying start in Piscopi. Before he left for this island, Sutherland approached Keith and asked him if he would care to take with him a bespectacled young American war correspondent named Donald Grant, who was then studying our activities.

'Well,' demurred Keith, 'I mean . . . will he *fight?*'

'Of course I'll fight,' said Donald Grant aggressively.

'Right you are,' said Keith. 'Here's a carbine.'

Arrived in Piscopi, Balsillie and Stefan Casulli, who was acting as interpreter, immediately contacted the mayor of Megalocorio, which, as its name implies, is the largest town.

'Why you not come and see me last time you here?' said the mayor aggrievedly. 'What you want . . . you want wine? . . . you want Germans?'

Keith said that he wanted Germans.

'I fix that easy,' said the mayor. 'I excellent relations with Germans. This Lootenant Urbanitz he think me very good friend. I introduce him to woman with disease, but he not know that yet. Ha! Ha! What you say I tell Urbanitz there is fat pig in this village? Then he come up with some men to get this pig and you shoot him . . . What you say, eh, feller?'

Keith said that he thought this idea positively brilliant.

'Right,' said the mayor. 'You wait here, in this path to-morrow. I go now and get cart—everything.'

Keith was mystified. 'What does he want a cart for?' he asked, when the mayor had left.

Stefan Casulli grinned. The ways of his compatriots were no mystery to him.

'Oh,' he said, 'I expect he wants the cart to take the bodies away when it's all over. Then he'll go down to the town with them and act as chief mourner.'

At dawn on the following day, Keith's patrol were lying in

the agreed position. The German officer, Urbanitz, had been told that pigs and other food supplies were available for him in a village at the other end of the island. He was a greedy man and his unwillingness to exist on normal army rations was his undoing. Shortly after eight o'clock he was seen coming up the path, followed by his quarter-master, his personal clerk, and another soldier, who was leading a mule.

When the German officer was some ten yards distant, Keith jumped up from behind a rock and ordered him to surrender. Perhaps a reflex action, perhaps a real intention to resist, made Urbanitz reach for his holster. Marine Hughes, behind the patrol Bren gun, was taking no chances. He emptied a whole magazine at the four men. The mule was the only survivor.

Almost everyone had fired at least one shot in this brief engagement but when it was over, Donald Grant was discovered sitting disconsolately on a rock. He had tried to fire but the safety-catch of his carbine had been pressed home. Perhaps, in view of his position as war correspondent, this was all for the best. Later, when Donald Grant got back to the States, he wrote an article about S.B.S.: it was entitled . . . 'They're tough . . . they wear no ties . . .' He was a nice young man. Unlike most war correspondents he was able to carry a heavy pack without complaint.

Three or four hours after this legalized murder, the mayor, with another party of Germans, collected the dead. At the funeral, the mayor made a most touching oration. He kept a copy of it for the next party of S.B.S. which should land.

David Sutherland had a splendid idea at this time. The island of Nisiros was linked with Cos by submarine telephone. Sutherland's idea was that a Beaufighter from Cyprus should dive over Nisiros and drop a smoke bomb in the sea, thus giving the impression that it had crashed. A few minutes later, Stefan Casulli, posing as a well-disposed citizen, would ring up Cos from Nisiros and declare that two British airmen had landed on the island by rubber boat. The Germans on Cos, who would have seen the supposed 'crash', would be invited to send a party to collect the stranded airmen. When the Germans entered the harbour, Ian

131

Patterson's exploit would be repeated on terms even more favourable to ourselves.

Unfortunately, the plan fell through, for the Germans put a garrison on Nisiros, thus placing the telephone beyond our reach. My patrol, which had been briefed for this job, was now diverted to Calino.

We were very fortunate in the main target assigned to us. This was a shipyard on the fringe of Calino town. Normally, this area was guarded by two fixed and one mobile sentry, but on the night of my attack (made with Hancock and Rifleman Lynch) there was no interference. Of fourteen caïques on the stocks for repairs of one kind or another, we selected ten as being of the most value to the enemy, one of these being a very trim little ship under charter to the Gestapo. Near the caïque yard was the cable station, surrounded by a great deal of imposing but rusty barbed wire. Very large charges fitted with various delays in the interests of German insomnia, were laid on all these targets. Explosions continued throughout the night. The sentries, who had been brewing-up coffee while we worked, were sent up into the hills after us. Unfortunately we did not know this until later, for we could have easily taken them prisoner.

Meanwhile, Sergeant Henderson and the American, Jarrell, had been sent to another part of the island with a Bren gun. They were to site their gun in some suitable position and a fire a single shot at the shutters of a German billet. The Germans, it was hoped, would believe this to be the act of some sniper in possession, at most, of a rifle. As they ran out of their billet, Henderson would open up in earnest.

This plan worked well up to a point. The Germans did run out of the billet and Henderson gave them several nutritious bursts. But the enemy reaction was very much more vigorous than had been expected, and they were evidently more numerous than our information had suggested. Henderson's fire was returned almost immediately. Six Germans actually began to work their way up the hill towards him.

For Germans to move at night in this way, and against unknown opposition, was quite unheard of and definitely against the rules of the game. Henderson and Jarrell were harried and chased for several miles, heavily handicapped by the weight of their gun and magazines. In their initial attack they had inflicted five casualties, though it was never discovered how many of these were killed.

By contrast, four men sent to Borio in the north of the island with orders to fire shots outside German billets in the hope of luring the occupants out had no success; even when, in desparation, they blew up telegraph poles inside the village itself. The Germans may have found it humiliating to sit quietly indoors, but they knew what we wanted and were learning wisdom.

All the raids described above followed each other in very quick succession. The pace was now being stepped up. Barely was a patrol back at base before it was out again to attack another target. Nobby Clarke, with Pomford and McAulay, was sent to Amorgos. This island lies far to the west, beyond the confines of the Dodecanese. Amorgos had been Greek since the liberation. Normally, the island possessed a German garrison, but when Nobby called there they were absent in Santorin. One man alone remained, who was living, paradoxically enough, with his mistress in a monastery. 'The morals of the Germans on this island,' said Nobby, 'were lax.' He pursued the solitary German through the town and eventually cornered him in a church. 'He seemed to imagine that this would afford him some kind of sanctuary,' said Nobby. 'Not wishing to fire in the church, I told him to come out. The man refused, whereupon I went in and got him, not having to fire at all. He was a stupid little man and he wasted a great deal of my time.' Nobby was beginning to get a little tired of the unspectacular jobs allotted to him. He need not have worried. Trouble was coming soon enough.

While Nobby was in Amorgos, Corporal Holmes of his patrol, with Privates Crouch and Sanders, was sent to Nisiros with instructions to find out what had been happening on that island since Patterson's raid. They discovered that there was now a garrison of not less than 150 men there. Led by an islander whose intelligence had been reckoned by previous parties as adequate, they took refuge for the night in a cave.

In the morning when he woke up, Corporal Holmes found a German entering the cave. Holmes was still in his sleeping-bag, without shoes or socks. He raised the Bren gun beside him and gave the German a burst through the head . . . 'Boy, you should have seen his brains spill out.' The noise woke Crouch and Sanders. They ran out of the cave naked, holding their carbines. Three more Germans were approaching. Crouch and Sanders killed two of them and caused the third to run away. Profiting by this lull, the party dressed hurriedly and made off. They were chased all day, and re-embarked under fire that night. The enterprise of the naval launches in coming in to take the men off under these conditions is beyond praise.

So far our losses, as you will have noticed, had been negligible; those of the enemy considerable. But now an operation was to be mounted which would cause us to pay dearly for a too prolonged penetration in enemy waters.

Lassen had done well in Calchi in January. Captain Bill Blyth, with Sergeant Miller and Privates Rice, Evans, and Jones, was now sent to that island with orders to find a suitable lying-up area for a caïque . . . for, a few weeks later, it was intended to knock out the radar posts on Scarpanto; and Calchi was a useful staging-point on the way there.

Bill Blyth had completed his business in Calchi and was re-embarking, when no less than four German 'P' lighters entered the inlet in which the caïque was hiding. That there had been a betrayal there could be no doubt: the informer was later caught and shot. The battle itself was brief, unequal, and bloody. Sub-Lieutenant Tuckey, R.N.V.R., the commander of the caïque, was taken prisoner with the survivors of his crew. Bill Blyth and his men slipped overboard, swam ashore, and hid in the hills.

The Germans searched for them in vain. Blyth was beginning to think that he had got away with it. As soon as the search-parties had gone, he made arrangements with a fisherman to be ferried across to Rhodes, which lay only four miles distant. From Rhodes, Blyth calculated that escape would be easy.

They never reached Rhodes as free men. Half-way across the channel the fishing-smack was stopped by a German patrol boat. Blyth and his party lay down in the bilges. They remained unnoticed during the examination of papers which followed. For some reason, however, the patrol boat remained suspicious. Closing with the fishing-smack again she fired a shot across her bows. Blyth, who had no wish to get the fisherman into further trouble, stood up, and was made prisoner with all his party.

Bill Blyth was well treated. He was flown to Athens, and from Athens to Germany. Within a week of his capture he was playing hockey in an Offlag. But what happened to Tuckey, to Miller, Rice, Evans, Jones and the naval ratings we never knew . . . and, it seems now that we never shall know. The war is over, but they remain listed as 'missing'.

Had the German garrison in Rhodes remained unchanged until its capitulation, we should have discovered supplementary information. Unfortunately, the garrison was changed and, in 1945, no longer resembled in any way the original command of von Klemann.

Were these men shot? I was taken prisoner myself later and have good cause to know with what fear and loathing our unit was regarded by the enemy, but I am still alive and my patrol, on that job, had caused the Germans severe losses. Bill Blyth and his men, through no fault of their own, did not shoot a single German and, moreover, were closely associated with naval prisoners, whom the Germans invariably treated correctly.

In these circumstances, most people are inclined to believe—since no further word was ever received from these men—that they perished either in an air crash or in a ship torpedoed by one of His Majesty's submarines.

If that is so, theirs was a hard and unmerited death, but more pleasant, perhaps, than that of the two Long Range Desert Group Signallers who were shot in cold blood in Istria thirteen months later; more pleasant, perhaps, than that of the nine 1st Special Air Service men who were shot in cold blood in a French wood; more pleasant, perhaps, that that of the twenty-two 2nd Special Air Service men, tortured and burnt to death in a German prison camp.

I have mentioned the occupational risks before.

CHAPTER SIXTEEN

One of the most exasperating features of raiding in the Aegean at that time was the frequent restriction in our choice of targets. There existed, in fact, another organisation which in view of its tradition of anonymity we will call Force X. This Force X was doing splendid work collecting and collating Intelligence, landing agents and distributing supplies to members of the Greek resistance on the mainland. Secrecy, however, was an essential of their trade, and secrecy could not very well be maintained if a S.B.S. raid brought a swarm of Gestapo men to some island where an agent was employed, say, in a study of the German gun positions.

Somebody had therefore to yield precedence, and the victims were more often than not S.B.S. This may seem a small matter, but pushed to its logical conclusions, the results were sometimes quite extraordinary. At one time, every single island in the Aegean, with the uninteresting exception of Pserimo, was out of bounds to S.B.S. for any purpose other than that of reconnaissance. Let us see how this could occur . . .

Well . . . a brigadier in Force X would announce to his immediate subordinate, a colonel, that an agent was to be landed, on, say, Syros, in the Cyclades on such and such a date.

'You might see that Jellicoe's bandits keep quiet during that time,' he would add. 'This fellow is valuable. I want him given time to settle in.'

The colonel would go away, brooding over the grave

137

words of his chief. Presently, an edict would be issued that Syros was out of bounds to S.B.S. for a period of two weeks. In due course this edict would pass to another department. This department would have no idea of the reason for the order, but it would be slow in noting that Syros lay in the centre of the Cyclades.

'Well, if they can't go there,' someone would say, 'it stands to reason that we can't have them mucking about in the neighbouring islands.' The entire group of twenty-three Cyclades would then be placed out of bounds to S.B.S. for a period of a fortnight. Two or three further pieces of hanky-panky of this nature and S.B.S. would be left with a couple of barren rocks, a dismantled lighthouse at one end and a disused goat-pen at the other.

On the famous occasion when David Sutherland's choice of targets was down to Pserimo, he sent an expedition there in desperation, captured a caïque and an Italian, and then complained in restrained but measured terms. The bans were lifted ... or when not lifted (dare I say it?) were circumvented:

('It's no use cursing me,' officers would say, 'I only went to the bloody island to reconnoitre. How could I help it if the German got in my way ... I mean, what would *you* do in my place?')

Such protestations of innocence, if insincere, were not infrequent.

Lassen was now back. The wound sustained in Calchi had turned septic. Lassen had spent two months in hospital in Alexandria with a disgusting little dog lurking under his bed. This dog, Lassen claimed, against all evidence, to be a Maltese terrier. Its habits, which Lassen encouraged, were lubricious and obscene. He arrived with it now in time for the raids on the Cyclades.

On all the outlying members of that group, the Germans maintained small garrisons, who consisted for the most part of young naval ratings, entrusted with a shipping watch. They also possessed radio transmitters with which to report the movement of hostile air and surface craft. Brigadier

Turnbull's plan, which was approved in early April 1944, was no less than the liquidation of these posts on a single night.

Sutherland's squadron was mobilized for this task. My patrol was given Mikonos, in many ways the easiest of the group to attack.

Lassen, with his own patrol, and Keith Balsillie's under his command, was to attack Santorin. Nobby Clarke was to visit first Ios and then Amorgos, where the enemy had recently re-established themselves.

These raids were successful, the various garrisons either being taken alive or liquidated, their radio sets destroyed, and the German information service paralysed for a long period to come.

Before the war, Mikinos was a tourist resort, deriving considerable prosperity from the Delphic ruins on near-by Delos. Its buildings were in consequence more modern and their sanitation more advanced than in those encountered throughout the Dodecanese. Mikinos is well populated. We landed on a dark night in conditions of secrecy, but not many hours had elapsed before the news of our arrival had spread. That day chanced to be a Sunday, the eve of the Greek National Festival of St. George. By ten o'clock in the morning I was receiving deputations who had come considerable distances in order to welcome us. The men, stiff in their festive clothes, with starched collars, saluted with dim memories of military service . . . the women, perched primly on mule back, gazed at us solemnly and threw flowers. It was all very touching. We were the first allied troops to visit Mikinos since the declaration of war.

It goes without saying that everybody knew of the arrival of the *Inglesi* with the exception of the Germans. There were nine Germans on Mikinos. Seven lived in the best villa in the town. Two were stationed in a lighthouse some distance away. Throughout the day their movements were reported to us. The Germans, it seemed, were getting drunk.

Next morning, at first light, we attacked the villa. Simultaneously, three young Greeks, who had volunteered to work for us, were sent up to the lighthouse to dispose of the two men there.

The German sentry at the villa was shot at once by Rifleman Lynch. The villa was then rushed, but the occupants had had time to collect their wits. They barricaded themselves in a single room, whilst one of their number threw grenades down the stairs at us. We now sent for the mayor of the town. This man spoke German and had a German wife. He was brought to the garden wall and told to order the garrison to surrender. The Germans made no reply. Although unable to stand up in their room without drawing a volley of shots, they could hear aircraft overhead and shrewdly guessed them to be friendly. They began to fire Very lights in the hope of attracting attention. The aircraft, which were in fact Junkers, escorting a convoy, did not see the Very lights.

The young Greeks now arrived with the two prisoners from the lighthouse. I took one of these prisoners to the garden wall and ordered him to tell his comrades that unless they surrendered immediately we would burn the house down with the aid of a dump of petrol in its grounds. This was a bluff, for it would have taken us the entire day to place that petrol in position. The Germans, however, had no means of knowing this. They surrendered immediately. The villa was delivered over to the exultant civilian population, who looted it efficiently. British and Germans adjourned to a local hotel for lunch.

On the first floor of the Bank of Athens, in Santorin town, was a billet containing forty-eight Italians and twenty Germans. There were other targets on Santorin but Lassen reserved this one for himself. He took with him Stefan Casulli and twelve men. Despite many sentries and police dogs, surprise was achieved. The billet, from which exit was impossible, became a death-trap for its occupants. 'There was,' wrote Lassen, 'a grand mix-up in the dark.'

He is too modest. In point of fact, Lassen, accompanied by Sergeant Nicholson, walked from room to room. They paid the greatest attention to detail. First, Nicholson would kick the door open . . . then Lassen would throw two grenades inside . . . then Nicholson, firing his Bren from the hip, would spray the walls and corners . . . finally, Lassen, with his pistol, would deal with any remaining signs of life.

Next day, of all the enemy in this billet, only four Germans and six Italians were seen by the townspeople.

Unhappily, this massacre, although almost complete, was not achieved without loss. Stefan Casulli . . . standing *in* a doorway instead of to one side of it . . . was shot through the chest. He died immediately. His companion, Sergeant Kingston, a medical orderly, received a bullet in the stomach, from which wound he succumbed on the following day. Marine Trafford and Guardsman Harris—the latter Bill Blyth's batman—were slightly wounded by the sentries outside the billet. They forgot their pain in the pleasure of watching four fear-crazed Italians jumping through the windows from a height of forty feet.

Two other attacks were taking place in Santorin at the same time as Lassen's. Sergeant B. Henderson, a physical training instructor, familiarly known as 'The Brown Body' in consequence of his nudist tendencies, was sent to investigate the house occupied by the German Commander and his orderly. Not unnaturally, Henderson now heard what he described as 'the murmur of voices issuing from the rear of the house.'

He dashed round just in time to find the German officer making an undignified escape through the back streets.

Keith Balsillie was fulfilling his mission thoroughly. Keith was fortunate in having with him on this job Corporal Karl Kahane, a fluent German speaker. Led by Kahane, the party entered the first German billet. They found a man asleep in bed.

'For you, my friend,' said Kahane, 'the war is over. Now be a good fellow . . . get dressed and lead us to your comrades.'

The German was so persuaded by the logic of Kahane's remarks—which admittedly were supported by considerable fire-power—that he immediately conducted Balsillie to a second house. Here, three more Germans were found asleep in bed. These Germans also allowed themselves to be convinced and the procession, now swollen in numbers,

141

moved on to a third house, where yet another trio of Germans were found asleep in bed. Here, at least, there was a little variety, for two of the Germans were in bed together. Only one German now remained in the area and he, hearing of the fate of his comrades, tamely presented himself of his own accord. Balsillie prepared the radio station for demolition and withdrew to contact Lassen.

Next day, as might be expected, there was considerable air activity over the island. Santorin is crescent-shaped, the spawn of that extinct volcano which affords its deep harbour moderate shelter. There is very little cover in Santorin and had the defending ground forces not been virtually exterminated, things might have gone badly for Lassen. Fortunately the enemy command in the larger island of Melos seem to have thought that the island had been captured. They did not appear with reinforcements for over forty-eight hours. Lassen was able to collect his scattered forces and to evacuate in comfort.

Subsequent events in Santorin throw interesting sidelights on the mentality of both Germans and Greeks. The Germans gave Stefan Casulli and Kingston a funeral with full military honours. On the same day they issued a proclamation demanding the names of those who had helped the British. Six Greeks, including the mayor of a village, presented themselves voluntarily. They were shot.

We must now turn to the third leg of this most successful experiment in concerted attack. Nobby Clarke and his patrol, had landed in Ios on 25th April. As on the other two islands, the Germans here were careless in the extreme . . . a state of affairs which must be attributed to the enemy's practice of censoring all news of our raids, with the result that all who had not actually suffered were unaware of the disasters that might come with the night.

Corporal Holmes, sent with a small party to collect three of the garrison, was unable to make the capture. The Germans, when approached, seized a number of children and held these unfortunate little creatures in front of them to cover their withdrawal.

Nobby Clarke, with Pomford and McClelland, was more

142

fortunate. Forcing their way into a house, they surprised two Germans who were undressing. These men were more courageous than their comrades. Refusing to surrender, they attacked the invaders with bare hands and were killed. A third German, who was visiting his mistress in another part of the town, was captured as he was about to get into bed with her. This man was most disconsolate. Had he known that his mistress, herself, had supplied the information concerning his whereabouts, he might have been more disconsolate still.

Nobby Clarke marched his captives along the quay. Presently, footsteps were heard. Two men were seen approaching. When challenged they opened fire. The British replied with grenades but the intruders succeeded in getting behind a house. Covered by the house they escaped to the hills.

Unperturbed by this setback, Clarke proceeded with the business of the evening. He blew up the telegraph and cable stations and detonated a dump of 75 mm. shells. In the harbour he sank one caïque and unloaded the food from a second, for distribution to the civilian population. On the following day he requested the mayor to send a messenger to the surviving Germans with orders that they report to him immediately, under pain of being hunted down without mercy. The credulous Germans, who might easily have remained hidden, surrendered half an hour later.

Clarke then sailed for Amorgos, where he was joined by Flying Officer Macris and five men of the Greek Sacred Squadron. There were ten Germans now on Amorgos, all living in a house in the chief town. That night the house was surrounded and fire opened upon it by two Bren guns. Macris and another Greek climbed up some trellis work and tossed grenades into various rooms. At a blast from Clarke's whistle, firing ceased and the Germans were invited to surrender. Instead of capitulating they made a sortie with arms in their hands. Eight of them were killed as they reached the open; the remaining pair escaped to the hills.

Thus concluded forty-eight hours of British intervention in the Cyclades. Casualties suffered by the enemy were forty-one killed, twenty-seven wounded and nineteen made prisoner. S.B.S. losses in the three operations were two killed and three slightly wounded, of a total expeditionary strength of thirty-nine men.

The list of stores and equipment of all kinds lost by the enemy I need not enumerate.

The immediate result of these raids was the distribution of large garrisons of German mountain troops throughout the Cyclades. Sutherland, however, remained sceptical as to the ability of the enemy to defend even his own living-quarters against determined infiltration. To prove his point, he dispatched Lassen and thirteen men to Paros, a large island lying only seventy miles from Athens. An air landing-strip had recently been completed on Paros. Workmen of the Todt organisation still slept in tents along its fringe.

Lassen, as was his custom, divided his party into small groups, each with a separate target. The main attack failed— the alarm being given almost at once by some unusually alert sentries—but the subsidiary expeditions were in each case successful. Private Perkins, accompanied by a Greek officer penetrated into one house to discover a German officer standing uncertainly in pyjamas and holding a Lüger.

'Hands up,' said Perkins, who spoke good German, 'everything is finished for you.'

The German officer does not appear to have believed this. He replied with an incredulous 'Was?' and a shot. The Greek killed him. In the next room the pair found and killed three private soldiers.

Sergeant Nicholson and Marine Williams, detailed to capture a second German officer, discovered their quarry hiding behind a door, clad in a flowered dressing-gown. He accompanied them without fuss. Several other German occupants of the house hid beneath beds and inside cupboards. They hoped to avoid capture. Nicholson and Williams who were perfectly well aware of the number of people in the house made no attempt to search it. Withdrawing, they threw phosphorus and fragmentation grenades through all the windows. Three of the men hidden were killed.

So, incidentally, was Nicholson's prisoner, hit first in the neck by one of his own snipers and subsequently in the chest by a grenade explosion. Nicholson, who had wasted several perfectly good field-dressings and mouthfuls of brandy in an endeavour to save the man, returned sadly to the rendezvous.

A strange, plump, freckled, kilted figure now enters the story. It is that of Captain Douglas Stobie, a very early member of Special Air Service, who had had the misfortune to break a leg in Tunisia; in consequence of which disaster he had been invalided home. He arrived back now, bringing with him a tommy-gun, the largest biceps and calf measurements in the Middle East, and a huge file of papers, apparently the result of some disagreement with the Army Pay Office. Stobie, it seemed, had not received his servant allowance or some such emolument for the period of his convalescence in the United Kingdom. He was determined that justice should be done to him. Briefed to accompany Nobby Clarke on a raid in Naxos, he took his file with him. During the intervals of planning and fighting, Stobie composed letters of complaint.

The Naxos operation was most successful. This was the first island in which guerillas were encountered and their assistance was invaluable. Clarke and Stobie found Naxos well guarded and in a state of considerable alertness following the raid on Paros. They decided to devote their attention to a single German garrison of one officer and seventeen men. The three houses in which this group lived were surrounded and progressively demolished by large explosive charges. All the Germans became casualties, though Clarke was obliged to leave the wounded behind, owing to the approach of an enemy relief column.

The final operations of Sutherland's squadron, prior to handing over to Lapraik, are of minor importance. Sutherland himself, who had been chafing at base for weeks, was now finally able to get out and, with a motley force, penetrated deep into the Cyclades, sinking a caïque in Siphnos and capturing a stray German in the same island.

Harold Chevalier, also with a scratch force, accompanied a naval patrol travelling north. Caïques of all sizes were stopped and searched in the waters between Samos and Chios. Eventually patience was rewarded by the appearance of a ship which could be commandeered with a clear conscience. The four Germans on board her were made prisoners.

Throughout this whole period, the naval liaison work, under Commander John Campbell, R.N.R., was a very high order. Motor launches carrying S.B.S. parties never hesitated to go close inshore, lay-off—sometimes for hours—within shouting distance of enemy observation posts and, in more than one case, re-embarked personnel under the immediate threat of air attack.

CHAPTER SEVENTEEN

The legacy awaiting Lapraik when he left Alexandria to take over the conduct of operations was unenviable. Patterson had stirred up the Dodecanese to such an extent that every garrison was now wide awake. Sutherland had intensified Patterson's policy and, with the additional advantage of fine weather, had caused nearly 4,000 German reinforcements to be transferred from the mainland to the Cyclades. In these two groups, no island remained which had not been visited at least once. Tactical surprise could still be achieved by the switching of patrols from one area to another, by simultaneous attacks in islands widely separated, by feints and carefully spread rumours. Gone for ever though, were the days when the German defenders would be found in bed. The German defenders now slept increasingly in slit trenches with barbed wire for their eiderdown.

Lapraik in person did not appear immediately. Like Mark Antony before him, he remained brooding upon certain splendours to come in Alexandria. In his absence, Stewart Macbeth assumed command of the squadron. Two or three abortive attacks in the Dodecanese quickly convinced Macbeth that here was a field rather more than well ploughed. He decided to try the Sporades, a small group lying close to the mainland and never before raided.

Macbeth's plan was an interesting and a novel one. A squadron of motor torpedo-boats was about to be sent to these waters to prey upon enemy shipping. S.B.S. personnel would act as the eyes and ears of the navy, ascertaining what anchorages were safe for them when they wished to lie up—providing shore guards and boarding-parties and, finally, attacking such opportunist targets as presented themselves.

Unfortunately, as far as the motor torpedo-boats were concerned, the plan miscarried owing to technical difficulties—but not before Captain James Lees, with three men, and Lieutenant Bob Bury, with Corporal Denham and two others, had sailed and were beyond recall. These two parties, working in different area, were for the next fortnight to have the varied and exciting time enjoyed by all troops who have the good fortune to be out of radio communication with their base.

Jimmy Lees landed on the small island of Strati on 22nd June 1944. He found no Germans, and was immediately caught up in the whirlpool of local politics. Strati was, in fact, under the control of E.A.M., the political movement later to prove so intransigent on the mainland. Emissaries of E.A.M. who were, at this epoch, friendly enough, presented themselves at Jimmy Lee's hide-out, a cave, and invited him to choose a less modest residence. Jimmy Lees installed his party in an empty villa. He was enjoying a well-earned sleep there when the chief of the local gendarmes called, soliciting an interview.

Would His Excellency the English officer be staying long? he inquired.

His Excellency the English officer replied vaguely that he liked the place and might possibly remain a few days.

In that case, said the gendarme, would His Excellency object very much if he and his men searched the villa? A pure formality, of course, but sooner or later the Germans would hear that His Excellency had been on the island. They would than inquire why the leader of the gendarmes had not chased the invaders? Further, if His Excellency could see his way to leaving a few cartridges and ... say ... a webbing belt about, matters would be greatly facilitated, for these objects could later be produced as evidence of thoroughness and zeal in respect of the search.

Jimmy Lees politely turned out of his billet and allowed it to be inspected.

Next day, the mayor and all the gendarmes returned and were even more exigent. They now demanded to be arrested and placed in 'custody'. Nothing less than this, they insisted, would ever satisfy the Germans. Without waiting for an answer they began to bind themselves with rope and chains which they had thoughtfully provided for this purpose. Finally, trussed and powerless, they lay at Jimmy's feet, groaning with all the fervour of men about to be hurried to summary execution. The large number of islanders who had gathered to watch this curious exhibition had not had so much fun for years.

Jimmy Lees, however, was now beginning to weary of farce. He had commandeered two caïques and he informed the officials that if their intentions were really above suspicion, they would accompany him to Turkey and there place themselves at the disposal of the British authorities. The officials agreed, but insisted upon bringing their wives, their families, and their more remote relatives. Jimmy Lees' fleet then sailed, leaving Strati seriously depopulated.

Bob Bury, meanwhile, was laboriously canvassing the northern islands of the Sporades in search of Germans. He drew a blank in Skopelos, the largest of them, and another blank in Yioura. Finally, towing a number of captured caïques, and bored and irritated by the Greeks who perpetually mistook him for the enemy, he was informed that a small German garrison existed on Pelagos. Bury decided to attack it.

The Germans, Bury was told, kept no watch at night; a statement which he received with scepticism. He approached the building, a monastery, with care. Outside it a figure was standing, whom Bury's guide declared reverently to be a monk. Doubts were resolved when the 'monk' threw a grenade at the advancing party with most unecclesiastical precision. The grenade failed to explode and the sentry was killed before he could gain cover. Bury now retreated to a safe distance and sent up a prearranged Very light to his armed caïque in the bay below. The multiple Browning machine-guns on the caïque poured a stream of incendiary bullets on to the monastery and the gorse-covered area around it. The whole headland was soon ablaze, the Germans completely silenced, and those who were not roasted inside the house, dealt with by Bury's party as they emerged.

Captain Charles Bimrose, with Sergeant Waite and ten attempting to embark for Cythera, was less successful than his famous precursors. Unable, owing to bad weather, to land in Cythera, the party finally made port in the Peloponnese, where they were attended by one misfortune after another. First, the accidental explosion of a grenade put three men out of action . . . then the partisan authorities, unable to believe, or unwilling to believe that they were British, held them under arrest for a week . . . finally, when their identity was at last established, they were chased all down the coast by one of the periodical drives by which the enemy maintained his tottering New European order. Bimrose did succeed in taking two prisoners, but these he was forced to hand over to the partisans, who first tortured them and then shot them.

The results of these raids not having been altogether satisfactory, Macbeth decided to make a reconnaissance of Calino, which was reported to have been heavily reinforced following the raid by my patrol in April. Jimmy Lees was selected for the job and took with him ten, under Sergeant Horsfield. The reconnaissance established that no less than sixty Germans were now stationed in the Vathi Bay area, previously unoccupied, and Horsfield, pursuing his investigations too closely, ran into trouble.

'I was looking down at the enemy positions,' he said, 'when I saw a boy approaching, followed by two Germans. The latter said something to the boy, who pointed towards our hiding-place. When the Germans came within ten yards of us, we stood up and fired . . .'

One German was killed outright: the other, in his attempts to escape, fell over a cliff.

Macbeth now determined that Calino should be attacked in force, and for the first time in S.B.S. history command was given to a Greek officer, Major Kasakopoulos, who with fourteen of his own compatriots from the Sacred Squadron and ten of our men under Sergeant Dryden, landed at the end of June. Major Richard Lea travelled with the party as liaison officer.

Calino was a Pyrrhic victory. 'The approach and attack,' wrote Lapraik, who seldom minced his words, 'were reasonably sound. The withdrawal, however, I do not consider to have been in any way satisfactory.' These strictures must not be taken as a condemnation of either Majors Kasakopoulos or Lea. Both these officers behaved with exemplary valour during the action, but they were confronted throughout it by language difficulties and the task of co-ordinating two very differently trained sets of men.

The attack on the Vathi Bay area had been designed for three patrols. By 2200 hours on 1st July these were in position and all telephone lines leading from the area had been cut. At 2247 hours the first shot was fired, killed a German sentry who patrolled a key position. S.B.S., with hand grenades and tommy-guns, forced entrance into the enclosure between the main German billets, and deadly scuffling, in which friends were not easy to distinguish from enemy, took place in the dark. A Greek patrol, attacking from another direction, came within grenade-throwing distance of the houses but was held up by wire and accurate small-arms fire. A second Greek patrol, operating a Piat gun, sent several projectiles into the target which began to blaze.

The German reaction was immediate. The whole valley was lit and remained illuminated by Very lights while from a point some distance away, heavy mortar fire was directed on the battle area in the form of a box barrage round the besieged houses. The defenders of these, however, to the number of eighteen, were now beyond all mortal help.

Much had been achieved, but in the face of German reinforcements arriving from all sides, Major Kasakopoulos gave the order to withdraw. While this delicate manoeuvre was being executed, Sergeant Dryden and Privates Fishwick and Jackson were wounded by a mortar burst. Jackson managed to make his way to safety but Dryden, who might have done so, was given a morphia injection which left him in so comatose a condition that he could barely move. Private Doughty, a medical orderly, very gallantly decided to remain with his patrol leader and the more gravely wounded Fishwick. The trio were conducted to a Greek house and there concealed for the night. Next morning, since neither wounded man was fit to march, the local population decided, after much heart-searching, to reveal their presence to the enemy.

Throughout that night the enemy remained in a state of great tension. Long after all patrols had withdrawn they continued to mortar the valley, destroying some dozens of their own reinforcements in the process. Searchlights swept the eastern shore, and at dawn, fighter planes made their appearance as if in expectation of a major landing.

What became of the three prisoners? Of Doughty, nothing was known until he suddenly turned up again, having released himself in Greece.

Dryden, I saw myself in the Averoff prison at Athens, some two months later. Although very weak from loss of blood, the Germans had forced him to lose more in a transfusion to Fishwick, who died while the pair were under interrogation in Leros. Every conceivable threat and form of intimidation, short of physical violence, were used in an effort to make Dryden give information. When we met in Athens—doubling up and down a prison courtyard—his morale was low, but his determination to remain silent quite unimpaired. Dryden had then been for nine weeks in solitary confinement, on short rations, with the threat of execution hanging over him. Later, he too escaped.

Meanwhile, Lapraik had arrived at Yedi Atala and the reason for his delay became apparent. The greatest operation ever attempted by S.B.S. was to be mounted; an operation revolutionary in conception, involving not only the liquidation of an enemy garrison or an island, but also its capture.

The island—as everyone acquainted with Lapraik could have guessed—was Simi. . .

CHAPTER EIGHTEEN

The Simi operation had been considered for some time, but as long as the enemy possessed destroyers in the Aegean, it had never looked practicable. Destroyers can interfere with landing operations, even at long range and at short notice. At the beginning of the year, there had been four destroyers in the Eastern Mediterranean. Only very gradually were they eliminated.

The German navy in those waters seldom put to sea.

In March, one of these ships was damaged by a British submarine. Later, a second received a bomb amidships from a Beaufighter. Two remained lurking in Leros. In this emergency, Brigadier Turnbull requested London to send him out a small party of Royal Marine Boom Commando troops. A wise move, for though there were still many men in S.B.S. to whom folboating was second nature, the art of infiltration by canoe had undoubtedly declined since the days of 'Tug' Wilson. Folboats, when used at all, were now used to land personnel, their role being no more aggressive than that of a gondola.

When Turnbull's marines first arrived in Middle East the experts were inclined to scoff. Their attitude of condescension was abandoned when it was seen with what precision the newcomers handled their craft. In mid-June they went into Portolago Harbour, Leros, crossed two booms, sank the surviving destroyers with limpet charges and emerged without loss.

The way was now clear for Simi.

On 6th July Stewart Macbeth returned to base. He had made a personal reconnaissance of the island and pinpointed the enemy dispositions. Two days later the striking force, under Brigadier Turnbull himself, comprising ten motor launches, two schooners, eighty-one members of S.B.S. and one hundred and thirty-nine from the Greek Sacred Squadron were concentrated in Penzik Bay, Turkey, under camouflage. Three parties were constituted: Main Force, under the Brigadier with Lapraik deputizing; West Force, under Captain Charles Clynes; and South Force, under Macbeth. On the night of 13th July the landings were made, and despite great enemy vigilance, passed everywhere unobserved. The only casualties suffered consisted of two Greek officers who fell into the water with heavy packs. They were drowned.

The approach marches were difficult but all three forces were lying up and overlooking their targets before dawn. At first light a barrage was opened upon Simi Castle—the main enemy stronghold—by mortars and multiple machine-guns. Two Germans 'Ems' barges which had left harbour a few minutes before zero hour now came scuttling back. They had sighted the force of five British launches which was coming in to bombard the castle. Both motor launches and S.B.S. opened fire on these ships. Presently, large white flags could be seen waving from their bridges before they ran ashore and were captured in good working order.

'Stud' Stellin was clearing Molo Point. He had taken his first objective without opposition. Ahead of him, Germans were running up the hill to man their machine-gun posts.

'I took a shot with my carbine,' said 'Stud', 'but misfired. I therefore called upon Private Whalen to give them the works. We strolled in with grenades, and I think that everybody went a little mad. Soon, all the enemy were either down and dead, or up and waving their hands.'

Stellin locked these prisoners in a church, left a sentry outside it and moved on to his next objective.

Clynes, scheduled to attack gun positions, gave them three minutes softening from his Brens and then ordered his Greeks to charge. 'All I can remember, then,' he said, 'is a general surge up the slope and two small and pathetic white handkerchiefs waving at the top of it. I ordered a 'Cease fire' all round, and began to count my prisoners.'

By 0900 hours, Main Force Headquarters and the Vickers machine-gun and mortar troops had advanced to within 800 yards of the castle. Fire was intensified upon this target from all sides, mortar projectiles crashing on the battlements and nine-millimetre tracer searching every embrasure. The enemy reaction was spirited and indicated that they had by no means abandoned hope. Stellin, moving his patrol to clear some caïque yards, received most of the attention.

'The stuff started to whizz about. We had to cross a bridge. Somebody in the castle had a very accurate bead on that bridge. We doubled, but Lance-Corporal Roberts, Private Majury, and Marine Kinghorn became pinned down under a low parapet, the slightest movement causing fire to be brought upon them. I told them to stay there . . .'

They did. They were not able to get up until the castle surrendered three hours later. Roberts, who attempted to while away the time by lighting a cigarette, raised his head an inch or two. He received a bullet graze from the temple to the neck.

Clynes had also been send down to the caïque yard with orders to clear it. On the way he met Lieutenant Betts-Gray, who throughout the action did excellent liaison work. Betts-Gray was hugging the rocks, pursued by a hail of fire. Clynes and his patrol were presently pinned down in their turn. Private Bromley was hit in the arm, and Betts-Gray, who had had miraculous escapes all day, in the buttocks once, and in the back twice, was assisted into a house and put to bed.

To the south, Macbeth and Bury, with their forces, had assaulted a monastery position after considerable mortar preparation. The surviving enemy were driven down a promontory towards the extremity of the island, where Macbeth called upon them to surrender. The first demand written by Bob Bury, was rejected haughtily by the defenders as illegible. It was rewritten with the aid of a young Greek girl, who volunteered to carry it through the lines. This civilian armistice commission was successful and thirty-three more of the enemy laid down their arms.

Around the castle, the situation had developed into a stalemate, with mortar fire causing the garrison casualties and discomfort, but not sufficient in itself to bring about their surrender. Neither Brigadier Turnbull nor Lapraik considered that the position could be taken by direct assault. They decided to consolidate, make the maximum display of force at their disposal and institute surrender parleys.

Accordingly, Brigadier Turnbull sent a German petty-officer, commanding one of the 'Ems' barges, up under escort, with instructions to inform the enemy that they were completely surrounded, that the rest of the island was in British hands, and that further resistance on their part was as senseless as it was likely to prove costly.

The petty-officer returned an hour later. It appeared that the enemy were prepared to talk business. Lieutenant Kenneth Fox, a German speaker, now returned to the castle with the same man. A further hour elapsed during which the only incident was the emergence of a party of Italian *carabinieri* from the stronghold, weeping, and waving a Red Cross flag.

'I thought I recognized one of these fellows,' said Lapraik, 'and sure enough it was the old rascal who had given us so much trouble during our previous occupation of Simi. He grew very pale when he saw me . . .'

Lieutenant-Commander Ramsayer, the naval liaison officer, was then sent up to expedite matters. He found Fox and the German Commander in agitated conference and himself in imminent danger from our mortar fire. At last, the capitulation was arranged and the garrison marched out. They had barely been collected and counted when three Messerschmitts flew over the port and dropped anti-personnel bombs.

'Too bad,' the German Commander is reported to have said, shaking his head. 'You see, that's what comes of being late. I thought they had forgotten about us. I radioed for them five hours ago.'

Prisoners taken in this action totalled 151, of whom seventeen were wounded. Twenty-one Germans and Italians had been killed. S.B.S. and Sacred Squadron losses were as usual microscopic, and, apart from the two Greek officers drowned, not a single man was killed. Six were wounded.

As soon as the Messerschmitts had disappeared, tea was taken by both armies in the caïque yards. Sausages were fried and an ox, provided by the delighted population, roasted on a bowsprit. As for the prisoners, they were so delighted to find themselves treated deferentially instead of being shot out of hand, that they revealed the existence of many a cache of wine in their living-quarters. Bottles were transferred to S.B.S. packs, to be drunk at base.

Meanwhile, Lapraik, Macbeth, and Stellin, well known on the island, were borne to the town hall, where many speeches were made. The town jail was thrown open to the accompaniment of a furore which would have done credit to the storming of the Bastille. Unfortunately, only one prisoner was found inside and he, a Fascist, refused to be liberated.

'I admired these islanders,' said Lapraik, 'intensely; for they well knew that we could not remain and were rightly apprehensive of reprisals. But this did not diminish in any way their enthusiasm, though they were aware that hostile eyes were watching them, recording every incident. In the end, we caused them immense relief by taking the fifteen foremost quislings away with us.'

General demolitions were begun by Bill Crumper and installations as varied as 75-mm. gun emplacements, diesel fuel pumps and cable-heads, received generous charges. Ammunition and explosive dumps provided fireworks to suit the occasion. In the harbour, nineteen German caïques, some displacing as much as 150 tons, were sunk. At midnight the whole force sailed, the prisoners being crowded into the two 'Ems' barges. Stellin, with his patrol and Captain Pyke, Civil Affairs Officer, remained behind as rear party, with instructions to report subsequent events on Simi, and to distribute nearly thirty tons of food which had been brought in for the relief of the civilian population.

The German reaction was as expected, and followed the traditional pattern of attempted intimidation preceding assault. On the following morning the town was heavily

157

bombed. Stellin and his men sat tight in their slit trenches. When it was all over they emerged to find, as they had hoped, that two enemy motor launches were attempting to enter the harbour. Such accurate fire was opened on these ships that they withdrew, blazing. So did Stellin, whose keen ear had detected the approach of more bombers, and who knew that this was the prelude to reoccupation of the island.

At three o'clock, from one of the more remote mountains, he watched the German flag hoisted over the citadel. But Stellin's adventures were not yet over; that night the launch re-embarking his party, encountered an 'E' boat on the return journey. So many and so various were Stellin's store of captured weapons that every man in his patrol was able to take a personal hand in the battle with a machine-gun. The 'E' boat was left in a sinking condition.

The great raid on Simi marked the end of S.B.S. intervention in the Aegean. It had always been intended that the Sacred Squadron should take over this, their natural theatre of operations, as soon as they were fully trained and in a position to assume the heavy commitments involved. That happy state of affairs had now been achieved and Lapraik, instructed by Brigadier Turnbull, was able to write to the Greek Commander: 'Your group will operate in the Aegean until further notice. For the present, you will confine yourself to reconnaissance, but in September, raiding activities will be resumed upon a much larger scale. Sergeant Dale, S.B.S., will remain attached to you for Intelligence purposes.'

Lapraik, with his men, his prisoners, and his booty, withdrew to Castelrosso, and from Castelrosso to Beirut for a well-deserved holiday. Here they were met by the news that S.B.S. had been asked for in Italy for the purpose of attacking targets in Jugoslavia and Albania. Turkish waters would see them no more.

But it is not possible to leave those waters without some description of extraordinary life led by all ranks there when not on operations.

Picture the deep, indented Gulf of Cos, with uninhabited shores and sullen, fir-covered mountains rising abruptly from the water's edge. In this two hundred miles of coastline it would not be easy for you to find S.B.S., but if you were wise, you would look for some bay screened by small islands suitable for training purposes. Again, if you were wise, you would consult your map in search of one of the few streams from which drinkable water might be drawn.

Entering this bay, you would at first judge it to be empty. Closer inspection would show you a large, squat, ugly schooner lying close to one shore, with her gang-plank down and a horde of dories, folboats, rubber dinghies, and rafts nuzzling one flank like kittens about the teats of her mother. Farther off, a full mile away, lie five or six motor launches and an M.T.B. under camouflage, and within gun-and-lime distance of them a sleeker, trimmer, cleaner caïque, which is obviously naval property. In this area, too, are other subsidiary caïques. The intervening water is dotted with small boats from which men are fishing . . . mostly with grenades.

Let us approach the large and ugly schooner. She is the *Tewfik* of Port Said, S.B.S. depot ship. In her vast stern a naked figure is crouching, and whittling at something with a knife. It is Lassen, and he is making a bow with which to shoot pigs. Down below, in the murky cabin at the foot of the steep companionway, David Sutherland, pipe in mouth, is writing an operational order. Beside him are rum bottles, magnums of champagne from Nisiros reserved for special occasions, and a neat list showing the casualties inflicted on the enemy during the current month . . . and our own.

'Blyth, Captain H. W., plus 4—OUT—4.4.44. Due in 12.4.44. Overdue. Target, CALCHI.'

Presently, Sutherland reaches a difficult point in his work. He takes the pipe from his mouth and shouts:

'Corporal Morris.'

A tall, angular, serious, and bespectacled figure comes bowling down the companionway with a file in his hand. Curiously enough, it is the file which Sutherland wants, for Morris possesses second sight. Morris retires. His typewriter, seldom silent, begins clicking again in the distance.

Just forrard of the poop, Sergeant Jenkins, known colloquially as 'The Soldier's Friend' by reason of his claims to satisfy everyone, is trying to do three things at once. Sergeant Jenkins is accusing one S.B.S. man of pinching a tin of sausage meat, endeavouring to prevent another from doing the same thing under his very nose, and issuing orders to the Greek cooks concerning dinner.

'Not octupus again,' he begs them. 'Not octopus, *please.*'

On the hatch beside him, Nobby Clarke, his magnificent moustache stained by indelible pencil marks, is endeavouring to write an operational report under difficult conditions. Two American war correspondents recline on the same hatch in deck-chairs. They are polishing recently acquired Lügers.

Farther forward, Guardsmen O'Reilly, Conby, and D'Arcy, mugs of rum and tea in their hands, are discussing the good old days in Libya. In the black hole behind them which is the main men's quarters, the severe and well-cropped head of Staff-Sergeant-Major John Riley can be seen. Riley, oblivious of the noisy and vulgar game of pontoon going on in his immediate neighbourhood, is playing bridge.

In the forepeak, German prisoners, poking their heads up inquisitively, are being given cigarettes by almsgivers.

Towards dusk, the scene becomes more animated, and the immense capacity of the British soldier for slumber less noticeable. The headquarter signallers are pursued, for they alone have news of what is going on in the latest raids. Perhaps a motor launch returns with the personnel from one of these raids . . . another is almost certainly setting out to continue them. Men who have been bathing, fishing, bartering with the local Turks, return, demanding supper loudly. Aft, Paddy Errett, Cumper's deputy, is cursing and producing perfectly packed explosive charges at two minutes' notice.

A motor boat chugs alongside, and Sutherland is whisked away to Levant Schooner 9, where Lieutenant-Commander Campbell, sherry glass in hand, is entertaining a couple of M.T.B. skippers with the details of their coming patrol, which, to-night, will be north of Cos. 'E' boats are expected.

Sutherland and Campbell confer, confide, plot, send signals . . .

Keith Balsillie is zero-ing a German sniper's rifle found in Piscopi.

Marine Hughes is eating a tin of peaches . . .

'Brown Body' Henderson is unable to find any volunteers for P.T.

South of Samos, Harold Chevalier, two days out from base, has just ordered a German caïque to heave-to.

CHAPTER NINETEEN

After serving with S.B.S. for over six months, the little Greek had just been incorporated in the British Army and issued with a brand-new paybook. He was a very brave little Greek and the smug complacency of his compatriots in the Cairo bar irritated him.

'You,' he said disdainfully, after his third glass of oyzo. 'You, why don't you fight for your country like the Sacred Squadron, or even E.L.A.S.? You . . . I am sick of you.'

'You talk very big, my little friend,' said a fat Cypriot who was leaning agaisnt the *zinc*. 'You talk like Ulysees, but how do we know that you are not guarding a bomb store on the canal?'

'Know this, then,' said the little Greek, 'that in a short time from now I and my comrades intend to blow up every petrol dump in Crete.'

'That is very interesting,' said the Cypriot. 'Since you are so well informed I suppose you could even give us the exact date?'

'I could,' said the little Greek scornfully, 'but I have no intention of so doing. In the military life there must be secrecy.'

'Of course,' said the Cypriot. 'Indeed, I am well aware of it.'

The convoy bowled along the scarred and pitted desert road. A lonely road now, this, from which even the base wallahs had departed; their place being taken by a few dusky

162

Basutos and the Egyptian Frontier Force. So strange, so odd, that the blood of the fallen and the maggots which lived upon their corpses could do so little to nourish this barren soil. At El Alamein, freshly painted signs indicated mine-free tracks to the cemeteries. The dew had made the barbed-wire entanglements rusty, but they were good for another ten years. So were the death-dealing, acrobatic Teller mines beneath them; for Bill Crumper, who had collected thousands, had no further interest here.

Some of us who had not fought in the desert felt rather humble as we passed through the manifold relics of this forgotten Armageddon. But those of us who had been here during carnival times, leant from the jolting backs of their trucks and studied the familiar landmarks.

'God,' said Ronnie Govier, who had served with Stirling as a sergeant, who had been commissioned and posted to S.B.S., 'God, it's good to be back in the desert.'

But even among old comrades he was listened to with polite incredulity. Nor, in his heart, did he believe what he said. Passchendaele itself had charms when flavoured with the juice of reminiscence.

We de-bussed at Mersa Matruh, where Cleopatra, and even more recent Royalty, frolicked in days of peace. Our billets were uncomfortable but they comprised the only undamaged houses in this once pretty town. Jellicoe and Ian Patterson arrived from Cairo. Officers were summoned and briefed:

'Crete . . . third year in succession . . . German shortage of petrol . . . a resounding blow . . . co-ordination of attacks . . . last job before we leave Eastern Mediterranean . . . much is expected of you . . . your target is . . .'

The plaster was peeling from the wall, but an energetic sergeant had finally succeeded in pinning up a map of the island. It looked big. It looked formidable. David Clark, who was to do best on it, was in his corner asleep. Ronnie Govier, who was to do second best, was paring his nails.

'Any questions?'

No, there were none. What questions could there be? It was a good job. It had been long and well planned, too, and

163

Patterson would head the eastern party.

Those of us who were to make the initial reconnaissance left Mersa Matruh for Tobruk by motor launch. The others would follow in a fortnight.

In Tobruk, on the eve of departure, it was my wife's birthday. I remember celebrating it with some really dreadful brandy. Dick Harden, with his mucker, Marine Clark, was there; both as silent and as efficient as ever. Ian Patterson was wondering whether he would have sufficient time in Crete to grow a beard. In the Dodecanese he had grown a lovely beard, a Worthington-tinged Imperial.

The following morning the three motor launches set sail: Patterson's to the east, Harden's to the centre, my own to the west of the island. We sailed simultaneously. It was curious to see the boats diverging upon their various courses. Soon, the others were out of sight. My sergeant, Asbery, a muscular little Scot who, in peace-time, kept birds, was sharpening his fighting knife. 'You never know, it may come in useful,' he said gloomily.

'The general tone for security throughout this operation,' wrote Patterson, 'was set on the arrival of the advance party in the east of the island by the totally necessary appearance of twenty-three mules and their attendant villagers.'

That sabotage was about to take place had already been guessed by several Greeks, who knew from changes in the orders for boats that secret parties were due. These Greeks told others. Some of these others told the Germans. The enemy could quite well have taken advantage of this and protected his petrol dumps, but he did no such thing. In spite of the experiences of the past two years, he was over-confident. Besides, the mistake was made of believing that we were after airfields.

When, therefore, Harden, Ian Patterson, Sergeant Summers and myself made our surveys of the target areas, we noticed increased defensive measures, but none that we were not confident of overcoming. By a strange coincidence, the Germans were standing-to when we landed: a convoy of British motor launches had been observed in the Straits of Scarpanto, and the enemy imagined this to be the prelude to

Crete 1944-1945

↑ *S.B.S. Landing points*

The Eastern Aegean

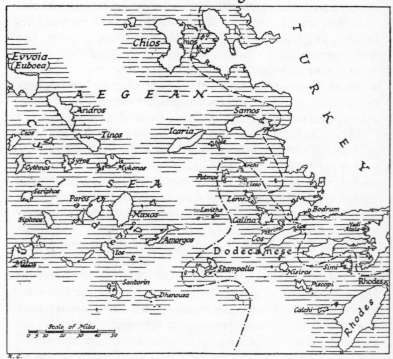

the long-threatened invasion.

Oh, those hills, those fir and gorse-covered hills of Crete. Crickets sang in the hazy afternoon air. The water point was always three miles away; forty minutes' march by Cretan reckoning, ninety by ours. Moving along the valleys at night one would tread upon a bush. But it was not a bush. It was a Cretan, sleeping out for fear of German perquisitions. The guide would explain our presence, our clothes, our cocked sub-machine guns in measured, ambassadorial terms. Chocolate and cigarettes would change hands. So would rabbits and *Rexina*. It was bad for security but good for inter-allied relations.

I think that there were none of us who did not love those Cretans. We lived in their mountain hiding-places, presided over by officers of Force 133, sleeping within sight of their burnt and ransacked villages, walking, when the mood moved us, to the disused mine-shafts down which the bodies of captured Germans had been thrown. Dick Harden and Jock Asbery, tireless as panthers and as agile, captured their imagination in particular.

When the target areas had been assessed, the main parties landed. Andy Anderson, accompanied by Ronnie Govier, took over my end of the island. Ian Patterson was reinforced by David Clark, Freddie Birkett and their patrols. Everything was now ready for the attack and, on 23rd July 1944, it took place; 165,000 gallons of German petrol in seven separate dumps, were destroyed. Thirty-two Germans were killed and three wounded. Staff cars and trucks to the number of seven were wrecked. Our losses were one officer and one other rank, prisoner of war.

David Clark's report, laconic, factual, conveys that night's proceedings with clarity. 'The target was surrounded by Dannert wire. We cut this and walked inside. I stopped to listen for guards and heard two coming towards us down a petrol bay. There was no time for concealment so I jumped up and attempted to take them prisoner. One of them, however, shouted something so I shot him twice with my carbine. Corporal Bentley shot the second man. It was all highly unpleasant and inconvenient . . .'

It certainly was. The whole area, which was well guarded, was now aroused. David Clark, however, did not allow this to perturb him. He remained in the dump for fifty-five minutes laying bombs. One of the parties under his command contained a Greek officer. At a crucial moment of the approach, this man trod on what he took to be a snake. He let out a shrill scream which so unnerved the sentries in this vicinity that they ran away. Bomb-laying then proceeded unimpeded.

Patterson's own party, which was numerous, were rallied and manœuvred into position round this target by a succession of unearthly howls which Patterson proudly maintained to be shepherds' calls: 'Woo-oo-oo-oo.'

And as Germans stirred uneasily beneath their blankets, thinking of ghosts, a group of men would steal forward.

'Woo-oo-oo-oo.'

Another group, and with them Patterson on tiptoe, bearded, brandishing a pistol and a knobbled stick. Disaster nearly overtook him as he was crouching outside the perimeter wire. Two Germans who, ironically enough, were leaving the dump with tins of petrol for sale on the black market spotted him and asked who he was. The Greek who accompanied him was quick-witted.

'It is a sheep,' he said.

The bomb-laying was accomplished without further interference. Patterson withdrew, leaving three men whom he instructed to begin shooting as soon as the alarm should be given. When the first dump went up, the German guard duly ran out of their barracks. They were sharply silhouetted against the blazing petrol. The rearguard killed ten and seriously wounded two before slipping away.

The irrepressible Summers, working with Corporal McKenzie and a man after his own heart in Gunner Jones, a fellow-Cockney, was equally fortunate, varying his attack with a generous distribution of tyre bursters on the road from which the German reinforcements must come.

'We had a good guide,' said Summers. 'I couldn't speak his lingo but somehow he seemed to understand me. The Greeks are all right,' he conceded generously.

167

When Summers had disposed of all his bombs he crawled to the German guardhouse and laid a block-buster on the window-sill.

'I thought we might as well add to the general confusion,' he said.

Curious as ever, he could not resist an impulse to look inside: 'Three Germans were asleep under very inferior-looking mosquito nets,' he said contempuously. 'One was reading a newspaper. I could see no loot.'

As they made their final exit, Summers' party were seen and fired upon.

'Only a few rounds were let off,' he said. 'I didn't bother to reply. The bombs would get them anyway, I thought.'

The bombs did, for this particular dump lay in a thick olive grove and several of the guard were burnt to death.

Dick Harden, accompanied by Signaller Stephenson, arrived above his target in the centre of the island to discover that the enemy were evacuating the petrol. Undismayed, he contacted the local population with a view to finding another objective. Presently he was introduced to a Russian (it had never been sufficiently emphasized how many Russians there *were* in the German army) who, in return for a safe-conduct to Egypt, offered to lead him at a favourable moment into a post containing eleven Germans. To this Harden agreed: the Germans were surprised in a confined space at supper and killed. On the following morning the little party, reinforced by the now enthusiastic Russian, held up and killed the occupants of a staff car.

'Unfortunately,' wrote Harden, 'though Germans, they were only sergeants. I had been hoping for at least a *Hauptmann*.'

'The only incident which might be described as in the least untoward in my target,' said Govier, 'is that while I was laying some bombs a man came out of the guard-room and urinated within a foot of my nose. Otherwise, we were not hampered in any way and our bombs were disposed of to the best advantage.'

His target, Voukolies, was indeed one of the most spectacular blazes of that eventful evening.

There were mines beneath our wire and I had brought two home-made ladders with me in order to scale it. I was rather proud of these ladders and also of the charges—some of them with quite fantastic delays—that I had instructed Greeks to scatter around suitable objects on the coastal plain with a view to misleading the Germans.

'Captain Lodwick and Bombadier Nixon went over the wire first,' wrote Sergeant Asbery, 'Private Stewart and I followed. We found the first row of bays and Lodwick set to work on them, while Nixon stood guard over him with a Schmeisser. Stewart and I moved off to the left, but before we had gone far we made a slight noise. Almost immediately, five guards came down the road from about twenty yards away, where I am sure they had been waiting for us. As they raised their rifles to fire I fired, too, with my pistol, and Stewart opened up with his carbine. We were now spread out a bit . . .'

We were indeed. Nixon and I, unsighted, and some distance away from the hubbub, had now laid our charges. We retreated to the wire with the intention of working our way round it towards the original entrance-point.

Meanwhile, a man with a fixed bayonet was attempting to hold up Private Stewart.

'I grabbed his rifle with my left hand and shot him five times in the stomach with my carbine. Jock Asbery hit two of the other sentries. The rest scuttled.'

Asbery and Stewart had now become separated. Each thought that a dying German who was groaning horribly in a clearing was the other. A German sniper appears to have made the same mistake for from behind a tree, he fired shot after shot at his agonizing comrade. Asbery made good his escape but as Stewart was crawling through the wire, a sentry leapt on top of him, shouting.

'We struggled for some time,' said Stewart. 'After a while, I managed to draw my knife. I put it in his stomach and he fell, but still shouting.'

Stewart and Asbery got through the now alert cordon of Germans, though not without difficulty. Nixon and I were captured the following morning. We were lying-up, well concealed, when a police dog scented us, and attracted every German in the area with its infernal barking. Our hiding-place was quickly surrounded.

Our subsequent adventures are not, it seems to me, germane to this book. I shall, therefore, relate them only briefly.

We were kept in solitary confinement, without exercise, for over a month in Crete. Threats to shoot us were frequent, and I had the unusual and unpleasant experience of mock execution. This treatment, if designed to make us talk, was, I have always considered, a psychological error on the part of the enemy; for in what appeared to be our final moments we were far too frightened and resigned to our fate to reflect that we might obtain a temporary reprieve by imparting some trivial pieces of information. And when thrust back into our cells and solaced by another of the eternal bowls of thin soup, we very naturally assumed that our captors, having bluffed in this, were bluffing in all things.

We were transferred by sea to Athens, by way of Santorin . . . an alarming journey, hag-ridden by thoughts of British torpedoes. From the well-appointed Averoff penitentiary in Athens to the Gestapo hostel in Salonika (more psychology) from Salonika and Skopjlie and Mitrovitza in Serbia, near which latter place we finally escaped, and, joining a local Chetnik band got a little of our own back, first by derailing a train and finally paralysing the railroad for good and all by the destruction of a bridge.

When the advancing Bulgarian armies neared our mountain refuge we went down to meet them and were rewarded by two cheerful and unforgettable weeks in Sofia.

I remember a hole which I bored with a spoon in the wall between our adjoining cells in Salonika . . . I remember Nixon, a big man, doing his exercises religiously every day and suffering acute hunger from the shortage of bread . . . a young and comely tart, mistress of the German commander in the same prison, who made eyes at Nixon but gave me the cigarettes . . . I remember an Alsatian whom we persuaded to desert, and another whom we induced to sell almost all the kit we had in order to provide us and himself with contraband *raki* . . . the eternal political arguments with depressed but garrulous sentries . . . the knowledge that every time we were moved it was because S.B.S. were coming a little closer to us.

Oh, yes, prison life can have its moments . . . once you know that you will eventually escape. After 134 days we returned to the unit.

'Ah, you're back,' said Jellicoe. 'Damned slow about it, weren't you?'

CHAPTER TWENTY

The town of Monte St. Angelo, at 2,500 feet of altitude, is situated in the hinterland of the Gargano peninsula, that barren waste of granite and virgin forest which provides only topographical relief in 800 miles of Italian Adriatic coastline. Dante, who once wrote of Apulia that 'forgotten by God, it had remained neglected by man', must surely have had Monte St. Angelo in mind. Within those insanitary confines, 25,000 people live in squalor, their sole occupation the painting of political slogans upon walls. At Monte St. Angelo, the black market alone flourishes. Divided in their political allegiance, the citizens of this town are united only in their hatred of the *carabinieri* and their determination to avoid military service.

Never very fortunate in the training areas placed at their disposal, S.B.S. moved to Monte St. Angelo in August 1944, having travelled by sea from Suez. In this new theatre of operations, the central Mediterranean, they came under the overall command of Land Forces, Adriatic (Brigadier Davy). Turnbull, with a much diminished raiding force, consisting of mostly Greeks, continued to play the Aegean. His only important recruits from S.B.S. were Lapraik and Dick Harden.

Jellicoe was not slow in finding employment under the new management. An important railway bridge at Karasovici, in Jugoslavia, had been marked down for destruction. Lassen, with the Irish patrol and Lieutenant J. C. Henshaw, a newcomer, was landed by sea. His report is

172

brief; so brief, in fact, that Jellicoe, who read it, disapprovingly ordered it to be destroyed and rewritten.

'But vat is it you vant me to say?' grumbled Lassen. 'Ve landed. Ve reached ze bridge. Ve destroyed it. Zat is all . . . no?'

Actually it was by no means all. Slight opposition was encountered at the bridge itself. This was overcome. The raiders withdrew to a partisan hide-out, and were there attacked by no less than 400 Ustachi and Germans, who closed in from all sides.

'Lassen,' wrote Henshaw, 'ran about throwing grenades and praising the Ustachi to everybody he met:

'Zey are damned good soldiers . . . damned good.'

However, this did not prevent him killing several of them. Finally, the enemy withdrew, and the party were to re-embark safely.

David Sutherland's squadron were now infiltrated into Jugoslavia and Albania in force, some parachuting and some arriving by sea. The parachutists were the less fortunate, the aircraft and the methods taken to deliver them being, in some cases, distinctly unconventional. Rifleman Lynch, for example, made his exit from the belly turret of an American Fortress with his static line secured to the frail aluminium chair of a radio operator. This is dangerous.

These parties, led by 'Stud' Stellin and Nobby Clarke, with Sutherland co-ordinating, were not over-successful. Many small shoot-ups and ambushes were carried out, but in general their activities were rather hampered than assisted by the presence of strong partisan formations in the same areas.

The partisan attitude, which will be encountered progressively from this period onwards, may be synthesized as follows: 'This is my country, where I have been fighting for years. I agree that my resistance has been greatly facilitated by the supplies of arms and clothing which you have dropped me from time to time. I am grateful for these, but do not expect me to kiss your Anglo-Saxon feet; for, after all, you sent them to me in your own interest as well as in mine, and my small struggle has helped your larger struggle. The moment of liberation is now at hand. You are sending me troops in much larger numbers than the one or two liaison officers, who have been with me for months. I am content to have these troops with me, but I do not intend that they shall snatch from me the fruits of local victory for which I have laboured so long. This victory must be my victory. Besides, I am inclined to distrust your political motives. Why are you here, in point of fact, and how long do you intend to stay?'

To this declaration, which was heard only too frequently, the British answer was as follows: 'Please understand, once and for all, that we are merely soldiers. We understand nothing of politics and we care less. We come here for one purpose alone, and that purpose is to kill and embarrass the Germans.

'We are quite willing to abide by decisions resulting from your wider experience of this stretch of country, so long as these decisions—as we have found so often—do not preclude us from making attacks upon the enemy. In the last few days you have gone so far, seeing our determination to strike, as to give us false information concerning enemy movements, with a view to nullifying any offensive action which we might take. This attitude is not that which we expect from an ally. Can you blame us that we attribute it to your fear that, by success greater than your own, we may too far impress the civilian population from whom you requisition your food?'

These points of view do not appear irreconcilable. If they were made so, it was by reason of the inability of Slavs to express their thoughts and their grievances frankly. 'The Greeks,' a German officer once replied, when I asked him which of the Balkan peoples he preferred. 'The Greeks,' he said, 'may be violent and unreliable, but at least they are open, even when they are your enemies.' Coming from this quarter the opinion may not seem much recommendation, but confronted by some sulky, ignorant, and double-dealing commissar many an Englishman and American has shared it.

It is particularly trying to be subtly insulted by a stubble-chinned doctrinaire who is wearing your own national uniform, and who has read Marx in a simplified edition.

If anyone overcame those difficulties on that occasion it

was Lieutenant Ambrose McGonigal who with Sergeant Flavell and his patrol operated for over two months in southern Jugoslavia. This McGonigal was a real Irishman inasmuch as he actually lived in Ireland, and did not base his claim, like so many people, upon a hypothetical Hibernian grandmother. McGonigal, with his mucker, Lieutenant Ian Smith, a regular soldier, had just come out from England, where they had taken part in many pre-invasion excursions from Newhaven to the French coast. Both were vastly experienced men who felt no shame at being, in Lady Astor's too-famous phrase, 'D-Day Dodgers'.

'France,' Ian Smith would exclaim contemptuously, 'why, we got tired of France last year . . .'

There was much truth in this. As armies mass for stupendous offensives, the value of raiding men, who have done so much of the groundwork, declines. With S.B.S., Smith and McGonigal were in their element again.

McGonigal landed on 28th August 1944. A few days later, having persuaded the partisans to accompany him by the simple method of moving off, so that they were obliged to follow in order to see what he was doing, he attacked a railway tunnel. The tunnel was guarded by fifteen Chetniks, whom McGonigal dispersed with Bren gunfire. He then laid charges in a manhole inside the tunnel, at the points of three sidings, in a near-by station, and on a large water-tank. Presently shots were heard. Investigation revealed trigger-happy partisans shooting at bushes.

'This whole area,' wrote McGonigal, 'was very thoroughly controlled by Mihailovitch Chetniks on behalf of the Germans. Movement by day was impossible.' The Chetniks made several daylight attacks on the British party, but were driven off on each occasion with such severe casualties that soon they left McGonigal in peace.

Having now, unlike his fellow-officers, thoroughly grasped the principle that the best way in which to deal with the partisans was to tell them abolutely nothing about his plans, McGonigal began to enjoy a measure of success. He attacked and destroyed a number of trucks laden with Germans, one of them in full view of an enemy-held village.

A battery from this village opened fire on the S.B.S. as they scrambled among the cargo of cigarettes and chocolate. McGonigal was unable to attack and destroy the occupants of a second truck, which had come to the aid of the first.

He now put himself in touch with the Austrian driver of the German Commander at Bar. This man offered 'in return for a consideration' to drive his superior into a prepared ambush. Unfortunately, the Gestapo heard of these arrangements. McGonigal was almost captured. The Austrian was arrested and tortured. Inhabitants of the entire area were ordered to congregate and to live in one of three villages; arrangements, no doubt, intended to prevent them passing information to the pernicious English.

McGonigal remained undisturbed. He assumed, correctly, that the Germans would be obliged to send patrols to these villages in order to enforce their order. With the eight men under his command, he waylaid forty-five of the enemy in a defile, killing about twenty without loss to himself.

'The remainder,' he said, 'threw arms, ammunition, even water-bottles away, and ran as hard as possible.'

His deputy and very able interpreter, Captain Eden, now became interested in a secondary railway along which it was rumoured that a troop train would pass within a day or two. The train was derailed, and the surviving Germans machine-gunned from close range. Casualties totalling thirty-seven were inflicted and wagons containing hay, cement, and flour set on fire. In the mêlée Private Howells of S.B.S. was killed. The local population to a man attended his funeral as a mark of respect.

So ended McGonigal's first adventures with S.B.S. They had not been without result. When he arrived, a well-disciplined force had faced him. When he left, German officers were no longer able to control their men, who were selling all they possessed. The garrison of the area was kept ready to move out at an hour's notice. Through an intermediary Eden was receiving daily applications from those who wished to desert.

We must now leave Jugoslavia.

The island of Cythera had been seized, and Lassen, who

had just taken over Lapraik's squadron, was dispatched with all urgency to reconnoitre the sea approaches to Athens. He put Douglas Stobie ashore on Aiyina island, within 15 miles of Piræus. Stobie indignantly reported that the place was a hornet's nest, full of drunken and disgruntled Germans recently evacuated from Crete. Nevertheless, he made his reconnaissance, and it was largely due to the information supplied by his concerning minefields that the Navy were later able to enter Piræus with so few losses.

On 26th August Rumania was out of the war, and the repercussions upon German dispositions in the Balkans were only too apparent. S.B.S. had arrived in Italy at precisely the right moment, for they were now to enjoy their greatest triumphs.

By the end of September 1944, in consequence of the Rumanian defection and of decisions made by von List at Salonika, the German evacuation of the Peloponnese and southern Greece had reached an advanced stage. Garrisons, when they still existed, were thin on the ground and confined to the coastal strips. A proposal was therefore made by Balkan Air Force that an airfield should be seized in the Peloponnese, from which fighter cover could be provided for subsequent land operations. The airfield selected was Araxos, in the north-west corner of the great peninsula. Patterson's squadron was directed to secure it, after an initial reconnaissance had been made by Charles Bimrose and his patrol. Jellicoe, now a lieutenant-colonel, was named overall commander of an operation which, planned and mounted on the lightest possible scale, was to snowball its way from Patras to Salonika.

Thus 'Bucketforce' was conceived and, almost casually, the re-conquest of Greece began.

On 24th September, Ian Patterson and fifty-eight dropped successfully on Araxos field without opposition from the enemy, who were retiring rapidly northward towards Patras. The scene on the ground resembled that on an Egyptian station when a troop train is pulling out. Determined knots of Greeks ran forward pressing nuts, lemonade, and oyzo upon their startled liberators. Other Greeks, in the background, comprehensively looted the neglected parachute containers. Only when their curiosity had been thus satisfied did they set to work to clear the runways.

Next day Jellicoe himself landed by Dakota. He brought stores, and that same evening the sea component of the force under Squadron-Leader Wynne, R.A.F. Regiment, was disembarked at Katakolon, a near-by port, of which Jellicoe, who had read history at Cambridge, remarked donnishly that 'it had been much used by former Frankish invaders'.

Two patrols under David Clark were now pushed forward along the coastal road towards Patras. They found that the town was being somewhat lackadaisically and euphemistically invested by partisans. Inside it and on the surrounding heights, 865 Germans and 1,600 members of a Greek collaborationist security battalion watched the arrival of the British uneasily. Patterson joined Clark and, setting up his headquarters outside the town, proceeded to contact the local representative of the Swedish Red Cross, a certain Herr Ornstroder.

'I wish,' said Patterson, 'to enter Patras.'

'But, my dear sir,' protested the horrified Swede, 'such a procedure is quite impossible. Surely you appreciate the risks you would run?'

'You mistake me, I think,' said Patterson. 'I shall enter under the protection of your flag. What, after all, is the Red Cross for? There are certain matters which I must discuss with the German Commander. My forces are moving up to surround the area. I am sure that my opponent would deprecate heavy loss of life as much as I would myself.'

In point of fact, Patterson's forces numbered sixty-two men. He employed them as producers do a stage army, transferring patrols from one height to the next in creditable imitation of perpetual movement. From a wooden ridge, David Clark made a brave show with his mortars.

'Up a trifle, Sergeant Chambers . . . no, no, you hit a cowshed then . . . left a trifle.'

Mortars had never played an important part in S.B.S. weapon-training curriculum.

179

Herr Ornstoder, however, who knew none of these facts, readily agreed to afford Ian Patterson his protection. The latter entered the town in a jeep, a figure as unlike that of a peace emissary as it would be possible to imagine. German soldiers off duty regarded him with amazement. So did the naval Captain Magnus, the enemy commander.

'It is advisable for you, I think, to surrender this town,' declared Patterson.

The German declared that while he, personally, was willing to accept this course of action, approval for it would first have to be obtained from Athens.

'Why wait?' asked Patterson arrogantly. 'Athens itself will have fallen in a few days; and, as if to lend emphasis to his argument, he pointed to the outer harbour, where a German minesweeper and an 'E' boat were being shelled by R.A.F. Regiment six-pounders and harassed by S.B.S. Brownings, mounted on jeeps.

The interview, none the less, was inconclusive, and Patterson reported to Jellicoe that the Germans, in his opinion, were playing for time. Jellicoe determined to leave them to their own devices, under our mortaring, and to secure instead the surrender of the Greek security battalion.

'These negotiations,' he wrote, 'conducted through Captain Gray, an officer of Force 133, who had been in the area for over a year, dragged on in a way peculiar to Greece in general, and the Peloponnese in particular . . .'

The security battalion was frightened of the partisans. They would surrender to the British, they said, but not to their fellow-countrymen: furthermore, they required a guarantee of subsequent fair treatment. Jellicoe had no fear of the partisans, but he was anxious to prevent a general massacre in Patras, a town known to be strongly anti-E.L.A.S. With his hands tied in a variety of ways by the orders of superior offficers and by various political agreements, he continued the negotiations. Finally, he issued an ultimatum that all security battalion personnel who wished to do so must surrender before a certain hour. He was far from sanguine as to the results.

Great, therefore, was his surprise . . . and embarrassment

. . . when he found that, unknown to the Germans, he had scored a minor diplomatic triumph. At the appointed hour the 1,600 Greeks presented themselves to a man, and laid down their arms, presenting Jellicoe with the problems of feeding them and educating them, and, in the meantime, of preserving them from molestation by the partisans.

He locked them all up in a barren peninsula, and obtained a promise from his erratic allies that they would not be attacked.

So well conducted had been the security battalion defection, that the Germans were not even aware of it. The whole eastern perimeter of Patras lay exposed, and Patterson, who saw his opportunity, asked for and received permission to exploit it.

Two mixed patrols of S.B.S. and R.A.F. Regiment penetrated into the sleeping town. They were rather less than twenty men all told, and they travelled in two armoured cars and a few jeeps. The Germans, taken completely off their guard, did not realize what had happened until the invaders had reached the central market-place and were rip-roaring up and down the adjoining side-streets. Patterson prudently withdrew, but not before he had caused an unknown but heavy number of casualties.

Throughout the following day S.B.S. handling their mortars with greater precision, maintained an intense, harassing fire on the enemy outworks; while Squadron-Leader Wynne and his men jabbed at the suburban defences from the south. These R.A.F. Regiment lads, whose first experience of action this was, showed an admirable dash and initiative.

That evening it became apparent to Jellicoe that the enemy—still more than eight times stronger than his own forces—were preparing to evacuate. He immediately ordered Patterson and Wynne to close in and to reach the port area at all costs with a view to preventing its demolition. Daringly led by Patterson, S.B.S. drove the Germans from a hill feature overlooking the town. At dawn they turned a captured 77-millimetre gun on the port. A Siebel ferry loaded with Germans troops was hit and sunk, but so intense was the return fire, that the engagement had to be broken off.

But down below Patras was falling. One of the first in—almost a little *too* soon—was Ronnie Govier. Having cleared two streets, Govier was sniped at by a German in a doorway, who had seen his shadow. This German kept Govier crouching in a gutter for five full minutes until matters were adjusted. David Clark, advancing, came face to face with another German in a slit trench, who held him covered. In such situations one must think quickly.

'Poor fellow,' commiserated David Clark, 'so your comrades have all left you? What swine . . .'

The German surrendered without further demur.

By dawn Patras was clear of the enemy. Prepared charges laid in the port area were captured intact. Seventy-one prisoners were taken. 'The centre of military gravity,' wrote Jellicoe, 'now shifted from harassing Germans to the more difficult task of maintaining order in a Greek town, freed after three years of occupation.' Fortunately, private resentments and jealousies were sublimated for the time being in the tumultuous resentment afforded to the liberators. Jellicoe, whose status as an English *milord* made him a particularly inviting target, was kissed into stupefaction. Govier, who also seemed to exercise some special attraction, was carried about garlanded with flowers.

But in spite of these diversions little time was lost. Patterson, never a cautious driver at the best of times, now rocked crazily along the precipitous mountain roads in his jeep, behind which he towed the captured field-gun. The fleeing Germans were located as they made for the Corinth Canal. Fire from the field-gun was opened upon them.

'It was not altogether satisfactory,' wrote Patterson, 'as the Germans had removed the sights. However, by a process of hit or miss, we succeeded in inflicting casualties; many of them due, I have no doubt, to shock.'

German demolitions along the coastal road were thorough. Progress was therefore slow. On 7th October, Govier's patrol entered Corinth and accepted the surrender of a further security battalion. Fire was exchanged across the canal as the enemy demolished their pontoons. Patterson and the main force succeeded at last in finding a ferry and, pressing on, made contact again at Megara.

Here, Bimrose, with three patrols, was sent north into the hills towards Thebes. He moved rapidly, and on foot, mining and ambushing the main roads at frequent intervals until, having overcome all other opposition, he made contact with the northbound rearguard. A pitched battle ensued, and Bimrose, after causing casualties and himself losing Lance-Corporal Carmichael, killed, withdrew. On this same day Patterson determined to outflank the enemy, even if it still further reduced his main force, commandeered a caïque and sent Keith Balsillie with Sergeant Long and the marine patrol to reconnoitre the Bay of Salamis. Interpreting his orders freely, Balsillie landed and, whatever claims were subsequently made in respect of Athens, was definitely the first Englishman into Piræus.

At Megara, a stalemate had ensued, for Patterson, weakened by the absence of the R.A.F. Regiment (who were securing the surrender of the remaining security battalions in the Peloponnese), was not in sufficient force to attack the strongly held German positions.

The road here runs through wooded country close to sandy beaches and the sea. The enemy, who had previously so much over-estimated S.B.S. strength, now seem to have arrived at the true conclusion regarding it. They became aggressive. Fighting patrols, seldom comprising less than thirty men, were sent forward to probe our thinly held lines. Undismayed, Patterson allowed the Germans to come through and then surrounded them by superior use of fieldcraft. Twenty-four prisoners were taken.

The bluff maintained by 70 men on over 700 could not, however, have been maintained indefinitely. It was with relief that Patterson heard from Jellicoe that a company of the 4th Independent Parachute Brigade was scheduled to drop on the landing-strip behind him. The drop took place in a wind approaching gale force. One-third of the valuable reinforcements became casualties. Nevertheless, the sight of them landing was sufficient to deflate the last German hopes of an orderly withdrawal from Athens. The force holding

Megara slipped away in the night. Patterson's convoy of jeeps drove on towards the capital.

Jellicoe himself had devoted these few days to the thankless and difficult task of preventing partisan excesses against the defenceless population. Having now worked out a *modus vivendi* with the leaders of E.L.A.S., and received a reply to his not unreasonable request that no private citizen should be executed without fair trial by the legal government, he arrived at Megara, where he placed himself under the orders of Lieutenant-Colonel Coxon, of the Parachute Brigade.

He was ordered to proceed at once to Athens, and to investigate the position in that city.

With the faithful Milner-Barry at his heels and a Mr. Sedgwick of *The New York Times* as interpreter, Jellicoe embarked by caïque and landed at a small quay in Scaramanga, on the outskirts of the city. Patterson's force and Patterson himself sailed with him.

At Scaramanga the only transport available consisted of two bicycles captured by the Germans at Megara. Jellicoe and Patterson mounted them and cycled into Athens as the last Germans withdrew from the northern suburbs. By nightfall the whole S.B.S. force of fifty-five men was installed in the Grande-Bretagne, the capital's most luxurious hotel.

'Parties,' said Jellicoe, 'and politics then ensued.'

'Bucketforce,' originally planned with the modest intention of securing Araxos airfield, had captured half Greece.

CHAPTER TWENTY-ONE

I remember an American, a tank man, who had been among the first to enter Rome. This American was a Catholic. Rome, to him, was the eternal city. For two months he had lived in the paddy-fields of Anzio. During this time he thought about Rome. When he got there he stayed four hours: they gave him a bottle of *Berbera* and sent him off towards Grossetto in pursuit of the beaten enemy. The American returned to Rome three months later on leave (that would be after the Gothic Line, if a minor battle like that strikes a chord in your memory). The American was not able to get near the Pope, who was surrounded by war correspondents and ladies of the auxiliary forces.

Who now remembers the first men into Yorktown, into Moscow, into Tereul? The answer is 'No one'. The quartermasters, the field cashiers, the deputy assistant provost marshals, the able-bodied but non-combatant redcaps, the young officers with the suède shoes and bedroom manners, move in. They install themselves comfortably. They signal for blanco and button-polish and issue orders enforcing the use of these articles. Boots, they declare, must be polished. Unfortunately, the boots of S.B.S., when they did eventually return to Athens, were worn to shreds. It was not possible to polish them, and their wearers were looked at askance in clubs and cafés . . .

Though not, of course, by the Athenian population.

Two days after the occupation of Athens, David Clark was sent forward by caïque with his patrol to maintain contact

185

with the retreating army. At the same time, largely owing to Jellicoe's insistence, it was decided that a larger force must immediately follow and harass the enemy during their withdrawal.

'A mad expedition,' declared engineers of the recently constituted Third Corps. They parted, most reluctantly, with fresh jeeps.

The motley army was known ironically as 'Pompforce'. It comprised 4th Independent Parachute Battalion (Lieutenant-Colonel Coxon), S.B.S., attached paratroop engineers, an R.A.F. Regimental contingent, and a battery of 75-millimetre guns—in all a total of 950 men, under the command of Jellicoe.

Strafed from time to time by their own Spitfires, the column made contact with the enemy north of Lamia. The road here was well cratered. In many places it was almost impassable. The German is thorough in his demolitions. In Jugoslavia I once took the trouble to examine a kilometre of railway. There were fifty-two cuts in the line. The German is thorough in other respects, too, as the burnt and shattered villages, mementoes of his summer drive against the partisans showed only too clearly. Strange that such a race, such a *tidy* race, who invariably move their dead if there is still time to do so, should have left so much litter along this insignificant Greek road. There were packs, there were water-bottles, there were gas-expanded dead mules.

Evidently the Spitfires had found the right target in the end.

Arriving within sight of the enemy, 'Pompforce' split into two parts. 'Coxforce' (Lieutenant-Colonel Coxon) moved off towards Florina to cut off their retreat; 'Patforce' (Ian Patterson), comprising S.B.S., R.A.F. Regiment elements, a battery of field-guns and a battalion of parachutists, moved forward to make a frontal attack. They found the Germans protecting their retreat with several strong outposts south of the town of Kozani. A mountain called, like all prominent Greek features, after the Prophet Elias, was also held by the enemy.

Patterson at once attempted to secure the surrender of the

local security battalion, using the methods employed at Patras. He was unsuccessful, though not for want of cajoling. The security battalion stood firm, to its eventual cost, for in the end they were murdered by E.L.A.S. Patterson now made a reconnaissance of the hostile positions in his usual mode of transport—a jeep. Under the Prophet Elias's hill, the jeep came under heavy fire. Two men in the back of it jumped out and hid behind an embankment, where they pretended without great conviction to be fulfilling a natural need. Patterson strolled to and fro unconcernedly, noting the bad marksmanship of the enemy, the situation of their emplacemens and the prospect of the weather for the morrow.

He mounted his attack at first light. On the right, the Parachute Battalion went in and captured or killed the seventy Germans on Prophet Elias's hill at the cost of fifteen casualties to themselves. S.B.S., who were to have attacked the remaining enemy posts, were spotted as they advanced, and subjected to violent machine-gun unpleasantness on an exposed terrain. Freddie Birkett and Sergeant Hessell, leading the assault, were pinned down behind some minute rocks for over two hours. David Clark and Sergeant Chambers crawled down over the ridge to their assistance.

'Are you all right, Freddie?'

'Fine, thanks, but my neck's cricked. Can you get a mortar on the bastards?'

David Clark and Chambers looked back at the slope. There was some 80 yards of it without cover. Spandau bullets were exploring the heather like a dog-comb in the coat of a spaniel. They ran for their lives, and by so doing preserved them.

The first shot from the mortar was one of those miracles for which men under shell-fire pray fervently. It landed plumb on a German post, demolishing it. Freddie Birkett was able to advance.

The battery of field-guns, towed with immense trouble from Athens, now went into action against a German barracks west of the town. Their marksmanship was far from distinguished, and was further prejudiced by the failure of radio intercommunication, due to a downpour of rain. The enemy replied with a more accurate bombardment of the recently captured Prophet Elias's hill. This was, however, a Parthian shoot, for their outer posts had fallen, and they were already withdrawing.

R.A.F. Regiment, armoured cars, and S.B.S. in jeeps pursued them out of Kozani. Casualties were inflicted, but in a final engagement Flying-Officer Dennis, standing in the turret of his vehicle, was killed by a shell-burst.

S.B.S. drove westwards. They linked with 'Coxforce'. They entered Florina. They caught up with the enemy again on the Jugoslav frontier. Here, the conditions for long-range attack were ideal. The German column, on foot and in horse-drawn vehicles, was moving through a narrow defile. The jeeps, with their Brownings, the 75-millimetres, were drawn up on the covering slopes. It took a long time, later, to count the German dead.

At Florina an order was received forbidding British troops to cross into Jugoslav territory. Patterson's squadron stared wistfully across the frontier, drank in all good faith the health of Marshal Tito, and returned to deal with such questions as the release of two American airmen held as hostages by a local security battalion. Milner-Barry set off bravely into the unknown hazard of Moslem Albania. He succeeded in contacting David Sutherland at his headquarters, in the town of Korce.

The two Balkan squadrons had now joined hands.

Meanwhile, Lassen, who had just received his major's insignia and command of the third squadron, was raiding the coast and off-lying islands of Greece from the sea. Despite his training as a sailor, Lassen had no great love of the second element, which he regarded at that time as an impediment placed deliberately between himself and the enemy.

He said as much to Jellicoe in Athens:

'Vy do Patterson and Sutherland get all zee work vile I vaste my time on ze water?'

'You bloody well do what you're told,' said Jellicoe menacingly, 'or I'll take your crown away.'

This was no idle threat. Jellicoe had a habit of relieving his more trusted subordinates of their commands. It was, I suspect, his method of keeping them in order. At Patras, Patterson had twice been deprived of authority in this manner for some too liberal interpretation of instructions. His dumbfounded squadron, hearing the news, had crept round to condole with their leader. They had found him having tea with Jellicoe. The two men were discussing the campaigns of Belisarius, their quarrel already forgotten.

On 22nd October, Lassen, with forty, embarked at Piræus on two motor launches and proceeded towards the Sporades. His first call was at Skopelos, which will be remembered as the scene of Bob Bury's exploit. Skopelos was found to be empty of the enemy, but only very recently so, for on the previous day 250 Germans had been ferried across to the mainland after destroying their coastal defence guns.

'Having drawn a blank there,' said Lieutenant Martin Solomon, Lassen's naval liaison officer and old Beirut drinking partner, 'we decided to try Sciathos.'

They were about to capture this island, which was unoccupied, when an indignant motor launch, carrying members of Turnbull's raiding forces, approached, demanding through its outhailer what the hell they were doing.

'I say, you can't land here. This is our area.'

A brief consultation took place. It was finally decided that representatives of Brigadier Turnbull should land a few minutes in advance of Lassen's party. These niceties of behaviour were lost on the local population, who were determined to welcome all allied soldiers on whom they could lay their hands. They were also lost on Lassen. A service of thanksgiving was held. With unbelievable speed cakes were baked and covered with indigestible icing denoting the divers colours of the United Nations. Loud political oratory followed. Here, Lassen made a speech which, perhaps fortunately, was never recorded for history.

Martin Solomon was then diverted to Volos in a local caïque. Here, again, he discovered that the enemy had just left, having inexplicably abandoned a number of schooners and a merchant ship displacing over 500 tons. To show that they were still in the area, however, the Germans shelled the port from long distance. They did not hit it. While this bombardment was proceeding, the British party were approached by an immacuately clad British major.

'He had come down from some mountain or other,' said Solomon, 'where he had been sitting, apparently forgotten, for over a year. He seemed unsurprised to see us and said, "Hullo, Navy, just the fellows I want to see. I have got 10,000 Italians I want you to take off my hands at once. When can you embark them?"'

Martin Solomon pointed to his tiny caïque and said diffidently that he could manage four if that would be any help.

'How long have you had these men?' he asked curiously.

'Oh, since the armistice with Italy, old boy. Damned nuisance they are, too. Still, can't let them starve, I suppose.' Producing a particularly filthy flask of oyzo from his pocket, the major offered Solomon a nip.

Wondering how the major could have fed, clothed, and hidden what amounted to the strength of an infantry division in enemy-occupied country for over a year, Solomon asked him if he spoke Italian.

'Good God, no, old boy,' he replied, looking insulted. 'I'm a sapper.'

Bob Bury, in another caïque, had also been diverted for coastal reconnaissance.

'We approached a large bay which was known to be held by Royalist guerillas,' wrote his sergeant. 'From what we learnt later, these partisans were expecting an attack by their rivals and deadly enemies, E.L.A.S. At any rate, they opened fire upon us.'

The helmsman on the caïque was hit. Despite the complete absence of cover, Bob Bury jumped up and took his place. He possessed no recognition signals and no means of making his identity known, except by shouting. He steered a course which would bring him close to the point of fire. While doing so, he was mortally wounded.

So perished, one of the most able, most devoted and most

unselfish officers who ever served in S.B.S. Bury was twenty-four years old when this happened. All of his adult life had been spent in warfare. For a very long time he had refused a commission, although his abilities entitled him to one. Certain reputations seem diminished when the documentary evidence is examined in its entirety. Bury's seems enhanced.

He was buried next day by the men who had killed him in error.

Before these pages close you will see more clearly that I write no silly platitude when I say that the best were always taken.

Two schooners arrived to join Lassen's force. They bore a jeep for his personal use and orders that he carry out a reconnaissance of the Salonika area.

Nothing could have pleased Lassen more. He was becoming bored with unoccupied islands. He sailed immediately, escorted for a part of the way by the two motor launches, and with his usual boldness entered the Potidhia Canal, some 30 miles from the city. This area was still occupied by the enemy, but as Lassen rightly assumed, his schooners attracted no attention, concealed as they were among a fleet of harmless Greek shipping. Through field-glasses he watched the Germans evacuating gun positions about two miles away. That same morning, the enemy hospital ship *Gradisca*, carrying able-bodied men from Leros, sailed past within a few hundred yards of the canal entrance.

Lassen without transport would have been aggressive enough, but Lassen with a jeep and petrol spelt chaos in the area.

'I knew what was coming,' said Martin Solomon, 'I prepared myself for it all night with prayer and solemn reflection. We set off at seven o'clock at too-high speed, and made an eight-mile tour in country which we had no reason to suppose was not infested with the enemy.'

Actually, E.L.A.S. and not the Germans, were now in control of the hinterland. Their commander, a Colonel Papathanasion, instructed his troops to be as unhelpful as possible. In a brief interview, Lassen so pulverized this man that he relinquished his command and was not heard of again.

'Venn I vish to see zee the German positions, I vill do so . . . you understand? Vy are you not attacking them yourself?'

It was true. The opposing forces, though in some cases only a few hundred yards apart, showed distinct reluctance to clash. When the Germans left a given area the partisans moved into it. The area would then be described as 'liberated'.

'Lassen,' wrote Solomon, 'impressed the partisans so much that their tone changed considerably. Everywhere we went the people, at first thinking we were Germans, would slink frightened into their houses. Children, on occasions, ran in terror. But as soon as they realized we were British their enthusiasm was incredible . . .'

On that evening Solomon left for another coastal reconnaissance towards a battery which the Germans were reputed to be evacuating. He had with him Lieutenant J. C. Henshaw, an old Guardsman, and Lassen's second-in-command. The battery, they discovered, was still in existence, but due to be removed the next day. Having ambushed a truck carrying supplies to it, they decided optimistically that they would bluff the Germans into surrender. Henshaw, who spoke German, wrote a note informing the enemy commander that he was completely surrounded by British troops, and would do well to give up the unequal struggle immediately, unless he wished to be starved and bombed out. The note was entrusted to a young Frenchman, a slave worker.

While awaiting a reply to this curious document, Henshaw and Solomon were casually joined by two German soldiers who had been drinking oyzo in a café and who mistook them for comrades.

The Germans were taken prisoner.

It would seem, though, that the German commander was doubtful concerning the information contained in the note. In any case, he possessed the means to assert his scepticism. While Henshaw and Solomon waited for an answer, they saw to their amazement, two tanks, six self-propelled guns, and six lorry-loads of troops approaching. Abandoning their jeep and driving their prisoners in front of them, the two men made a hurried escape.

When they had recovered their nerve somewhat, the awful realization of what they had just done dawned upon them. The vengeance which Lassen would take for the loss of his beloved transport far exceeded in frightfulness anything which the Germans might contrive. Henshaw and Solomon sat shivering in a wood all night with their prisoners. Just before dawn the former crept down. He found the jeep still intact. A hundred yards away the Germans were demolishing their emplacements. Under cover of the explosions Solomon drove the vehicle away. At base, Lassen listened to the story of their adventures.

'You have done vell,' he said, 'but had you not brought ze jeep back I would have slit your throat.'

'I believe he would have done so too,' wrote Solomon with fervour.

The Germans were now retreating in earnest. With his usual genius for the improbable, Lassen procured four fire-engines for the entry himself and his troops into Salonika. The western half of the town was undefended, and here the forces of E.L.A.S. were content to call a halt. Lassen, however, declared that British prestige must be maintained. He drove on. In the distance explosions could be heard as German engineers demolished the petrol installations.

The fire-engines screamed to a stop, and Greek citizens who had leapt on board in the first flush of liberation ran hastily for cover. Lassen's men went into the action for which they had waited. The German rearguard, without adequate protection, without leaders, was taken completely by surprise. The rules of the gentle name, played so long with the mountain guerrillas, were now to be broken.

Henshaw, who distinguished himself, killed eleven Germans personally; Lassen, eight. In all, the enemy casualties were over sixty, and S.B.S. did not lose a man. When they returned, many of the red flags which had been hung out to celebrate the liberation of Salonika were strangely absent. They had been replaced by Union Jacks.

It may be asked what purpose was served by this expedition to Salonika? Here is what a highly placed officer said of it:

'But for Lassen and his band, Salonika would not have been evacuated as soon as 30th October 1944. The town would have suffered greater destruction. His solitary jeep and few troops were seen everywhere; behind the enemy's lines, with E.L.A.S., and in the mountains. Their numbers and strength were magnified into many hundreds of men and automatic weapons. Prisoners taken confirmed this, their estimate never being less than one thousand men.'

'I have the honour to report,' wrote Lassen, 'that I am in Salonika.'

'Give your estimated time of arrival Athens,' replied Jellicoe curtly.

Meanwhile, raiding forces, with Bill Cumper and Lapraik commanding in the field, were capturing one island in the Aegean after another. Such landmarks in this story as Amorgos, Cos, Mikonos, Simi, and Stampalia fell, some after naval bombardment and on opposed landing, some without a fight.

In Syros, Bill Cumper established a benevolent dictatorship, eventually to embrace the entire Cyclades. When a fractious E.L.A.S. commander in Tenos refused to submit to this central authority, Cumper ordered him to report to Syros immediately. The man reported. In Lemnos, Lapraik finding the garrison about to embark, was offered the chance of a lifetime. He took it. Two Siebel ferries were sunk by his naval escort with heavy loss of life. Over 375 prisoners were taken. The fish accounted for many more.

We were eating our thin vegetable soup in Mitrovica, Nixon and I, when the German Intelligence Colonel entered. He was a very young colonel, and we remembered him well from Salonika. Nor were we particularly surprised to see him, for although only twenty-four hours had elapsed, we had heard the news of that city's fall already, from our Albanian grapevine.

'I hope that you are enjoying your soup,' said the colonel

benevolently. 'It is the last which you will eat here, for now we must move you to the Fatherland . . . ours, I regret to say, for the moment . . . not yours.'

We said nothing.

The German colonel toyed with his cigar. He smiled:

'You will no doubt be interested to hear that some of your units are now in Salonika, while others are on the Jugoslav frontier.'

Again we said nothing.

'Yes,' pursued the German colonel after a slight pause, 'yes, they are in Salonika. We had hoped to give ourselves the pleasure of capturing your commander there—Captain Jellicoe, is it not? Unfortunately, we did not have time.'

'You did not have time,' we echoed.

The German positively grinned. He bore the misfortunes of his country with composure, for he had long foreseen them.

'What is happening in the Aegean?' we asked.

'Oh, the Aegean,' said the German colonel nonchalantly, as though we were unaware that his work had lain in that area for over two years. 'Well, to be frank, we have suffered reverses. Circumstances have obliged us to evacuate most of the islands, but the garrisons of Crete, Cos, Leros, and Rhodes remain. These will continue to keep a grip on the Aegean for us.'

'Perhaps because you are unable to evacuate them?' suggested Nixon in his innocent way.

'Dear me, Nixon, how *can* you say such a thing,' expostulated the German colonel.

And to do him credit, he laughed . . . perhaps because his English was so excessively good.

I well remember that he also gave us a cigar apiece with which to celebrate the news.

CHAPTER TWENTY-TWO

'Do not,' I was warned when I began this book, 'make too detailed reference to the fleshpots of Egypt and the Levant.'

If I have refrained from so doing it must not be imagined that men did not occasionally go on leave. They did go on leave. They went, the frivolously minded, to Cairo, the students of ancient civilization to Tyre and to Baalbek, and those ambiguously in search of something 'different' to Aleppo, Tel Aviv, and the King David Hotel at Jerusalem.

'Stud' Stellin, Ronnie Govier, Sergeant Pomford, were students in this latter category. Particularly Sergeant Pomford. In Alexandria, in a photographer's window in a certain main thoroughfare, there used to hang a huge picture of Sergeant Pomford. In this picture Pomford looked tired.

But Athens was a very different glass of oyzo to the tawdry amusements of *Mittel-Osten*. To understand S.B.S. you must remember that they had been fighting with Greeks and in Greek territory for over a year. Nearly every British soldier has a smattering of Arabic, but to S.B.S. Greek was almost a second language: a language vilely pronounced, grammatically tortured, it is true, but somehow universally understood.

S.B.S. liked the Greeks. The Greeks liked S.B.S. The two had, in fact, many things in common: a certain individual tendency to anarchy, an untidiness in dress, a disrespect for authority, a deep belief in the black market. When Lassen's and Patterson's squadrons returned to the capital, the Athenians had not forgotten the beige beret, the strange insignia, and the corduroy trousers. The sounds of revelry by night were many, and by no means always harmonious. Several marital engagements were announced, and other liaisons of a more irregular nature contracted. 'It was,' said a corporal, who had perhaps forgotten that British pubs observe strict opening and shutting hours, 'almost like being home.'

Athens was very much in the news in that November of 1944, and, not unnatually, many war correspondents were present. 'A strong platoon of these gentlemen,' wrote Jellicoe, 'had landed with us at Patras and had gradually swollen in numbers until, at last, no detail of my private life remained secret.' The full glare of publicity was, in fact, turned upon the unit after years of semi-secrecy and whispering in newsrooms. References to the 'long-haired boys', to 'secret raiders of the Aegean' and to 'iron rings' round this or that island became fashionable in the home press. Many a man who had formerly yearned for some small small measure of notoriety now sighed again: this time for oblivion.

Von Klemann, an avid student of our newspapers, must have smiled ironically as he read the garbled accounts of raids of which he alone knew all the details. Von Klemann had left Rhodes, and having earned that promotion which comes, in the German Army, to generals who box cleverly, was now defending Budapest. The ranks of our distinguished opponents had indeed been strangely thinned. Driven from Salonika, von List had been superseded by Baron von Weichs, to whom the final evacuation of the cursed Balkans was entrusted.

Even in beleaguered Crete there were changes. One General, the notable coprophile, having denuded his island of its best effectives, had also departed, and was now commanding an infantry division in southern Serbia. This man will, it is hoped, one day be brought to trial. He wantonly slaughtered more Greeks than any other enemy general.

By the middle of November the enemy garrison in Crete, once able to put less than seven infantry divisions in the field, had been reduced to a matter of 13,000 ill-disciplined and

197

hungry troops. From the sea a complete blockade was maintained, but it remained possible to evacuate small numbers of effectives by air. Officers of Force 133 had always been particularly active and well chosen in this island and, when towards the middle of the month they reported that the enemy were likely to withdraw to a smaller perimetre, Jellicoe was instructed to send a force to watch over and report upon this recoil.

Lassen's squadron, reinforced by an artillery section of the Raiding Support Regiment, was chosen. His primary purpose, as stated, was not offensive, but merely to observe the enemy and to protect the landing of food supplies for the civilian population at the port of Heraklion.

The Germans did, in fact, abandon large portions of Crete amounting to four-fifths of the total area. They retired to a small coastal strip in the north-west corner, twenty miles in length and some ten in depth. The nodal points of this perimeter were the airfield of Maleme—at which a solitary Junkers 52 arrived nightly, carrying mail from Vienna—the town of Chanea and the now useless haven of Suda Bay, in which the wreck of British shipping—notably that of the cruiser *York*—remained to remind them of happier days.

Lassen landed at Heraklion on 3rd December and established his headquarters in the town. The patrols at his disposal were leap-frogged forward in order to provide due warning of any move by the enemy to retrieve his lost territory. Within two days, Ian Smith, with the Irishmen and Bimrose, were spotting targets inside the perimeter for air attack. They found the perimeter itself loosely blockaded by formations of Greek Andartes who were not above selling food to their opponents, and who invariably retired gracefully when the famished Germans emerged in sheep-rustling expeditions. Smith put a stop to this nonsense, but reported that black market caïques were undoubtedly still trading between Rethimnon and Chanea.

Henshaw, sent still farther forward, had the honour of an interview with the German police chief, the ostensible purpose of which was to arrange an exchange of prisoners. The German welcomed Henshaw ironically to the island

and trusted that he would enjoy his stay.

'It is a pity you are so few,' he added. 'Otherwise we might have considered surrendering to you. As it is, with these wild men . . . these Andartes . . . all about us, to give up our arms would be suicide.'

Henshaw remarked that if the Andartes were not now kindly disposed towards their late overlords, these latter had only themselves to blame.

'Now you are making propaganda, my friend,' said the German. 'But please . . . to be serious . . . why do you not cease your stupid bombing? We do no harm. We cannot escape. Let us sit here in peace until the end of the war.'

Henshaw said that since the Germans found the bombing inconvenient he would take steps to see that it was redoubled.

The German now suggested a football match: 'We have an excellent team. Doubtless you yourselves are strong. You English are so sporting.'

Henshaw said that he did not think that his commanding officer would be likely to favour this idea. He was right: Lassen, who until now had been devoting much of his time to the acquisition of new and odoriferous dogs for his collection, became inarticulate with rage at the very proposal.

But the German, of course, was not to know this. 'We could have a neutral referee,' he said. 'The Bishop of Chanea in his cassock. That would be a droll sight, would it not?'

The two officers drank tea together. They parted on good terms. Returning to his own lines, Henshaw persuaded the Andartes to put in a night attack and ordered the S.B.S. Bren-gunners to support it. Things began to look more lively on this forgotten front.

The tragedy which had overtaken Bob Bury was now to be repeated in the case of another S.B.S. officer. In this case, however, no doubt was to be left but that the attack was deliberate and undertaken with malice aforethought.

Having business requiring attention in Rethimnon, Captain Charles Clynes left Heraklion in a jeep, accompanied by Bimrose and a Captain Oakie, with Private

Cornthwaite as motor-cyclist outrider. There had previously been disturbances between the two main armed political parties E.L.A.S. and E.O.K., respectively Left and Right in their sympathies. To these disturbances, however, S.B.S. had not been a party; Lassen's policy being to work with all forces prepared to undertake attacks upon the enemy.

The jeep was travelling at a slow speed in order that there should be no question of its identity. Moreover, the men inside it were unarmed, as proof of their pacific intentions while crossing country where the rival factions were quarrelling bitterly.

Suddenly, two rifle shots were fired. The first killed the outrider, Cornthwaite, the second, traversing Bimrose's calf, passed clean through Clyne's body. Only Oakie was unhurt.

Clynes died a week later, in Athens, Bimrose, whose third wound this was, recovered rapidly. The man who had fired the shots, an E.L.A.S. sympathizer, was later arrested and tried by a Greek court. He was pronounced guilty but insane. Lassen, although obliged to remain in Crete for some time longer, maintained henceforward barely formal relations with either Greek party.

If this was a dirty business, still dirtier was to follow. In Athens the honeymoon was over. The rival parties, in their manipulations for power, had reached a point where a solution could be found only by violence. Lieutenant-General Scobie, senior British officer in Greece, had fixed 8th December 1944 as the final date by which all arms in the possession of guerrilla forces were to be handed over. On that date the organization, E.L.A.S., rose in rebellion. For a while it was hoped that British troops would not be involved in the disturbances. These hopes proved vain. Patterson's squadron was actually standing on Kalamaki airfield, kit packed, waiting for transport to Italy, when it was recalled urgently to the city to take up battle positions.

Let us be frank: the obstructionist tactics of E.L.A.S. during the German occupation, their reluctance to attack the enemy themselves, their known hoarding against civil war of arms given them for quite another purpose, their massacres without trial of men who may or may not have been collaborators, their wholesale requisitioning of food, their gagging of all criticism and their fanatical belief in a single party system which appeared to resemble only too closely that which they professed to abhor, were not such as had recommended them to S.B.S.

On the other hand, it was hard indeed for S.B.S to have to fire upon Greeks ... just how hard those senior officers perhaps realized who noticed that, in the first few days, S.B.S. fought only when attacked. This reluctance was not finally broken down until the methods employed by their opponents became apparent. Then, their determination to fight the battle out was reinforced by the realization that the great majority of the Greek people were with them.

Picture central London divided into two hostile camps. start at the bottom of the Haymarket, walk up to Piccadilly Circus, thence to Oxford Circus. Outside Waring & Gillow's there are barbed wire barricades. This is the frontier. Don't linger too long or you will be sniped. Expeditons to Fleet Street, for example, or to Hyde Park Corner, are at present quite impossible—unless you want your throat cut. You must find the food and the lodging you need in Regent Street.

Freddie Birkett, Sergeant Hessell and their patrol were dead out of luck. When S.B.S. returned to the city and took up their positions, Birkett was assigned to the city waterworks. He shared the guard of this ugly edifice with a platoon of E.L.A.S. troops. One morning—this was before the fighting became general—Birkett was lying on his bed reading a novel. The E.L.A.S. commander entered, and requested him politely to give up his arms.

Birkett and his men were marched north towards Thebes. They were not ill-treated. It is, in fact, very difficult to ill-treat British soldiers because, when threatened, they become so derisive that their persecutors feel guilty, imagining that they have transgressed in some secret way the magic British code of 'fair play'. Thus, on the third morning of the march, somebody attempted to remove the boots of Corporal James Webster, formerly a London policeman.

'Here,' protested Webster, 'you can't do that.'

'Oh, yes I can,' said the man.

'Look here, you bloody well shut up,' said Webster, cuffing his tormentor. 'I'm a prisoner I am. Prisoners have got to be treated with respect. It says so in the Geneva Convention.'

'What is this Convention?' inquired the bootless man. He was puzzled.

Webster outlined a version of the famous protocol extremely favourable to his circumstances. He kept his boots. From this moment onwards, the man clung to him demanding further evidence of higher education.

E.L.A.S. had planned to disarm the bulk of British troops in a similar way and thus neutralize them. They failed. No other S.B.S. patrol was caught napping, and the Independent Parachute Battalion, upon which the defence of the perimeter largely devoted, established barricades and road blocks at the first sign of danger.

After the first week of fighting the British held, in Piræus, the greater part of the Callipopis peninsula, and the north coast of Phaleron Bay with its seaplane base. In the central area of Athens they held what corresponded roughly to the Whitehall and Mayfair areas of London; the British Embassy, the infantry barracks south-east of Lijavitos hill, the eastern peak of this same hill and the Acropolis. In eastern Athens they held part of the Kaisariani suburb and the battered Goudhi barracks. Communications between all these districts was possible, though seldom accomplished without interference. Aircraft bringing supplies, reinforcements, and brass hats could land freely at Kalamaki airfield. Armoured cars conveyed the brass hats to Athens. They conveyed, at various times, Messieurs Churchill and Eden and Field-Marshal Alexander.

There is a squaddie's story that when Alexander's armoured car was speeding through hostile streets, fire was opened upon it.

'They can't do this,' said the field-marshal and, leaping out, revolver in hand, he ordered his startled conducting officers to charge the offending house.

This story is probably untrue. I do not care very much if it is untrue, for it illustrates what squaddies thought of the best-loved and most brilliant British commander of that war.

In the Hotel Grande Bretagne, the war correspondents crouched over the cocktail bar.

'A well-informed person told me yesterday that . . .'

'Smith says that every third man on the E.L.A.S. side is a Bulgarian or a German . . .'

'I am speaking from a bullet-proof room in a hotel in central Athens. Outside I can hear the noise of fighting . . .'

He could indeed. Let us go outside and study some of this fighting: the little sector held by Sergeant Asbery, Corporal Stewart and their men will provide us, I think, with a fair cross-section of a day's work in Athens at that time.

Sergeant Asbery was living at this time in a luxurious flat . . . not so luxurious now, as a matter of fact, for both water and electricity had been cut off. Not very far from this flat lay Sergeant Asbery's road block, manned by his patrol. This was the frontier of the British perimeter in that neighbourhood. Beyond lay deserted streets. From the houses in these streets the muffled sounds of tunnelling could be heard. Each two or three minutes a distant Bren gun would stammer.

For S.B.S. were using Bren guns now to the exclusion of every other weapon except the Piat. Why waste a carbine bullet on a man crossing a street junction 600 yards away? Give him a Bren gun burst and the ricochets will get him even if the nickel fails. Perhaps you think this is a little hard . . . perhaps you think that this man 600 yards away may have been some harmless civilian? At first, it is true, he might have been, but when harmless civilians took to approaching British barricades, only to pull out a gun and to fire it, a curfew was imposed. Harmless civilians, henceforth, could emerge only between midday and two o'clock in the afternoon. Sergeant Asbery, who had lost two men wounded through such treachery, began to know where he stood.

And it was about time: it is difficult enought to fight an enemy who observes none of the few rules of warfare, who wears civilian clothes, who can only be identified as a friend or as an opponent by the absence or presence of a bulge in some part of his suiting and who uses women to cover his withdrawals and attacks. It was difficult enough in these circumstances, God and Sergeant Asbery knew. He did not desire the additional responsibility of killing those who were neutral.

Five of Asbery's ten men were wounded during those thirty-one days. In street-fighting enduring through weeks, such casualties are not high. S.B.S. lost twelve wounded and three killed in all; about one-quarter of their strength engaged. Ian Patterson, now at the zenith of his reputation and military talent, spent much time closeted with General Scobie. In his absence, the inspection and co-ordination of S.B.S. outposts devolved largely upon Keith Balsillie. Thin, quiet, steady old Keith, never until then perhaps adjudged at his true worth, was seen everywhere . . .

Ronnie Govier, attached to an armoured car unit, was responsible for keeping open the road to Kalamaki. He spent most of his nights lifting 'S' mines on the Piræus avenue.

David Clark, sniped as he was sitting in a certain intimate office, was sniped again as he crossed the street to find a substitute for it. Uncomfortable and bilious, he abandoned the attempt altogether.

Webster, the policeman, was released, together with the remainder of Birkett's men when E.L.A.S. finally withdrew from Athens on 8th January 1945.

Signaller Stephenson who, all this time, had been conducting a tender correspondence with a young lady on the wrong side of the barricades, was now able to rejoin her.

The sounds of revelry by night were resumed.

CHAPTER TWENTY-THREE

The wounded men were passed into the Dakota transport plane on stretchers. Medical orderlies moved among them with field service syringes of morphia. Two of the wounded men were cases of leg gangrene. Morphia was of little help to these. Beneath the gauze and the bandages their multiple lacerations bubbled. The smell was very evil.

When all the wounded had been loaded, the other passengers followed. Last to enter was Ian Patterson. He carried a brief-case with the contents of which he was proposed to while away the long journey to Italy. As the Dakota taxied down the runway Patterson studied his papers: there were recommendations for decoration, for promotions, for the future employment of his squadron. He did not look out over Athens, even when the Dakota circled over the Acropolis. He did not now regard Athens as the cradle of civilization.

The weather was not good. A depression centred over the Straits of Otranto was moving westwards. A warm front near Malta would produce complicated meteorological conditions with ground mist and rain. The pilot, who was flying on a radio directional beam from Bari airport, placed his ship on the automatic control and drank some coffee.

They were approaching Brindisi when Patterson first realized that trouble lay ahead. Something was going wrong with the radio beam . . . he could hear the pilot and navigator discussing the matter, debating whether they were not now receiving course direction from Foggia. A few minutes later the wireless operator asked Bari for his position and was given it. The position received did not coincide with the navigator's own estimate, based on air-speed, course, and time airborne. He ignored it.

Patterson, declared the only survivor, was asleep when the end came. The Dakota hit an olive-tree beside a lonely farm, proceeded 200 more yards with waning momentum, and crashed on a hillside.

Another—and this time a senior S.B.S. officer—had gone.

Stewart Macbeth, in Bari, did not learn of the disaster until over twenty-four hours later. He arrived just in time to prevent Ian Patterson from being buried in a communal grave . . .

> 'Courage, dead soul, now learn to wield
> The weight of an immortal shield . . .'

The British soldier is not by nature a great believer in the After-life. The more surprising, therefore, this snatch of conversation, which I overheard some months later:

'Garn . . . you can't get away from 'im. Patterson's up there watching you. 'E knows what's going on 'e does.'

The other soldier, who was contemplating a transaction of which Ian Patterson would have strongly disapproved—namely the illegal disposal of an Army blanket—looked impressed.

'I believe you're right,' he said in an awed voice.

Neither of them could believe, in point of fact, that the activities of that restless, brilliant, violent man could have come to an end with anything so ordinary as the crash of an aeroplane.

'George is going . . .'

'What?'

The Lord's leaving.'

A military canteen is normally a noisy place, but when these words were pronounced you could have heard even the tiny clicking sound as Sergeant Henderson, P., adjusted the position of his false teeth.

To many, the idea that George Jellicoe—'the belted Earl',

'Curly', 'His Reverence', to employ only some of his innumerable nicknames—might leave S.B.S. appeared utterly inconceivable. True, he was now of comparatively exalted rank, and had even for a few weeks been a brigadier, but the reason announced for his departure—that he had been called to Haifa to follow a staff course—was greeted with knowing winks.

''E's up to something, you bet.'

'Oh, 'e'll be back, you just wait and see.'

Many good commanding officers have a certain mystical reputation with their men, but with Jellicoe this was carried to extraordinary lengths. It was known, for example, that prior to the Cairo conference, Churchill had consulted him concerning certain Aegean problems. It was known that he had the ear, occasionally, of the mighty, and always of the influential. It was known that his actual military rank bore no relation to the great esteem in which his abilities were held; that his remarkable facility for securing employment for his forces in the right place, at the right time, were by no means an accident, but rather the fruits of an acute mind, and of much study.

Jellicoe left S.B.S. in mid-December 1944, when the European war had still some months to run. He was succeeded—and indeed could have only been succeeded—by David Sutherland, now senior member of the unit, not only in rank, but also in length of service.

The problems confronting Sutherland were manifold.

He had, for some months, been a partisan of intervention behind the enemy lines in Istria where, he argued, much soft-skinned prey in the shape of transport and inadequately protected columns would be found. This operation—dear to his heart perhaps because it offered an opportunity of leading the unit in the field himself—Sutherland was obliged to postpone for some weeks. Meanwhile, he was requested to put a squadron in the field, based on Zara, with a view to attacks upon the German-held Adriatic islands.

We shall deal presently with these attacks.

In early January 1945 I went down to Rodi-Garganico,

where some recruits from an artillery depot were training on the magnificent beach. After a gruelling half-hour of contortions presided over by 'Brown Body' Henderson, they were now being initiated into the 'battle-crouch' and other trade secrets by Marine Hughes.

Douglas Stobie, kilted, knobkerry in hand, plumper than ever, stood by, surveying his charges with gloomy boredom.

'Training,' he exclaimed disgustedly, 'why the devil do I have to do training?'

'Somebody has to do it, Douglas.'

'But why *me* . . . why should I have to do it . . . training indeed.' He snorted.

'Because you're good at it, Douglas,' I said soothingly.

'Oh, let's go and have a drink, for God's sake,' said Douglas Stobie.

At Monte St. Angelo, Lassen was reorganizing his squadron. When asked what type of training he intended to give them he, too, snorted.

'Zey vill *marsch*,' he declared briefly.

'And when they have finished their march?'

'Zey will *marsch* again . . .'

Fortunately, quite apart from his large and unique collection of dogs, Lassen now had a new toy, his interest in which prevented him from fully implementing these threats. During a brief visit to Albania he had acquired, and somehow succeeded in evacuating, a German *Volkswagen* motor-car. He drove about in this vehicle all over Italy until finally it was seized and impounded by the military police.

Lassen was bored with raiding, he declared. Like all specialists he had an inordinate respect for those who do not specialize; and, in particular, for the infantry. 'Ve must go to ze *big* war,' he said continually. Lassen was not quite certain what 'the big war' would be like, nor what his own role would be in it, but he knew that it involved great feats of organization and administrative ability. Lassen was very much impressed by organization. The organization, for example, required to move a division from one point to another, to throw parts of it into battle and to maintain other parts in reserve, excited his warmest admiration.

'Look at von Rundstedt,' he would say.

Lassen's almost international reputation for violence in the night ensured that his proposals should receive attentive hearing in high places. When the spring offensive in Italy was being planned and certain operations became necessary before it could be begun, he was called for.

But this, too, we will come to again later.

'Where did you spend your leave, Corporal Stewart?'

'In Rome, sir.'

'And did you enjoy it?'

'I did, sir.'

'Business was good, then?'

'Business was *very* good, sir.'

The officer walked off, making a mental note to ask the quarter-master when Corporal Stewart had last drawn his pay.

From the mail-bag:

From Mrs. J. Runcible, 77 Black Street, Walsall, to Corporal Arthur Runcible, Special Boat Service, C.M.F.

'Dear Arthur,

'I am glad you had a good Christmas. You must be well dug in, out there, I expect. Jack was home last week. He spent his Christmas in Holland. The fighting's terrible there, by all accounts. In spite of what the neighbours say about our boys in B.L.A. and so on, I can't help feeling pleased that you're safe in Italy. Molly Taverton says . . . etc.'

From Corporal Arthur Runcible, Special Boat Service, C.M.F., to Mrs J. Runcible, 77 Black Street, Walsall:

'Dear Nell,

'We had a dance last night, first I've been able to get to for quite a while. The girls out here are all right, but not a patch on you, Nell dear. You should have seen one of our officers, "Stud" Stellin at this dance. He was a scream. Don't ask me why he's called that, either, 'cos I shan't tell you. I'm

glad old Jack's got back safely. How long has he been abroad
. . . six months, isn't it? I wish they'd give *us* home leave out
here, but I suppose with this shipping shortage they can't
manage it. Still, I've done my four years now, and it won't be
much longer, dear . . . etc.'

From Private Ronald Rivers, Special Boat Service, to
Miss Euridice Kambanos, 43 Korai Street, Athens:

'My darling Sweetheart,
'No hope, it seems, of getting back to you for the
moment. But don't worry darling. I'll manage it somehow,
even if we have to wait until after the war. I'll never forget,
darling, the way you saved my life that day the sniper got a
bead on me. How's your Mum getting on? She certainly
makes an apple-pie just like we get back at home . . . etc.'

From Lloyds Bank Ltd., to Captain Dion Stellin, M.C.,
Special Boat Service, C.M.F.

'Sir,
'We write to inform you that your account is once again
overdrawn . . . etc.'

From Lieutenant-Colonel D. G. E. Sutherland, M.C., to
Mrs. R. Potts, 27 Butler Road, Macclesfield:

'Dear Madam,
'It is with very great regret that I must confirm the War
Office report which you have received that your son, Private
Richard Potts, was killed in action recently, under my
command. I wish to tell you . . . etc.'

From Captain S. F. Macbeth, Special Boat Service,
C.M.F. to Messrs. Raymond and Machard, Tailors, 94
Bruton Street, London, W.1:

'Dear Sirs,
'The riding breeches which you made for me recently to
a pre-war measurement do not fit me . . . etc.'

From Captain I. N. Swan, No. 15 Commando, B.L.A.,
to Major Anders Lassen, M.C., Special Boat Service, C.M.F.:

'Dear Andy,
'. . . having reasonable time here. Did a job on you-can-guess-where last week. Much booty but not really like the old times. What are you up to in your part of the world? We never hear of you nowadays . . . etc.'

From Orders:
'The practice of wearing unit headgear at other than the regulation angle will cease forthwith . . .

'Material Captured, Enemy: Articles of Enemy personal apparel, toilet items, cameras etc. will in future be described in the correct terminology. They will *not* be referred to as "liberated".'

CHAPTER TWENTY-FOUR

The township of Zara, which owes its origins and development to the settlement of Venetian colonists, lies in the somewhat exiguous Dalmatian coastal plain, screened from the open sea by a number of splinter-shaped islands. By virtue of its former Venetian ownership, Zara was allotted to Italy in the Versailles arrangements of 1919. By virtue of its garrison of Germans, it was bombed in 1944 with such great efficacy that no more than the shells of its many beautiful houses now remain.

At the beginning of 1945, Zara was a naval base for coastal forces operating as far north as Pola. It was also used as a clearing house and disembarkation point for stores landed in the name of that philanthropic organization, the avowed intention of which is the relief and rehabilitation of starving peoples. The population of Zara itself, who, one would think, would be the first to benefit from this distribution of largesse were, as a matter of fact, in no position to do so; for, being for most part Italians, they had already been marched away to inland concentration camps by their Slav liberators.

Zara in early 1945: soldiers who are not British but who wear British battle-dress, walk the quays in pairs. They carry rusty Mauser rifles with a certain swagger as they pass the anti-aircraft cruiser *Colombo*, which is moored alongside the docks. They inspect with a certain arrogance the bales of flour and clothing which are being unloaded for their compatriots. British personnel, whether naval or military,

The Eastern Adriatic

SPRING '45

213

are forbidden to penetrate farther into the town than the dockside. The imitation of the Russian manner by lesser peoples is not as amusing as propagandists would have one believe.

. Nobby Clarke had succeeded to the command of Sutherland's squadron on the latter's promotion. He arrived with his men in Zara in early February, and finding the town to be insanitary and his reception not such as to which he was accustomed, he transferred his quarters to the near-by island of Ulyan, where the lodgings were more civilized and the inhabitants, correspondingly, more friendly.

Clarke did not rely entirely upon his own forces, for Jellicoe, in his time, disproving the proverb, had gathered much moss. The latest semi-independent recruits to S.B.S. were some twenty men of the R.A.F. Regiment. These men had been briefed at one period for a drop on the Brenner Pass. The operation had been cancelled and, finding themselves without either employment or influence, the survivors had drifted within the S.B.S. orbit.

S.B.S. were now about to resume operations in their traditional island-hopping manner. The present islands, however, were very different from those encountered in the Aegean, and so, for that matter, were the Germans who garrisoned them. Naxos is spherical, Santorin a tattered crescent, Paros a rhomboid: but all these are small. Those in the Adriatic, from the euphoniously named Krk to barren Pag are uniformly narrow. Woods, a feature unknown in the Aegean, are to be seen on their summits. Communications are good, particularly with the mainland. Roads are metalled. The peace-time standard of life is high.

When defeat came to the Germans in the Aegean they scuttled many of their ships. Some, however, preserved by the presence of mind or the obstinacy of their commanders, remained. These sailed for Pola, Fiume, or Trieste; that triumvirate of ports in the northern Adriatic which was all that now remained to the enemy in the Mediterranean basin.

The Germans who held these islands in numbers, never hitherto encountered by us, had, curiously enough, been drawn largely from the evacuated Aegean garrisons.

Consequently they were in the fullest sense of the word *avertis*. They expected to be attacked and they knew who would lead the attack when it came. Their emplacements, their dug-outs, the hundreds of yards of wire and mines with which they surrounded their living-quarters, were soon discovered by our reconnaissance parties.

Another hazard existed in the Adriatic which had been absent in the Aegean ... mines, not the vast, horned monsters which sink merchant shipping either magnetically or by contact, but little mines, laid only a few feet beneath the surface and designed to sink coastal craft. Mines had been laid in the northern Adriatic since the outbreak of the war. They had been laid by the Italians, the British, the Germans, even the Jugoslavs. Some of the minefields were charted, but many more were not. Others had drifted from their former known positions.

Mines are not nice. Ronnie Govier who, with his desert experience, knew as much about them as anybody, had once stepped on a German 'S' land mine. When this happens and the prospective victim hears the clockwork ticking, he can pursue one of two courses: he can leave his foot on the mine, in which case it will be blown off, or he can fling himself flat on the ground, in which position he has nine chances out of ten of being irreparably maimed as the mine jumps. Govier chose the latter position and, miraculously, was completely unhurt. In 1945, Govier was passenger on a P.T. boat following its flotilla leader through another kind of minefield in the Adriatic. A brief and sharp explosion and the flotilla leader blew up. Seventeen men, drinking coffee in her fo'c'sle, were killed. The only survivors were the two officers who, standing on the bridge, were thrown clear. Noticing this, Govier moved cautiously on to the bridge of his own craft.

'Information concerning the islands,' wrote Nobby Clarke, 'was scarce and for the most part inaccurate.' He decided that he would carry out very thorough reconnaissances of each before making an attack, and to this end he sent his Intelligence Officer to the small island of Olib with instructions to collect data concerning Lussin and

215

Cherso, reported to be strongly held by the enemy. Meanwhile, McGonigal and Rifleman Lynch cross-checked this information from the somewhat larger island of Unie.

Exceeding his instructions in the interests of truth, McGonigal had himself ferried by rowing-boat to Lussin itself.

'I watched a somewhat slovenly parade outside a house occupied by Germans,' he wrote, 'but otherwise saw very little.'

Clarke then sent 'Stud' Stellin with a large party including Sergeant Flavell, the American Jarrell, and Private Watler to mop up a small post on Cherso Island, reputedly held by Italian Fascists. Fire was opened from the Piats and Brens on the billet and the occupants, numbering twelve in all, surrendered without further demur. A powerful radio transmitter and many code books were seized.

A very much more difficult objective was now engaged. At Villa Punta, on Lussin, existed a strongly held post housing no less than forty-five men. These men were Germans. Under McGonigal an expedition sailed to attack this post. Jimmy Lees and two newcomers, Lieutenants Thomason and Jones-Parry, led sections. The striking force totalled twenty-one.

Landing unobserved and with local inhabitants acting as guides, the raiders approached the target area. Here, McGonigal ordered Jones-Parry and his patrol to advance along the seashore to the south of the villa. Unfortunately, Jones-Parry was observed, challenged by a sentry and fired upon.

Since all chance of surprise had now been lost, McGonigal ordered the general attack. The enemy, who at first had attempted to make a sortie, were driven back into their billet.

The billet was surrounded.

Jones-Parry, Jimmy Lees, and Thomason, with their men, were now sent into the house with orders to clear it room by room if necessary: Jimmy Lees, on the first floor, had almost accomplished his part of this task when he was hit and fatally wounded by a man firing from behind a sofa. He died in German hands the next day, never having recovered consciousness.

Elsewhere: 'I saw,' stated Jones-Parry, 'two or more persons moving about in the corridor. I threw a grenade, but it was a dud, so I threw a phosphorus bomb and opened fire. I went in. I went up to a door and listened. No sound, very dark. Rushed in, paused. No movement. I went into a second room. Marine Kitchingham, following me, covered my back. Sergeant McDougal covered the corridor. Suddenly, Kitchingham asked, 'Are you all right, sir?' I replied, 'Yes'. At that moment there was a burst of machine-gun fire from some point in the room which we must have overlooked. I was hit in the arm and chest. Kitchingham collapsed. He had received the burst through his head. My thinking then began to get a bit confused. I changed my magazine and slung my tommy-gun round my neck to make myself more stable. Then I opened fire on the point from which the burst had come, traversing along the wall and floor. I am certain I got the man as there was no reply, only groans. I reported to Captain McGonigal, who sent me on to the road for dressing. Very weak now, so lay down until told wounded were to move. Finally, walked back to motor launch.'

This report was dictated by Jones-Parry from a hospital bed. If this officer survived to sleep between sheets again it is owing to his courage and endurance in walking two miles to the embarkation point with a shattered arm and a bullet in his spleen.

Meanwhile, McGonigal, with all available remaining men, made the decisive assault. The enemy fire slackened. Finally it ceased altogether. With their house wrecked by Lewis bombs and on fire, it seemed unlikely that many of the garrison had survived. S.B.S. casualties, though, had not been light for, apart from Jimmy Lees and Marine Kitchingham dead, eight men, including Jones-Parry, had been more or less severely wounded.

Opinions differed concerning the results obtained on this raid. Some maintained that the price had been too costly and this argument was reinforced when it became known that no less than twenty of the enemy had escaped unhurt by hiding in cellars or in the garden. The truth is perhaps that it is extraordinarily difficult to manœuvre and deploy more than fifteen men, under night conditions, and against a fixed objective, when more than one officer is involved. There were too many officers at Villa Panta, and though they led the attack with considerable verve and dash they were frequently at cross-purposes. Both Jones-Parry and Thomason, for example, had at various times to send messages out to other patrols begging them to cease fire into parts of the villa which friendly personnel were clearing.

Villa Punta must stand as an indecisive action . . . and in S.B.S. an indecisive action is synonymous with a defeat. The loss of Jimmy Lees and of Kitchingham were particularly grievous, for both these men had served with the unit for a long time and with great distinction. Modest and unassuming almost to a fault, Jimmy Lees had always been unlucky in the operations allotted to him. The spectacular captures, the actions which draw immediate attention, had never, somehow, come his way.

One indirect result of this raid, nevertheless, was a startling decline in the morale of Italian Fascists throughout the area. Courage was required to be a Fascist in the attenuated Empire under Mussolini's control in 1945. Defections from their numbers had therefore not been considered very likely; particularly when it was learnt that elements of the 'Sud Fronte' division, which had fought well against the Americans, were being employed as reinforcements.

But when Lieutenant Alan Lucas, accompanied by Lance-Corporal Hancock, landed on Lussin, he was informed that no less than twelve Italians desired to surrender. The detention and evacuation of prisoners being no part of Lucas's programme, he endeavoured to avoid these men. In this he was singularly unsuccessful, for when the Italians discovered that no notice was being taken of them, they came of their own accord to Lucas's camp and laid down their arms. Germans being in strength in the neighbourhood, Lucas ordered the Italians to leave him in peace. But the Italians were adamant . . . their desires were centred on a comfortable prison cage and they would be content with nothing less: and to prove their goodwill, they brought with them as captive their officer. The officer, who did not share the feelings of his men and who, perhaps, feared court proceedings in Italy, took out a Beretta and shot himself.

Lucas evacuated the others.

McGonigal with an even larger party (thirty-eight men this time) was instructed to try it again, and the target on this occasion was of the first importance. The islands of Cherso and Lussin, in reality a single entity, are linked by a bridge at the village of Ossero. Repeated bombardments by naval forces and by Balkan Air Force had failed to destroy this bridge, essential to the maintenance of enemy communications. That the Germans appreciated its importance is shown by the fact that they maintained a garrison of no less than eighty men to guard it, and endowed these men with numerous light anti-aircraft and machine guns.

Ossero was awkward: even high authorities admitted that. Heavy casualties were expected and the inclusion of no less than three medical orderlies in the party did not pass unnoticed.

'Got any brandy on you, chum? Don't give me no bleedin' morphia if I cop one.'

'Grr! I'd rather be bandaged by a Jerry than 'im.'

'They ought to do the thing proper-like. Why don't they bring a sky-pilot?'

McGonigal had pondered deeply since Villa Punta and he was determined that on this occasion there should be no cases of mistaken identity, no confusion, and above all, no early and disastrous challenges from outlying sentries. His plan was well conceived and involved the approach of numerous patrols in such a manner that they could not possibly come into conflict with one another. For the first time for a very long while in S.B.S. history, a separate folboat party (under Sergeant Holmes) was briefed to land. From the moment of disembarkation of the main party, no enemy forces, however small, were to be allowed to remain alive behind the axis of advance towards the target.

The expedition left Zara at dusk on 18th March 1945, in two motor launches. Off Ossero point, Holmes and Rifleman Lecomber were dropped off. Soon, their folboat was but a grey streak against the general darkness. The main force landed farther up the coast in a small bay and began their tiring three-hour march towards the bridge.

In keeping with McGonigal's policy of peeling off the outer defences as one removes the leaves off an artichoke, Ian Smith, with Sergeant Henderson's patrol, was sent to investigate a reported machine-gun position in a church. They found the emplacement tidily arranged, obviously in continuous use, but abandoned for the night. They disarranged it and removed the machine-gun.

At a cross-roads, Captain Anderson and a small party broke off to attack the German guard-house from the jetty.

The first sign of enemy alertness was encountered when a patrol under Sergeant Wright observed a party of five Germans approaching from the north. They opened fire. Four of the Germans were killed. The fifth escaped.

This scuffle, though successful, resulted in the general alarm being sounded throughout the German positions. Once again, McGonigal was obliged to launch an assault before his troops were thoroughly ready and in position. The situation was saved by Henshaw who, running forward in the lead, distracted enemy attention to himself while others advanced. The way to the German positions was well covered by wire. Eight enemy machine-guns directed their aim upon this wire and upon the approaches to it. Indifferent to his danger, Henshaw attempted to cut his way through the obstacle. He was killed by a grenade.

At this stage, Anderson's patrol should have intervened on the flank, with results that might well have been decisive. But they, too, were held up by wire and high walls.

An intense engagement developed, in which the only advantage in S.B.S. favour was that the enemy were obliged to move occasionally in the open while bearing fish supplies of ammunition. Nine Germans were killed and two wounded while thus exposing themselves.

In return, S.B.S., who for all practical purposes had no cover at all, lost three further men, all wounded.

It became clear that the way through to the bridge could not be secured without the intervention of much heavier metal. McGonigal, accordingly, dispatched a message to the motor launches requesting them to open fire on the target area. A bombardment by Oerlikons commenced, but the Germans continued to resist stoutly and with admirable determination.

Thirty-five men, exposed, with light weapons and short supplies of ammunition cannot indefinitely engage eighty men well entrenched and with heavier armament. Realizing that the project of destroying the bridge must be abandoned, McGonigal concentrated his main effort upon sniping with a view to causing the maximum number of casualties. He was wise.

When small boys play Red Indians, the palefaces usually triumph in the end, for small boys (and they are not alone in this) like their military triumphs to be in terms of scalps and black and white. Similarly, when we write of our late enemies, it is with perhaps a natural desire to show them out-manoeuvred and out-fought. The Germans, however, have suffered so many humiliations in the course of this story that I find it easy to concede them their rare triumph. They defended Ossero with great bravery. They lost twenty-seven men in that action but they maintained the vital bridge intact. If five, or even fewer, of their number had surrendered, the result would have been very different. But no one man surrendered and, with dawn, S.B.S. were compelled to withdraw.

David Sutherland now intervened: 'In view of the strong precautionary measures being taken by the Germans almost everywhere,' he wrote, 'I decided that raids of this nature could only produce diminishing results. In future, attacks would be made exclusively upon transport and, in particular, upon the Cherso-Lussin road . . .'

With this in view, he dispatched Lucas with Sergeant Flavell's patrol to the tiny island of Levrera. Here they were to make their base, crossing every night by motor dory to Cherso to maintain a watch upon the road.

Lucas established his ambush at a track-junction. The first night's vigil was unfruitful. Just before dawn, on the second night, a staff car approached and was attacked. Of the two occupants, the driver was killed immediately, but the other man, a German *Kapitän-zur-See*, jumped out and endeavoured to defend himself with a diminutive pistol. He was disposed of by a grenade. The car was set on fire, after all papers had been removed from it. Tyre bursters were placed in the road.

Lucas returned to Levrera in a German motor barge which he had captured in a local fishing port. On this voyage he encountered a small caïque bound from Lussin to Pola with three Germans on board. He made them prisoners.

Two nights later, Lucas was back on Cherso in time to shoot up a truck containing Germans returning from a dance. He failed to stop this vehicle but received confirmation later from civilian sources that three of its occupants had been killed and nine wounded.

Ian Smith, instructed to proceed with the Irish patrol in order to establish the strength of a certain small garrison, became bored with these peaceful proceedings. Ossero lay near. He decided to go and take a look at it. In broad daylight, from a position half a mile distant, he fired eleven Bren gun magazines into the crowded court-yard where the Germans were sunning themselves. The Germans scattered, leaving nine of their number dead or too severely wounded to move

Aircraft of Balkan Air Force now began to fly over the islands, warning their garrisons that an offensive against them was imminent and that they would be well advised to surrender to British raiding parties if they wished to avoid a sterner doom at the hands of the partisans. Individual German desertions to us increased but, generally speaking, garrisons composed solely of Germans stood firm . . . a fact which seems less surprising when one remembers that their radio sets had been deliberately removed and that they were in consequence without authentic news of the fighting in Europe.

With Italian Fascist reinforcements brought direct from the mainland, the situation was quite otherwise. In their homeland, which they had left most reluctantly, these men had heard sinister rumours, forewarnings of the end of a now tiresome masquerade. Ian Smith became their shepherd and on various nights led large parties of crestfallen *Fascisti* to selected beaches. In their ransacked billets he left derisive notes addressed to the Germans who were quite powerless to prevent the exodus. From one post, some six kilometres from Cherso town, Smith rang up the German *Inselkommandant*. The German, who had been fetched from his bed, employed obscene and intemperate language when he discovered to whom he was speaking.

'Good-bye, my dear Major,' said Smith sweetly, 'I trust that we shall meet again.'

In the early spring, a successful but bloody partisan offensive had eliminated the enemy corridor of resistance round Sarajevo. Attacking now along the coast, the Jugoslav Fourth Army reached Senj, more than half-way to Fiume, and captured the important inland town of Ogulin, on the Zagreb plain. The islands now lay exposed. No time was lost in reducing them.

Supported by Royal Marines, British naval forces and the artillery of the Raiding Support Regiment, partisan battalions gained a footing on Pag, Rab, and Krk. All three islands fell within a week and a particular satisfaction was felt in the fall of the last-named, where 800 Croat *Ustachi*—perhaps the most brutal and unprincipled of all German satellite troops—were rounded up and delivered over to a well-merited fate.

The disappearance of all his targets, with the exception of Cherso, which was next on the list for assault, allowed Sutherland to realize the project which he had long cherished in secret: namely, the invasion of the Istrian Peninsula and the infiltration of S.B.S towards Trieste, there to link up with the Eighth Army.

'The war is ending,' he told officers. 'When the last day comes, S.B.S. must be in the field and not at base.'

CHAPTER TWENTY-FIVE

The Istrian Peninsula, containing the towns of Trieste, Pola, and Fiume, had been partially awarded to Italy by the settlement of Versailles. I say only partially because the ubiquitous President Wilson, with his habit of doodling with a pencil across the face of a continent, had drawn a line down the middle of Istria. Gabriel D'Annunzio, that scented poetaster but resolute soldier, removed this line by his premeditated rape of Fiume in the year 1922. Istria, and indeed country beyond its confines, was now wholly Italian and became, in fact, part of the province of Venezia Giulia. Carabinieri and the Ovra moved into it. The various and sometimes peculiar laws of Fascism were enforced.

This did nothing to alter the fact that, except in a few coastal areas and in the chief towns, the population was predominantly Slovene.

This population was what is known among earnest revolutionaries as 'politically uneducated'. That is to say that they did not care a damn who governed them, for they had experienced misrule at the hands of the Austrians and Italians, while a glance across the frontier was sufficient to persuade them of the disadvantages of joining the new Jugoslav federation.

In the early part of the war, Istrians had been recruited into the Italian Army. The Folgore Division, which fought with such valour at El Alamein, was largely Istrian in composition. When the British finally made the 'Folgore' Division prisoner, they acted with unusual wisdom. They separated the Istrians from the men of Lombardy, de-loused them, issued them with battle-dress and finally engaged them in their service as Jugoslav Commando troops. Ironically enough, these 'Jugoslavs' were sent to Italy. At the crossing of the river Garigliano they gained nineteen medals.

But the Istrian who had not been conscripted, who was permitted to continue tilling his barren soil, was apathetic about the war. He disliked equally the Germans and Italians, and he saw no hope of salvation in the *banditen* of Tito and Mihailovitch. Accordingly, when the former with his armies not far distant from the province, and certain most explicit instructions from another source in his pocket demanding its annexation, made overtures and distributed arms, he met with but a poor response. The Istrians were quite willing to receive a Lüger or an Italian carbine which they would subsequently hide beneath the floorboards of their houses, but they were supremely disinclined to dress up in motley uniform with a red star on their bonnet and the words of the great Engels in their mouths.

Sutherland sent Captain Daniel Riddiford, his chief Intelligence Officer, into Istria in early March, with a view to preparing the ground for us. This Riddiford—a New Zealander, but on the other hand not really a Kiwi, for he had been educated in England—was well equipped for his task. In 1943 he had been a German prisoner in the Tyrol. He had escaped and, while escaping, had made his way through the fringe of Istria. Riddiford spoke appalling Italian with great fluency. Here was an idealistic in the strictest sense of that term. As such I esteem him, though I disagree with him on almost every conceivable subject.

But there are, of course, very few idealists left nowadays . . .

Riddiford landed in Istria on 11th March 1945. He found that the Long Range Desert Group, which were working with us at that time, had already established an efficient shipping watch, by means of which the course and speed of enemy vessels was signalled to Balkan Air Force, who, in due course, destroyed them. A Captain John Olivey was largely responsible for this work. Olivey had been in S.B.S.

Riddiford had many indecisive but lengthy palavers with

225

officers of the local Partisan 43rd Division. 'This man had rank and engaging manners . . . this man has a clear, decisive mind, a soldierly bearing and a good grasp of military values and the main principle . . . this man kept very much in the background: I could not form any impression as to his character.'

From these conferences, conducted in mud huts on the scrub-covered mountain-side, from which the partisans very rarely sallied forth except to requisition food from the civilian population, it appeared that they would view British intervention with distinct benevolence. They were weak and their offensive record was poor. They were hungry and a tin of bully beef contains magic comfort for those who do not taste it every day.

Persuaded of their good-will—and who would not have been—Riddiford reconnoitred a suitable lying-up area for a squadron of S.B.S. Then he returned to David Sutherland to report.

The Istrian operation, which we all hoped would enable us to end the war in a fitting blaze of glory, was on.

McGonigal had taken over Patterson's squadron. No better choice could have been made. He and I landed with Sergeant Nixon and his patrol on the night of 12th April 1945. We had twice attempted to land previously but had been prevented from so doing by naval battles in the vicinity which made a nearer approach to the coast inadvisable. David Sutherland, already ashore, was becoming worried and irritable:

'Targets are being missed. Land,' he signalled.

'Landing,' replied McGonigal laconically.

But we were again foiled, this time by Lieutenant-Commander Timothy Bly, D.S.O., of the Royal Navy. This gentleman, in command of four Dogboats ('D' Class motor launches) was on patrol off Cape Promontore when his radar reported the approach of a flotilla of 'F' Lighters. In Dogboats, and indeed in all light surface craft nowadays, is installed an inter-communication system. By means of this system, if your own craft possesses it, you are able to follow the course of any action simply by hearing the individual

226

Istria

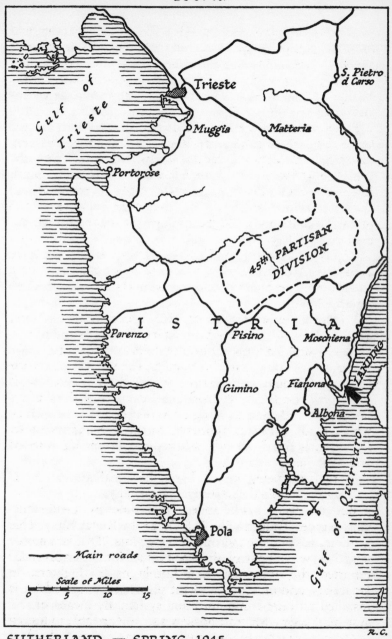

Gulf of Trieste

Trieste

S. Pietro d'Carso

Muggia

Matteria

Portorose

45th PARTISAN DIVISION

I S T R I A

Parenzo

Pisino

Moschiena

LANDING

Gimino

Fianona

Albona

Gulf of Quarnero

Pola

Main roads

Scale of Miles

0   5   10   15

R.C.

SUTHERLAND — SPRING 1945

commanders talking among themselves.

On that particular night we both heard and saw. Personally, I do not think I can remember any war experience so exhilarating and, at the same time, so particularly alarming. Our P.T. boat, with all engines stopped and twenty foreign bodies on board, lay rolling in the swell some 300 yards off the enemy island of Cherso, about five miles from our objective. Five miles away, too, the tracer and Very were streaming. Bly had made one unsuccessful run with torpedoes and was now urging his sister-ships to a second.

'Come on, boys . . . in once more . . . get the bastards . . . Green 45 . . . over.'

'Am in sinking condition . . . have many, repeat many casualties . . . Can you tow me?' came a faint response.

'Going in . . . will be back . . . plug your holes,' was the reply received.

Dogboats are fine craft but they are of wooden construction and no match for steel plate and 25-millimetre shells. Nor have the great speed. Bly finally withdrew, two of his ships disabled. The enemy did not follow him, and this is the true reflection of the casualties which they must have suffered.

The channel between Cherso and Istria was narrow. It was also mined to within a few hundred yards of the shore on either side. German convoys, evacuating personnel and stores from Fiume towards Pola passed through this channel. An ingenious system of lights on both shores was designed to warn these convoys of the presence of British raiding-craft. When this happened, the Germans lay up in a small cove until they judged the danger to be over.

This was all very well, but the cove selected as a refuge was the very one in which we wished to land: we were obliged to put in under towering cliffs a few hundred yards down the coast. Three 'E' boats, the advance party of the German convoy, must quite certainly have seen us. Luckily, they judged it prudent not to intervene. The Germans at that time were more concerned with surviving the melancholy business with a whole skin than with attacking an unknown number of British ships, who might quite easily radio for air support.

Ashore at last, we contacted David Sutherland and Riddiford, and installed ourselves in a village overlooking the coastal road. The Germans had evacuated this area, but they continued to patrol the road. On the following day we just failed to ambush a party of cyclists. The cyclists proceeded to the town of Fianona, where they found the partisans in charge. They disarmed them, cuffed them vigorously and warned them to behave themselves in future.

In Istria, the Germans did not take the partisans very seriously.

Nor did we, until we were about to set out to attack our various targets. We were climbing a particularly stiff mountain at the time. At the summit of this mountain a ragged but resolute Commissar, attended by three or four armed infants, all most certainly under the age of consent, informed us that, since permission for us to operate in Istria had not yet been received from Belgrade, we must refrain from offensive action and submit to internment.

'Considering that the whole incident would blow over in the minimum of time,' wrote Sutherland, 'I agreed to concentrate my force in the area chosen. We were very much stronger than they were, but they knew only too well that I did not desire an armed clash . . . and they played upon this to what they believed to be their own interest.'

The situation was, in fact, as follows: The Partisan Fourth Army was knocking a little nervously and without conspicuous success at the well-defended gates of Fiume. In Italy, the Anglo-American offensive had begun and it was not beyond the bounds of possibility that they would reach Trieste first. The whole of Istria, and in particular Trieste, were very dear to the Jugoslav heart. They had claimed the area, as they had claimed Carinthia, in 1918. They had been unsuccessful then, but they were determined to have it now. To win the hearts of the somewhat reluctant Istrians, however, the Jugoslavs must first liberate them by their own unaided efforts. In this province, far beyond their own front lines, they had at this time but two inefficient and timid guerrilla divisions. These divisions, in themselves were quite

229

incapable of driving out the Germans. Nor, indeed, did they particularly wish to do so; their role being rather to take over the area and the key-points of Pola, Pisino, and Trieste as the Germans showed signs of abandoning them.

The intervention—deeply distrusted, anyway, on political grounds—of even a few British troops could not, as the partisans saw it, be to their advantage. These few British troops might blow up railways. They would quite certainly attack German columns. No one had blown up railways or attack German columns in Istria before, and the population, who were feeding the tattered bands rather more than handsomely, might be inclined to ask certain awkward questions concerning their now conspicuous lack of activity.

Belgrade could not very well refuse to allow us to land in Istria, for this would have precipitated an international incident. They did, however, succeed in delaying our arrival and, once in, they determined secretly to prevent us from operating.

Outwardly, at first, the local Brusilovs were most amiable. The permission enabling us to move freely would come to-day, or, at the latest . . . to-morrow. Meanwhile, most obliging, they fed us with food requisitioned from the population.

Sutherland is, I think, one of the most patient and least excitable men whom I have ever met. In Istria, he bore some of the most tremendous responsibilities and withstood some of the most ardent temptations with which any military commander could be faced. He could, of course, have ignored the Partisan veto and operated without outside assistance. In this case he would have received false information, an utter lack of co-operation and, not improbably, a bullet in the back from someone 'who mistook him for a German' as he moved in to attack his first target.

'On 15th April Captain Brncic arrived. He was most apologetic for our being confined, but said he had to obey orders. He disclaimed all knowledge for the reason for the order . . .'

Riddiford, who believed in the good intentions of our hosts until the last: 'On 18th April a most offensive youth arrived with orders that we must pack up and leave forthwith. In his manner, bearing, and general obtuseness he strongly resembled a young Nazi. There were several unpleasant scenes . . .'

There most certainly were, and I do not think that the peculiar discipline of S.B.S. has ever been seen to better advantage than on that occasion. It is not amusing to see one's commanding officer, who possesses two decorations for bravery, ridiculed as the representative of a nation which has taken no active part in the war.

'The situation deteriorated. Although the partisans, generally speaking, avoided provoking incidents with us, they did their best to poison our relations with the civilian population. In spite of this, individual partisans seemed ashamed of their conduct . . .'

The question of our internment was now upon a high, indeed, an international level. We were, in fact, pawns in a far from pleasant game conducted by gentlemen in London who possessed an insufficient realization of the sacrifices which the British soldier can be asked to make. It would have given me great pleasure, I must admit, to have introduced the profanity of my Corporal Stewart into a Cabinet meeting at that time.

A month later, with the arrival of New Zealand troops in Trieste, the question of Istria was raised in deadly earnest. Both Britain and, I am happy to say, the United States, took an extremely firm line . . .

But that was too late for S.B.S. We could, and should, have been at Trieste at meet the Eighth Army. We could, and should, have taken thousands of German prisoners in Istria . . . they surrendered, in the final count, only to the armies of the Western Allies. We could, and should have laid waste the Istria plateau, but we were prevented from so doing.

Having gained their point . . . a reluctant permission to operate . . . those above us withdrew us. We were loading some mules in preparation for an attack upon a railway when the order to leave came through. Germans were on all but the seaward side of us, yet we had yet to fire one shot in anger against them.

231

'Copulating deadly, I call it,' was Corporal Stewart's comment.

We were evacuated in daylight. Partisan-manned Spitfires kept watch over us. As we passed by Cape Promontore, some two miles out at sea, the German coastal batteries opened fire upon us. Their aim was very poor.

In Trieste, a few weeks later, I had a conversation with Lieutenant Eddie Welles, an American, formerly in S.B.S., who had been attached to the Partisan Fourth Army.

'You can say what you like,' he said, 'but for the ordinary Partisan Joe who dies firing his rusty rifle while charging a strong-point held by Spandaus, I have nothing to respect.'

I said 'Yes', but don't forget the Commissars, the Piltdown men; secretive, assured, deceitful in what they are firmly convinced are the best interests of their country.

So there you are: you can take your choice. That may be the world you want. It is quite certainly the world you're going to get.

The Istrian fiasco was partially redeemed by Lieutenant-Commander Bly, with two Dogboats and one escorting Beaufighter. This officer met and accepted the surrender off Promontore of no less than forty German surface craft of all categories. The enemy were sullen at first and refused to capitulate. Certain of their officers wished to make a suicidal dash down the Adriatic, in the hope of seeking sanctuary in Spanish ports. Others wished to scuttle their ships; still others to blow Bly sky-high in one last glorious fling. By playing one faction off against the others, Bly secured the surrender of this valuable fleet intact.

CHAPTER TWENTY-SIX

Now I am approaching the end of this book. One operation alone remains to be described. A number of men have died in the course of these pages; some of them have belonged to S.B.S., some to the enemy. We must mourn them all. Outside Mersa Matruh, on the long road towards Sidi Barrani, there are three neat graves surmounting by German helmets. The men who occupy these graves died facing the final British onslaught on that well-mined citadel. They died without hope of succour, for their particular cause. In Leros, Private Fishwick and many others lie in not less shallow graves. They, too, died for a particular cause, without succour and without reinforcement.

War is most dreadfully unpleasant. We all of us admit this fact. We would indeed be lynched nowadays if we failed to do so. Naturally, we should like to abolish war. But we shall not abolish it. Even if we accept the evidence of the Bible, which maintains that the world was suddenly created in the year 4004 B.C., we must still set about the business of counting the thousand or more wars which have occurred since that time. We shall not abolish war bacause the desire to fight is ineradicable in human nature.

(Lassen, Bob Bury, Charlie Clynes, Stefan Casulli, Fishwick, Trooper Crouch, Sergeant Kingston, and a very great number of others died in this war. Personally, I am not at all sure that Lassen was destined to live. I believe that he was somewhat tired of the carnival. However, this you will presently be able to judge for yourself.)

The seven ages of man may begin in the cradle but they end in the gunsmith's: at four years, the first catapult; at six, the bow and arrow, at eight, the blank cartridge pistol; at ten, the entire armoury of stink bombs, manacles, air-guns and the first principles of chemical warfare.

Are Messrs. Hamley responsible for this state of affairs? They are not. This and other toy shops display upon their shelves a whole variety of innocent and peaceable baubles. Gladly they cater for the infant philatelist, the precocious ornithologist. But, alas, the true interest of childhood will never focus upon these harmless playthings. The tiny hand which demands to grasp the water pistol, will sooner or later wish to know the Lüger.

Men are attached to warfare because it offers them the one certain opportunity of discovering whether they are physically brave or physically craven. They seek in war the universal comradeship denied them elsewhere. They almost always find it. Both these desires are the inevitable result of that first water pistol.

A book such as this one, which might be said to exalt a certain type of warfare, may also be condemned as pernicious by good folk determined to propagate those ideas generally associated with the millennium. But I have laid no snares deliberately for the next generation: I shall be quite content if I have shown them how, in certain situations, some men—Lassen, for example—rise superior to themselves and to circumstance. Those situations only occur in war.

It is now time to make an end.

Lassen wanted to see the 'big' war. As usual, he obtained his wish. Normally, Lassen and his squadron would have taken over the island operations but when the islands began to capitulate, they was made clear for a move which he had long contemplated, and in which he was materially assisted by Brigadier Ronald Tod, of the 2nd Special Service Brigade.

In operations subsequent to the capture of the Gothic Line in the autumn of 1944, the Eighth Army had debouched upon the plain of Bologna, With great difficulty, before their offensive was spent, they had captured Forli, Ravenna, and finally, Faenza. Farther than this they did not succeed in penetrating. The Americans, in the foothills of the Appenines to the south-west, were similarly held in check.

The Lower Romagna is flat and marshy. Dykes, canals, and insignificant rivers intersect this area, which has frequently been compared with Holland to the latter country's advantage. The Lower Romagna, indeed, is far from beautiful. From its ponds and waterways, the breeding-ground of mosquitoes, stretches of great variety arise to pervade the atmosphere in summer. The Lower Romagna begins uncertainly below Argenta: it ends inconclusively in the many false shore lines of the shallow Adriatic.

It was here that the polyglot troops of the Eighth Army—Poles, British, New Zealanders, even a Jewish Brigade—spent the last cold and unpleasant winter of the war. The front line ran from Lake Comacchio on the coast, along the course of the Senio River, and thence to Castel Bolognese and Highway Twelve. Actually, to employ such a definition of the division between the rival armies is something of a courtesy. Patrols and outposts dug themselves in behind the steep banks of the river, it is true, but the main forces watched each other from a respectful distance. In flat country, where even a two-storied house is a dominant feature, it is not wise to concentrate too thickly.

Brigadier Tod and his force, comprising No. 9 and other Commandos, held the extreme right flank of this front. Nor was their presence in this apparently unpromising sector an accident. In front of them lay Lake Comacchio, on one side of the sea. Between the sea and the Comacchio Lagoon ran a narrow spit of scrub-covered sand-dune. The Germans had fortified and mined this spit heavily, but if a landing could be made behind them from across the lake, their fortifications would fall and their whole position in the plain to the west would become unbalanced, even outflanked. This operation was considered an essential preliminary to Field-Marshal Alexander's spring offensive. It was to be carried out by the Commando Brigade, with the co-operation of S.B.S.

Lassen and his men moved up to Ravenna by truck at the end of March. They carried with them many folboats, Goatley assault craft and rubber 'Jellicoe' Intruders. Lassen's collection of dogs, his *Volkswagen*, his many cooks and other Italian camp followers joined him by easy stages.

Lassen's first move was to signal for a dog which he had left behind him:

'Send Dog Tom.'

The reply came back: 'Dog Tom Dead.' Sergeant-Major Riley had profited by its master's absence to murder the wretched animal.

Installed in unusual conditions to comfort at Ravenna, Lassen went out in his jeep to inspect his area of operations and to interview senior officers. He interviewed a great number of senior officers. At one conference, with a bunch of them convened to discuss some administrative question, Lassen became bored with the mass of unfamiliar detail expounded for his benefit. He remembered that he had an appointment in a certain café. In the middle of a long speech by a colonel, he rose abruptly from his seat.

'I go now,' he announced.

It says much for the force of his personality that no one thought of recalling him.

But Brigadier Tod, who had known Lassen in England, was quite capable of handling the man. He called for him, explained carefully what he wanted done and gave him a free hand. The dogs were removed to a base area. The folboats were assembled. Work began.

Lake Comacchio is about the size of Lough Neagh in Northern Ireland. There, all resemblance ceases. Comacchio, in fact, is less of a lake than a flooded area. Even at its centre, there is no appreciable depth of water, while around its fringes, children would paddle for miles were they not inevitably overpowered by its smell and the danger of being sucked down by its mud.

From its shore, Comacchio seems a normal, unbroken, if somewhat stagnant stretch of water. But two feet is its average depth and this is exceeded only in the middle and in certain channels; some formed by the erosion of ages, some by human agency.

Few of these channels are charted and there is no reason why they should be, for in peace-time, Comacchio yields no fish except thin and tasteless eels. It contains, far out, a few small, wooded islands. The houses on these islands are in ruins. At that time they were used by the Germans as observation posts.

The difficulties of transporting upwards of a thousand heavy-laden men across four miles of this lake can be imagined. Only a fraction of it was in our hands, for one thing: the northern, western, and eastern shores were wholly German. On the south lay the neck of the spit, a strip of commando-held territory, then the high banks of the Senio river where it joined the lake. From behind these banks German sentries lay watching, their fingers upon Very light pistols.

They must not be alarmed by evidence of unusual movement. Nor must they hear the sound of motor engines, for these would reveal the nature of the project only too clearly. Consequently, every man who crossed that lake would have to *paddle* . . . at least until the moment when surprise no longer counted. They would have to paddle in Goatleys, Carley floats; in a dozen different kinds of embarkation normally reserved for the shipwrecked. The draught of a Goatley is one inch when unoccupied. When carrying ten fully equipped men, the draught of a Goatley is nearly two feet . . .

And two feet is the average depth of Comacchio.

Lassen's task, therefore, was to discover and chart channels of sufficient depth leading towards the chosen point of landing. When the attack finally took place he and his squadron would lead the assault, guiding the main force through these channels by means of lights and other signals.

All through the first week in April, Lassen was busy. The days he spent at Ravenna, the nights he spent on the lake. The large-scale map in Brigadier Tod's headquarters, once almost bare, became more and more closely annotated. Such annotations save lives, but Lassen seemed more than usually indifferent about his own. Returning from some long folboat sweep, in the course of which he had explored an island— fortunately unoccupied, but which might well have been held by the enemy—he would halt near the mouth of the Senio in order to listen to the German sentries chatting, and smoke a cigarette, in defiance of his own rules. Bimrose, who was devoted to him, was horrified.

'You bloody well shut up,' said Lassen. 'I do what I like . . . see?'

Lassen never went out without O'Reilly. He regarded it as a bad omen if he were obliged to leave the Guardsman behind. Two new officers, Turnbull and Michael Patteson, both very experienced men, fell completely under Lassen's spell but complained that they were not given sufficient work.

Patteson, a Hussar——

'*Seventh* Hussars, old boy, don't forget it'—had been in Alexander's Burma retreat of 1942. The Japanese had caught him and, after other refinements, had tied him to a stake on a cross-roads. British artillery was firing on the cross-roads. By some miracle, Patteson, instead of being killed, had his bonds freed by blast. He escaped and returned to his lines. He was not easily persuaded to tell this story but when he did so, people usually noticed that he wore the ribbon of the Military Cross.

'I suppose you got it for that?' they would say diffidently.

'Oh, no, old boy. Something quite different, you know. That's why I tell the story.'

Lassen was impressed by Patteson, but not quite by his insistence on employment.

'You bloody well shut up,' he said rudely. 'Take my dog out eef you're so keen on exercise.'

The attack on Comacchio took place on 9th April. The system devised to signal the assault craft in was completely successful. The spit of land was cleared to a depth of over four miles in heavy fighting. A Victoria Cross was won on that night in circumstances of great bravery by a Corporal in a Royal Marine Commando.

There is an unwritten rule concerning the Victoria Cross which precludes it from being awarded to two men in the same action. To win this decoration the recipient must, in the face of the enemy, exert a personal influence upon the course of an engagement. The circumstances may be those of retreat or advance; but it makes no matter which, but that personal influence must be exerted.

Few men have influenced the enemy and those under his own command to the same marvellous extent as Lassen. A second recommendation for the Victoria Cross was put forward after Comacchio. It bore the name of Anders Lassen, and it was successful. This is, I believe, unique in several respects, but you, who now know Lassen more intimately, will not wish me to enumerate them.

This is how Lassen died.

He had been ordered to make a diversion on the northern shore of Comacchio. He selected Turnbull for the job, but at the last moment decided to accompany this officer himself. O'Reilly, Crouch, Sergeant White and his patrol made up the remainder of the party.

The patrol landed and advanced along a road. The road was defended by pill-boxes set in echelon. Presently, very heavy machine-gun fire was opened upon the patrol. O'Reilly was severely wounded. Crouch was killed. The survivors took cover, dragging O'Reilly with them. Lassen, however, continued to advance. He silenced the machine-gun and the first pill-box with grenades. He then silenced a second, a third, and a fourth pill-box in the same manner, disposing with his revolver of men who continued to resist him. A fifth and penultimate pill-box, hung out a sheet in token of surrender. Lassen advanced to take the surrender and was shot at close quarters.

He did not die immediately. He crawled towards his own men who, inspired by his wonderful example, ran forward and completed the work which he had so nearly finished single-handed. When they returned, Lassen was still conscious.

'Leave me,' he ordered. 'I'm done for.'

They, nevertheless, continued to carry him until, feeling his body grow inert, and being themselves under heavy fire, they were obliged to leave him.

This happened on 9th April 1945. Lassen was then twenty-five years of age.

Lassen is buried not very far from where he fell. The

239

operation in which he died was the last undertaken by S.B.S. Neither the hostilities in Europe, nor the unit itself, survived him very long.

The remnants of the unit, united once more with Special Air Service, were about to embark for the Far East when the atomic bomb put a term to that conflict.

And that, I think, should be the end of the book . . .

Italy and Cornwall,
June–September 1945.